T0300258

Energy Management in Business

Energy Management in Business

The Manager's Guide to Maximising and Sustaining Energy Reduction

KIT OUNG

Routledge
Taylor & Francis Group

LONDON AND NEW YORK

First published 2013 by Gower Publishing

Published 2016 by Routledge
2 Park Square, Milton Park, Abingdon, Oxon OX14 4RN
711 Third Avenue, New York, NY 10017, USA

Routledge is an imprint of the Taylor & Francis Group, an informa business

British Library Cataloguing in Publication Data
Energy management in business : the manager's guide to
   maximising and sustaining energy reduction.
   1. Industries--Energy conservation. 2. Industries--Energy
   consumption--Management.
   I. Oung, Kit.
   658.2'6-dc23

Library of Congress Cataloging-in-Publication Data
Oung, Kit.
  Energy management in business : the manager's guide to maximising and sustaining
energy reduction / by Kit Oung.
     pages cm
  Includes bibliographical references and index.
  ISBN 978-1-4094-5245-4 (hbk) -- ISBN 978-1-4094-5246-1 (ebk)
  1. Industries--Energy conservation. I. Title.
  TJ163.3.O96 2013
  333.79'65--dc23

                                                                    2012025662

ISBN 13: 978-1-4094-5245-4 (hbk)

Contents

List of Figures

List of Tables

List of Case Studies

About the Author

Kit Oung is an energy consultant specialising in energy, carbon and water reduction services using low-cost, high-return strategies and management systems. He has 15 years experience in energy management, energy auditing and implementing projects for general industries and multinational blue chip companies.

A short list of clients includes the Ministry of the Environment (Singapore), the Ministry of Finance (Malaysia), ABB, Fonterra, Pan Century Oleochemicals, Diageo, Huntsman Tioxide, Huntsman Petrochemicals, BP Amoco, Petronas, GlaxoSmithKline, the British Broadcasting Corporation, Goldman Sachs (UK) and Johnson & Johnson.

He has also provided his services alongside professional service firms such as Deloitte Consulting, PA Consulting, Mott McDonalds and Johnson Controls Industries.

Kit is the British Standards Institute expert where he regularly reviews and provides input to European and International standards for energy and environmental management. Currently, he chairs two teams of experts for developing European and International standards for energy audits.

Kit graduated from the University of Sheffield in 1997 in BEng Chemical Process Engineering and Fuel Technology, and in 1998 MSc(Eng) Environmental and Energy Engineering. In 2011, he completed the Cambridge Executive Education General Management Certificate and Leading Professional Service Firms from Judge Business School, University of Cambridge.

Kit can be reached at uk.linkedin.com/in/kitoung

Foreword

Speaking as someone who has been working in the energy management consultancy business since the late 1970s, it is an interesting observation that the practice of energy management is still not part of mainstream business culture. Part of the reason for that is that energy costs may only be a few percent of operating costs for most organisations, the exception to this being energy intensive industries or large chains of, for example, supermarkets with hundreds of outlets and very high total costs.

In the last decade or so we have had an emphasis on climate change and the social responsibility to reduce carbon emissions. This has helped to engage more organisations, but a difficulty is the long-term nature of the problem. In the recent past security of supply, price rises and the shorter-term predictions of more to come have drawn greater attention to managing energy use and cost. Thus there is a gradual transition towards managing energy as a mainstream practice among all organisations – but there is still a long way to go.

Technology advances all the time and more energy-efficient devices and controls relating to energy are part of that process. This might relate to electric motors or motion detectors for lighting, as examples. The easy answer is to say 'no problem then, just rely on technology – no need to involve people'. But people are central to everything – many technologies do not work as they should or are not properly commissioned because the people involved do not have the right skills, degree of commitment or just time.

We take energy for granted, like the air we breathe. We need to engage employees with energy management in two ways. In a more general sense, for those using energy for normal working practice, awareness and behaviour change are key. For those with a more direct influence over energy-using systems, engagement is also key. These include equipment specifiers, purchasers, installers, commissioning engineers and servicing companies. In so many cases equipment is not properly commissioned and maintained. As long as it operates – that is all that matters.

ISO50001 is the new energy management systems standard, aimed at long-term sustainable energy performance improvement. This targets management commitment to address the above issues with technology and personnel. Its aim is to direct energy efficiency and management into mainstream management practice.

It is timely therefore for this book by Kit Oung to be written – aimed, as it is, at engaging mainstream business and public sector organisations with recognising the energy wastage that surrounds us and addressing the opportunities, which must become part of mainstream culture.

Kit is an experienced energy engineer now working in the energy management consultancy business. He also supports the British Standards Institute as the UK lead for the drafting of the new ISO Energy Auditing Standard.

Professor Martin Fry

Royal Academy of Engineering Visiting Professor at City University London
President of Energy Services and Technology Association
UK Lead for BSI Energy Management Systems Standards

Acknowledgements

As the saying goes, people never stop learning. I used to hate learning. Learning and information assimilation soon came with a vengeance. I seemed to be learning from everyone and everywhere – even during the most obscure conversations or in unexpected places. Ideas, knowledge, experience, insights and inspiration pulled my thoughts together.

Throughout my many years as an engineer, manager and consultant, some people have become my mentor, guided my career development, enduring my seemingly 'non-sense' questioning, ways of working, challenges and experiments. A significant majority of the ideas described in this book were tried, tested, discussed, debated, improved and incorporated into this book. Many more were found wanting.

Consequently, many people have, knowingly or unknowingly, helped me conceptualise and organise the ideas for this book. I would like to acknowledge them; without them, this book could not be published:

Professor Dame Sandra Dawson, Professor Jochen Runde, Professor Stefan Scholtes, Dr Mark de Rond, Dr Allegre Hadida, Dr Andy Neely, Michael Kitson, Barry Stirling, Allen Ormond, Duncan Woodcock, Ken Bell, Reg Crane, Dr Rob Terrell, Professor Martin Fry, Vilnis Vesma, Gopal Srinivasan, Graham Wooding, Rajvant Nijjhar, Nick Studdert-Kennedy, Michael Taylor, Kong Lee, Iain Paterson, Marcus Wyers, Lee Pannell, David Miller, Ron Buglass, Alexander Gutfreund, Biagio Lappena, Charlotte Karibuhoye, Chee Lim, Das Krishnadas, Eduardo Marques, Faisal Setoe, Fiorella Fiore, Hannes Gottwald, Ian Smythe, Johannes Keim, Nici Keeding, Sabine Disse, Stefan Kapoulas, Dr Tamas Havar, Warwick Pitts, Wayne McDermott, Yaninna Mella, Professor Ray Allen, Dr Kenneth Littlewood and Dr Keith Cliffe.

Finally, thanks go to Jonathan Norman and Adam Guppy at Gower Publishing, and to Maria Anson for all their help and support during publication.

Prologue:
Wesh Pharmaceutical – Energy Management

One midsummer evening, James (Jimbo) Brown, Managing Director at Wesh Pharmaceutical, was driving back, having just attended an all-day seminar organised by the Environment Agency – the environmental regulator in the UK. In the meeting, the regulator outlined the impending changes to energy regulation requiring a 2 per cent year-on-year reduction of greenhouse gas emissions.

Reflecting on the conversations during the seminar, the applicability of this regulation to Wesh Pharmaceutical would be synonymous with a 2 per cent reduction in energy consumption. Jimbo was worried about the long-term profitability of the business and the ability of Wesh Pharmaceutical to meet the tightened regulatory demands.

Results from two adhoc 'energy efficiency' campaigns in the last five years had resulted in little substantiated outcome. In fact, annual energy consumption had risen by 4 per cent year-on-year. Jimbo was becoming increasingly frustrated with the management team. He felt that real actions to reduce energy were not happening as fast as they should and suspected that his team had ulterior motives to delay his efforts. Jimbo was at a loss as to what needed to be done to turn this around.

Wesh Pharmaceutical

Wesh Pharmaceutical produces a range of generic medicinal products on eight independent production lines at their £8 billion factory in Wesh. Each line has a different throughput and consists of five basic unit operations. They consume approximately 73 million kWh of natural gas each year and approximately 17 million kWh of electricity each year. The trend of natural gas and electricity consumption over 24 months along with the production output is shown in Table P.1 and P.2 on the following pages.

Wesh Pharmaceutical was founded in the 1980s in the town of Wesh by the Wesh family and the Wesh town community after they purchased an existing manufacturing site from a reputable pharmaceutical company. At this time, the world-wide patent for the drug manufactured at the site by its predecessor was about to expire and they wanted to shutdown the site. The Wesh family

Table P.1 Production output over 24 months

Month	Availability	Performance	Production	Defects	Total Production	Percentage Defect	Quality	OEE
	(%)	(%)	(kg)	(kg)	(kg)	(%)	(%)	(%)
1	93	94	3,518	134	3,854	3	97	84
2	93	92	3,434	136	3,769	4	96	82
3	94	94	3,993	141	4,363	3	97	86
4	94	94	3,870	161	4,255	4	96	85
5	94	92	4,029	208	4,472	5	95	82
6	95	91	4,070	121	4,424	3	97	84
7	95	87	4,174	56	4,465	1	99	82
8	93	93	3,760	183	4,163	4	96	83
9	94	90	3,942	227	4,401	5	95	80
10	94	91	3,713	299	4,235	7	93	79
11	95	93	3,699	239	4,157	6	94	83
12	95	92	4,106	377	4,732	8	92	80
13	94	91	4,024	411	4,681	9	91	78
14	94	93	3,975	447	4,668	10	90	79
15	92	92	3,671	327	4,220	8	92	78
16	92	91	3,682	357	4,263	8	92	77
17	95	90	3,685	225	4,127	5	95	81
18	96	93	4,031	307	4,579	7	93	83
19	94	91	3,770	305	4,301	7	93	79
20	93	91	3,818	330	4,379	8	92	78
21	95	92	4,083	427	4,761	9	91	80
22	94	93	4,012	589	4,857	12	88	77
23	96	94	3,925	352	4,515	8	92	83
24	94	90	3,540	349	4,105	8	92	77

Table P.2 Energy consumption over 24 months

Month	Natural Gas		Electricity	
	Consumption	Specific Consumption	Consumption	Specific Consumption
	(kWh)	*(kWh/kg)*	*(kWh)*	*(kWh/kg)*
1	5,027,366	1,429.05	1,095,457	311.39
2	4,972,267	1,447.89	1,040,988	303.13
3	5,852,465	1,465.67	1,178,804	295.22
4	5,692,222	1,470.87	1,180,714	305.10
5	5,920,533	1,469.45	1,249,917	310.22
6	5,938,931	1,459.32	1,303,282	320.24
7	4,929,057	1,180.76	1,381,365	330.91
8	5,852,379	1,556.36	1,310,793	348.59
9	6,131,383	1,555.54	1,296,738	328.98
10	5,765,851	1,552.86	1,158,322	311.96
11	5,497,966	1,486.23	1,044,129	282.25
12	6,116,375	1,489.66	1,110,166	270.38
13	6,239,682	1,550.63	1,150,452	285.90
14	6,153,775	1,548.04	1,292,770	325.21
15	5,827,452	1,587.51	1,325,098	360.98
16	5,967,360	1,620.66	1,415,114	384.33
17	5,743,179	1,558.32	1,378,383	374.00
18	5,970,917	1,481.23	1,326,134	328.98
19	5,440,129	1,443.07	1,178,722	312.67
20	5,424,634	1,420.75	1,170,367	306.53
21	6,095,908	1,493.01	1,341,654	328.60
22	5,953,752	1,483.92	1,361,386	339.31
23	6,241,347	1,590.01	1,449,446	369.25
24	6,028,518	1,702.97	1,417,095	400.31

and the town community successfully rallied the authorities for the approval of licences and approval to continue operation under a different company.

The company relies heavily on local supplies for its raw materials and workforce. There has been little technology innovation in the company as the management practised management of the 'status quo'. Over the years, gradual improvements by its rivals meant that products sold by Wesh Pharmaceutical have the lowest profit margin in the generic industry.

The community in Wesh is a tight-knit community where everyone supports each other, including local businesses. Local businesses could always count on the community to support them and vice versa. In 1990, when there was a flood destroying 30 family homes, the whole community chipped in and worked round the clock to rebuild the lost homes with support from local businesses.

James Brown

Jimbo joined Wesh Pharmaceutical at the young age of 18 as an apprentice in 1980. He is a very hardworking, enthusiastic employee and displays a proficiency in operating and repairing mechanical machines. Like many of his co-workers at Wesh, he has worked in many different departments and is familiar with the operations at Wesh.

Over the years, Jimbo has demonstrated that he is a high achiever and excels in all of the challenges given to him. He has progressed from operations to maintenance, sales, logistics and finally into management. Jimbo's flair for machinery means that many of his colleagues continue to consult him on all matters relating to machinery and technology.

The previous Managing Director, Thomas Blair, a close friend of Jimbo, retired five years ago. At this time, Jimbo campaigned for the leadership position with a five-point plan to reduce production cost, increase profit margins and successfully compete with their rivals. He was appointed Managing Director a week later.

Jimbo's management team is shown in Figure P.1. In their current roles, each manager is responsible for and is measured on two objectives:

- site overall equipment effectiveness (OEE) – defined as the product of time available for production (per cent), time in actual production (per cent) and production that is right first time (per cent));
- reduction in site energy consumption.

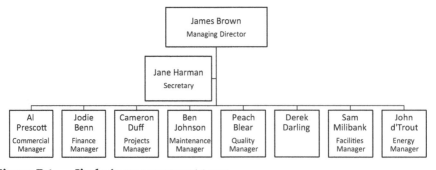

Figure P.1   **Jimbo's management team**

A Day in the Life of James Brown

On the next day, Jimbo arrives at work before anyone else and parks his car in his allocated space. It is very early and he drops his keys as he gets out of the car. However, he finds them easily, for dawn has already broken and the company has invested heavily in good car park flood lighting.

As Jimbo approaches his office, it is nice to see that the lights are on. He helps himself to a coffee from the coffee machine and notes that the contract cleaners have failed to empty his waste paper basket from the night before. It is a cool morning and Jimbo is pleased to find that his office is nice and warm. He checks his emails and does a little photocopying before he starts work, but as he approaches the copier he observes the out of paper warning is flashing.

Jimbo recalls the seminar the day before and also having read a magazine article a few months back: he vaguely remembers that the article was about ISO50001 – a newly published international standard on energy management. The article was written by a consultant on how companies like Wesh could implement ISO50001 and save energy. He recalls that he tore out that article and put it in an ever-expanding to be read pile of papers and makes a mental note to find this article before he goes home.

It is 7.30 am and in an hour or so the rest of the office staff will start to arrive. He had better get his head down and get some work done, for he has a meeting at 9.00 am sharp. Jane, Jimbo's secretary, called in to say that she would be late due to several accidents on the road, informed him that she baked an apple pie yesterday, had brought him a slice of his all-time favourite and reminded Jimbo of his meeting at 9.00 am.

At 9.00 am Jimbo joins his management team in the boardroom. Al (who had been entertaining late the night before) was slightly the worse for wear and closed the blinds to save his eyes from the morning sun. In fact he also felt a little too warm and asked for the air conditioning to be put on. The meeting had been called to discuss energy efficiency at Wesh Pharmaceutical and the investment in a new boiler.

The company has a cast iron rule for investments appraisal – a simple two-year payback or not at all. This has served the company well because investments that do not pay back in two years do not have an adequate rate of return. Obviously for larger investments the company takes account of reliability and production.

The existing boiler is 30 years old. Over the years, various improvements have been made – although the success is not very clear. The proposal as it stands is to spend nearly £250,000 on a new boiler (with an internal economiser) that will save almost 6.5 per cent, or repair and reinstate all the energy efficiency systems on the old boiler at a cost of approximately £70,000 with an expected annual saving of 2 per cent.

To everyone's surprise, Jodie, who has never seemed interested in the managements effort to reduce energy in the past five years, points out that gas prices are likely to be volatile in the future. The gas cost is likely to rise from 2 p/kWh to nearly 3 p/kWh in the New Year. The new boiler will have to operate reliably because production operates 24 hours a day – restarting a line is a major effort. Every hour of downtime costs the company £35,000.

The discussion regarding investment in the new boiler carried on among the management team. There appeared to be no firm decision on whether to replace the boiler or reuse the old boiler. The management team agreed to weigh the two proposals and make a decision at the next meeting. The meeting carried on with a discussion about the existing steam traps.

Historically, the company has invested in replacing the entire population of steam traps with purposed-designed orifice type steam traps. The purchase was recommended by Jimbo based on a presentation he saw at a conference when he was the maintenance manager. In the old days, technicians had to drill a hole through the steam trap before installing it to stop the steam trap from stalling.

The energy and operational benefits of these steam traps were widely contested by some of the management team. Cameron has been the loudest campaigner against these steam traps, claiming that since the replacement, steam trap blockage has risen by 50 per cent, leading to the need for more unplanned shutdowns.

Cameron has had several of his energy saving ideas rejected and later reintroduced by Jimbo at management meetings as his own ideas. This has led Cameron to openly and strongly oppose Jimbo during all meetings. He has recently blamed Jimbo for not changing the procedures to stop excessive sterilisation of production vessels between batches and during product changeover. Several unauthorised trials have shown that continuous steaming during these periods does not improve the sterility of the vessels. Cameron's calculation showed that a 33 per cent reduction in natural gas consumption could be achieved if his idea were implemented.

At this point in the meeting, a technician came into the room requesting Ben's assistance. Ben is the maintenance manager. He had to leave due to a burned-out chilled water pump. This pump has suffered many failures. Based on historical records, the pump failed every year. There are no spare parts for this particular pump. The standby pump had always provided coverage when the primary chilled water pump failed. Ben suspects that the increased failure rate for this pump is due to the compressor hot air exhausting towards the chilled water pump. The meeting continued without Ben.

At the end of the meeting, Jimbo decides to make his daily tour of the production areas. As he walked towards the production facility, he was stopped by Peach, the Quality Manager. She mentioned that she had difficulty opening the door to her office because of the excessive air flowing out from inside the room and that the temperature of the laboratory was too hot for her comfort. Jimbo walked past the chilled water valve from the laboratory ventilation system, opened the valve to maximum and continued to the production area.

Jimbo's first stop is to attend to Ben and another failed pump at the evaporator. The failure was caused by an overheating motor: the same motor has suffered an abnormally high number of bearing failures and he is determined to get to the bottom of the cause. The motors were procured from a local importer with a 30 per cent reduction in cost – a large saving for the company.

At this time, Thomas walked towards Jimbo declaring that he has partially solved the problem of the motor bearing failure. Thomas now works as a freelance consultant at Wesh Pharmaceutical when requested by Jimbo. He explained to Jimbo that the motor bearing failure can be solved by directing a small air hose (approximately 3 mm diameter) of compressed air onto the motors from a nearby compressed air line. To fit the small air hose, he has swapped all eight motors (originally at 15 kW) to slightly larger motors (now 22 kW each). This, according to Thomas, brings two additional benefits – the motors are lightly loaded and free up space in the warehouse. There is also no capital cost as the new motors are already in the warehouse.

The adjacent line is down for planned maintenance. Jimbo could barely hear himself think above the noise of a small hydraulic pack. It sounds as if the bearings in that motor have failed as well. Well, at least the waste extraction fan will function properly and he tests the suction by hand: this 22 kW motor was built and installed in the 1980s by a well-known manufacturer. He worries about the downtime on these lines, which amounts to nearly 6 per cent of all operational hours – he knows he must improve utilisation or lose out to the Brazilians, Russians, Indians, Chinese or South Africans.

Jimbo went over to Sam, the facilities manager, as he wanted to ask him about the loss of heat from the boiler. Standing between the two production lines, Jimbo could feel the heat even in summer. Derek came over and informed Jimbo that he has tweaked the pressure to improve operation. Although it looks 2 barg higher, Derek (whose job is unclear) promised that this would settle down over time. Derek is renowned in the factory for applying temporary fixes but has not really achieved very much. However, he tells a good story and Jimbo accepts the modifications made. Derek advises there is little point in insulating the steam valves, strainers and other fittings (although these constitute 20 per cent of all the steam pipes on the site) because they will need to be removed for annual inspections. Derek has also found that popping a little XE50 (a proprietary aerosol lubricant) onto squeaking belts quietens them down and improves the power transmission.

Sam, meanwhile, has had some success: he has identified 500 litres/hour of condensate that is not returned to the boiler – it is simply put to drain at 75°C. He elects to purchase a heat exchanger to recover the heat from this condensate and preheats the boiler's make-up water. The exchanger costs £10,000 to install.

In an attempt to curry favour with Jimbo and to improve efficiency, Sam indicates approximately 40 m of 2-inch condensate line that is not insulated. He proposes to insulate this immediately. Jimbo gives him a nod and Derek wanders off, leaving Jimbo alone with Sam.

Jimbo returned to his office for a meeting with John – his best friend at school and his best man. Nobody on the site knows exactly what John does, although he has identified suspected production problems. Whilst Jimbo left school after O-levels, John went on to obtain a PhD in biotechnology and worked for a large multinational R&D company. Due to a major rationalisation and reshuffling, he was made redundant and joined Wesh Pharmaceutical.

John is aware that, despite great effort to insulate the steam lines and to reduce energy consumption, this is not being achieved on some of the production lines. To him, insulation is not a big priority and he is looking for a way to determine which lines are least efficient. He could see no way of distinguishing between the performances of each of the eight lines. John wishes to ensure that the manufacturing costs are assessed and that resources are allocated properly. The stakes are high because even turning off one motor for a few hours when the lines are down saves several thousands of pounds in the year.

On this case, Jimbo disagrees with John. He thinks that there is sufficient data available from the £250,000 investment in a modern metering and automatic charting system. However, he is at loss as to what information he could obtain from this system and where he could gain further energy savings.

- What 'hard' and 'soft' issues are faced by Jimbo?
- In order to meet regulatory compliance, what options are open to Jimbo?
- Is Jimbo missing any tricks in reducing energy consumption?

Introduction

Energy savings is not a new concept. It has been in existence since World War Two under many names: energy conservation, energy management, global warming, climate change, carbon footprint, low carbon etc. Historically, they are a result of energy price increases and/or uncertainty in supply of energy sources.

The energy consumed is largely dependent on the company culture, its asset capacity and the output of the business in relation to its capacity. Regardless of the terminology used to describe energy savings, the underlying concept consist of two complementary concepts: (1) energy cost and (2) energy efficiency.

1. Energy cost is dependent on the cost to purchase energy from a supplier. In some businesses, the energy cost is a fixed tariff. If this is the case, the energy cost is simply a multiplication of the energy consumed by the energy tariff. In some businesses, there is a choice to either purchase energy from a defined tariff or to purchase from the energy markets. The ability to continuously find and purchase from the lowest energy supplier will ensure that the business continues to have the lowest energy cost.

2. Energy efficiency is concerned with the effectiveness of a business to use energy. It is a measure of energy consumed per unit of economic activity. In a manufacturing business, the economic activity is a unit of product. In a service industry, the unit output can be measured as a quantity of service provision.

Energy efficiency is a hot topic. Increasing energy efficiency may or may not reduce energy consumption. It does, however, reduce the total energy consumed per unit of output. When consultants, contractors, regulators and the media say increasing energy efficiency will reduce energy consumption, they are assuming that business output remains the same before and after implementing projects to increase energy efficiency.

If after implementing energy efficiency projects, a business increases its output, absolute energy consumption (and hence its cost) may increase beyond the levels before energy efficiency improvements.[1] This duality of energy efficiency – the phenomenon of increasing efficiency to reduce energy consumption vs. increasing energy efficiency leading to increasing energy consumption – has been studied by many macroeconomists, such as Daniel Khazzoom, Leonard Brookes and Henry Saunders. However, this phenomenon was first mentioned by a British macroeconomist, William Stanley Jevons, in 1865 and this phenomenon is known as the Jevons paradox.[2] The distinction between energy efficiency, energy consumption and the underlying assumptions made needs to be kept in mind at all times.

Assuming a fixed level of output, the business benefits of lower energy consumption are clear: lower energy costs, energy tax avoidance, selling excess CO_2 credits, immediate adding of savings to the bottom line and improved competitiveness.

Why Was this Book Written?

Universities and commercial institutions are constantly creating and launching new products that purport to be energy efficient. Consultants and suppliers are constantly launching new services to help businesses become more energy efficient. As more people become aware of the need to save energy, the general public has pushed for tighter regulation on energy consumption.

Over the last 15 years, many energy regulations and economic incentives have been introduced in the UK, the European Union (EU), the USA and many other countries. Some of these regulations and incentives introduced are climate change agreements, climate change levies, EU emissions trading, carbon reduction commitments (CRC), combined heat and power (CHP) directives, energy performance in buildings directives, energy efficiency service directives, renewable obligation, feed in tariff, renewable heat incentives etc.

In 2009, the European Committee for Standardization (CEN) and the European Committee for Electrotechnical Standardization (CENELEC) jointly published Europe's first unified energy management system (EN16001). This

---

1   For an interesting review on this topic, see Herring, 2006; Barker and Foxon, 2006; and Keay, 2011.

2   The Jevons paradox (sometimes known as the rebound effect or the Khazzoom-Brookes postulate) has polarised the view of energy efficiency into two factions, i.e., energy efficiency to reduce energy consumption or energy efficiency leading to increasing energy consumption. Very few people see the paradox from an economist's point of view – a profession that almost always provides two extreme pictures but rarely takes a firm stand on a single point of view.

was followed by the International Organization for Standardization (ISO) of the same management system (ISO50001).

Several surveys carried out between 2006 and 2008 found that nearly 80 per cent of respondents had not started to reduce the energy consumed in their businesses, but expect some form of regulation to enforce energy reduction by companies (Enkvist and Vanthournout, 2007; Enkvist, Naucler and Riese, 2008; Farrell and Remes, 2008; Ipos MORI, 2006). The Ipos MORI (2006) survey gave an insight into the inaction: 71 per cent of the respondents quoted a lack of resources to implement the energy reduction programme.

For those that do, energy reduction programmes are largely technology driven. There is a historical reason why this has been technology driven. Many political commentators and energy commentators credit this to the failure of President Jimmy Carter's re-election in 1980. President Jimmy Carter called on the US to conserve energy by equating it to 'morals and god'. His successor, Ronald Reagan, used a different approach by telling the nation that energy could be reduced by implementing better technology. Jimmy Carter's failure (or Ronald Reagan's success) has political, social and economic repercussions globally. It has driven the growth of energy efficient technology.

In the science-based and fact-based subjects, application of machines and new technology will result in an outcome that can be closely predicted to some form of accuracy. Unlike science and technology, the behaviour and choices that a person make is more complex and have more variables and is therefore less certain. This is the second reason for managers and engineers to favour technological solutions.

However, as the saying goes, 'Buildings don't use energy: people do'.[3] This applies to industry and processes too! In the present market, there are many different techniques available and marketed by various consultants, contractors and suppliers to help their clients reduce energy costs: energy benchmarking, energy audits, energy management, energy efficiency, energy savings, carbon offsetting, carbon trading and changing energy tariffs. The list of techniques continues. Each will require different skill sets and different demands for the energy reduction programme to be successful.

With a need to focus on day-to-day business management activities, implementing energy reduction programmes stretches the capabilities and know-how of each individual manager and engineer many fold. The ability of managers and engineers to implement energy reduction programmes will be limited to their available time, resources, interest and ability to grasp technical and managerial aspects of saving energy.

---

3   This phrase was first used as the title of a conference paper by Janda, 2009.

When wanting to reduce energy consumption, 79 per cent of managers and engineers seek and rely on the services of consultants, contractors and suppliers for information, recommendations and to implement energy reduction projects (Ipos MORI, 2006).

Therefore, managers and engineers need to know what to specify, what to buy, how to select the most appropriate supplier and must be able to check the work being carried out. The busy manager and engineer would rely on the suppliers to pull in the expert capabilities as and when required – a link and moderator between the business and the chosen techniques.

1.   Which technique should the manager and engineer choose when promoting an energy reduction programme?
2.   How do they know which programme is suitable for the company? How will they determine which recommendation will yield the highest returns on investment?
3.   Which consultants, contractors and suppliers are right for the business?
4.   How can they ensure that the quantum of energy saved and the speed of implementation will beat their business competitor?
5.   What resources will be required from the business? Will following all the recommendations result in all of the savings recommended by the consultants, contractors and suppliers?
6.   What does the manager and engineer look at to ensure the improvement projects are complete, achieving the results as agreed, and to sign off the project?

There are about 28,000 books published on the subject of energy conservation, 14,000 on energy management and 14,500 on energy efficiency. Of the available published material, approximately:

*   25 per cent are on energy risk management in the power generation and transmission sectors.
*   25 per cent on climate change, environmental protection and renewable energy.
*   25 per cent on the methodology, economics and politics of energy trading.
*   25 per cent on energy savings.

Of this 25 per cent, most of the books are written for buildings and/or specific technology. There are no books written to inform about and describe, at a high level, the basics of energy reduction, what happens in an improvement project, and what resources the business have to make available.

There is no book on the market that meets the requirements of busy managers. Managers find that the resources available in the market are too technical and delegate the task to technical personnel for various reasons.

1. Apart from petroleum refinery, petrochemical, chemical, power plant, metal, mineral, cement and ceramic industries, whose energy consumption represents a large portion (30 per cent–67 per cent) of total operations costs, the energy cost for a significant majority of business ranges from 2.5 per cent to 10 per cent. Because of the small contribution in the business, managers are inclined to put little or no priority on energy.

2. Since the 1980s, energy efficiency has been associated with the growth and innovation of technologies that use less energy. Managers have, to a large extent, left the development and implementation of energy efficiency to engineers and scientists.

3. Busy managers, predominantly educated in and tasked with managing business and administration, see the task of energy as 'technical' and not relevant to their roles. Many managers delegate the task to engineers, consultants and contractors.

4. Many tasks – such as management control, ensuring energy-efficient behaviours in staff, resolving internal and departmental conflicts and utilising data to make appropriate company decisions – require day-to-day managerial input and control to sustain and make things happen: many of these tasks require access to information and skills beyond the capabilities of engineers and scientists. All of these tasks also lie outside the capability of outsiders such as consultants and contractors to influence. Managers need to be involved in these tasks.

5. Experienced engineers, scientists, consultants and contractors are aware of the importance of managerial involvement. There are many consultancy services that provide training and consultancy services in the area of staff awareness, staff motivation and using data effectively to manage energy. However, writing on these non-tangible subjects (while tangible to the specific application) is very difficult to generalise and is almost always quantified retrospectively. This makes technically minded engineers, consultants and contractors unable to write at length on the subjects except for a quick mention over one or two paragraphs.

This book addresses the needs of a busy manager and busy engineer by bridging it with the technical contents available in the market without having a need to be well versed in the 'technical' and 'engineering' aspects. This allows busy managers to have minimum information to make good decisions and let the engineers execute the necessary works.

The Layout of this Book

Up to 25 per cent energy reductions can be achieved at relatively little or no cost and without significant lifestyle or business practice changes (Enkvist, Naucler and Riese, 2008).

This book is written on the basis of 'energy reduction'. It is written in four parts and distils practical concepts for sustainable energy management and energy efficiency. Each part is accompanied by real-life case studies chosen to build insight, illustrate and allow managers and engineers to relate to a broad range of energy reduction opportunities.

PART 1: STRATEGY

Part 1 sets the overall strategy for designing, implementing and maintaining long-term sustainable energy reduction. It describes the need for energy efficiency and energy reduction from a business perspective: economics, business drivers, operations management, environmental protection and competitive advantage. Then it reviews the reasons for inefficiencies and introduces a framework for sustainability in energy savings in existing and new organisations.

This part concludes with a review of the barriers a business faces when rolling out energy reduction programmes: organisational requirements; human resources; equipment design; operational losses; project limitations; wrong expectations; and stuck in perpetual cycle of perfectionism.

PART 2: TOOLS AND TECHNIQUES

Part 2 focuses on the tools and techniques for energy reduction. It begins with a non-scientific, non-engineering introduction on energy conservation, measurements to determine energy efficiency is developed along with some of the common terminologies used in the market.

The part then describes the five generic tools and techniques used by consultants and contractors when identifying opportunities, its features and scope of works.

It concludes with a means to quantify non-energy related savings, followed by a simple method to prioritise and finance energy efficiency.

PART 3: AVOIDABLE ENERGY LOSSES

Part 3 focuses purely on quick wins. It begins by introducing the maintenance cycle and the various tools to break away from a fire-fighting based maintenance regime.

The part continues with seven additional areas where quick win opportunities can be found: install correctly, sizing to match demand, turn off when not required, operate to match demand, start-ups and shut down, insulation and heat recovery.

This part finishes by highlighting items a manager and engineer should consider when choosing a consultant and contractor for the company.

PART 4: MANAGEMENT

Part 4 centres on the management activities that enable sustainable energy reduction programmes. It covers gaining commitment from senior management, myths of a perfect energy manager, energy management and its key features.

The part continues by exploring the rationality of an irrational mindset, the motivation for energy efficient behaviours, creating change teams and actions that involve all employees to sustain energy efficient behaviours.

This part concludes by highlighting the need for communication as a feedback process, tools that enable daily energy management and describe an intuitive management dashboard that gives timely and accurate data for informed decision making.

PROLOGUE AND EPILOGUE

The prologue introduces a fictitious case study of an operating manufacturing business. It poses three key questions about energy reduction. The epilogue concludes the book by pulling together all of the concepts covered by commenting on the case presented in the prologue and to give a possible method to move energy reduction forward. The purpose of this case study is to show how easy (or difficult) it is for managers and engineers to miss energy reduction opportunities on a day-to-day basis and how management input is absolutely critical to sustain long-term success.

PART 1
Strategy

In this global economy, businesses are continually striving to reduce their cost base, increase their profit margins and create value for their customers whilst meeting tough health, safety and environmental regulations in order to compete. To achieve this objective, many businesses are going leaner by implementing lean practices, complex quality control, 5S, kaizen, gemba, 6 Sigma, total production maintenance (TPM), Toyota manufacturing systems (TPS), energy efficiency, waste reduction, resource efficiency etc.

In theory, implementation of any of the above chosen techniques would represent a great opportunity to reduce costs and compete in the market. Within a lean organisation, managers and engineers invariably have multiple job functions and responsibilities, each requiring different skill sets and demands for attention. Managing energy is one of the tasks demanding the attention of a manager.

Managers know the importance of managing energy use by the business successfully. Several surveys found that 60 per cent of managers and senior executives recognise the need for, and importance of, energy efficiency and its contribution to their business: overall strategy, product development, investment planning and brand management (Ipos MORI, 2006; Enkvist and Vanthournout, 2007). For a significant majority of businesses, the primary cause of climate change is the emission of carbon dioxide (CO_2) as a result of using energy.

On a global scale, if all companies and individuals implement simple energy reduction projects between now and 2020, it would half the projected growth of energy demand, and keep CO_2 abatement levels at 450ppm – the generally accepted level to prevent a rise in global temperature. At a total cost of US$170 billion this would save 135 quadrillion BTU per year (64 million barrels of petroleum per day), providing an average return on investment of 17 per cent (Farrell and Remes, 2008).

1

We Need to Reduce Energy Use

In the majority of businesses, the primary purpose is to generate profit whilst simultaneously increasing return on investment and creating positive cash flow. In a manufacturing business, this is accomplished by converting raw material into saleable products and services. Almost all of these processes will involve the use of some, if not all, of the available forms of energy: electricity, fuel, steam, compressed air, cooling water, oxygen, nitrogen and water.

An efficiently managed and effective business would, ideally, produce products or services using the least amount of energy. In a competitive business environment, most manufacturing plants are far from running optimally, which is easy to ignore when they are working adequately. They may be working adequately, but if kept unchecked will cost a lot more than they should, reducing profit margins.

As an example, for a business operation with a 10 per cent gross profit margin, for every £1 saved on energy costs the business would have to sell an equivalent of £10 to make the same £1 of gross profit. Wasting £1,000 a year would thus need £10,000 worth of sales to achieve the same profit.

From a business perspective, the real reasons behind managing energy consumption and its efficiency consist of five major elements, listed below in order of priority and integrated into the entire business value chain. All five components are interrelated and none can be isolated from the others:

1.   Economics.
2.   Business drivers.
3.   Operations management.
4.   Environmental protection.
5.   Competitive advantage.

The principal purpose of a business entity is to make money. Thus economics, business drivers and operations management are listed before environmental protection. From a business perspective, energy savings must, first and foremost, be considered for business survival and business longevity.

A business must first have a good and fundamentally sound business plan and business vehicle. It must then be able to successfully operate this process safely, economically and to generate a profit. If this cannot be achieved, the business is not healthy and will be at risk of closure in a short period of time.

Economics

McKinsey and Co. predicts that global energy demand is likely to grow at a rate of 2.2 per cent until 2020. Europe's demand, consuming 17 per cent of the global energy supply, will grow at a slower rate of 1.2 per cent until 2010 (Bressans et al., 2007; Hartmann et al., 2008). With a growth of energy efficiency estimated at 1 per cent until 2020 (Hartmann et al., 2008), a 'business as usual' scenario means that the demand for energy outweighs the rate of energy efficiency by approximately 1.2 per cent.

With the average cost of bringing new oil wells online having risen by 100 per cent over the past decade (Dobbs et al., 2011), the implication is that global energy prices will continue to rise and will remain volatile, peaking in the winter seasons. It is estimated by many energy economists that energy prices are likely to remain high for some years to come.

Some business analysts place a lot of emphasis on the meaning of energy consumption vs. GDP as an indicator of efficiency. Such data is widely available from the internet. However, the use of such figures for comparative studies needs some degree of caution for several reasons.

- While all costs used to generate economic figures are in a single currency, energy expenditure is not a true indicator of energy efficiency, and the cost of energy is different for different countries.
- Countries with many heavy industries will skew the energy expenditure and GDP figure. Some examples of such industries are refineries, LNG plants etc.
- GDP is only one of two economic figures driving growth. The other figure is the rate of productivity improvement. On average, this rate is approximately 2 per cent per annum. This means that on average, even when there is no change in GDP people will find better ways, more efficient ways or new ways to generate the same economic output with 2 per cent less input.

Present projections indicate that there will be a shortfall of oil in the latter half of the twenty-first century. The long-term value of fossil fuel resources will continue to increase as scarcity increases. This cycle will continue to spiral upwards unless a new source of energy is found, so the inevitable solution is to preserve and prolong reserves that are presently available. Energy efficiency and sustainability will become more important.

Several economic instruments have been developed and used in most of the first world countries. Two of the commonly used instruments are taxation (levy) and carbon cap-and-trade (emissions trading). In some countries these schemes are voluntary, while in others they are mandatory. The careful utilisation of these instruments can and will benefit business operations by generating additional monetary benefits and reducing the cost of production. Coupled with good and sustainable energy reduction initiatives, this can enhance the returns of a project – a 'bonus' for the investment.

If the investment is not technically and economically feasible on its own but is feasible after considering these economic instruments, these investments should only be sanctioned after careful planning and further detailed studies to reduce any risk and/or uncertainty associated with the project.

In addition, despite the western media 'naming and shaming' China and India for 'burning more fuel', China and India are able to be energy efficient and less dependent on fossil fuel. They have become the two largest exporters of certified carbon credits, providing over 60 per cent of global demand (*The Economist*, 2009; Business Line, 2011). In effect, China and India control the carbon credit price. As more and more businesses buy carbon credits, the availability of carbon credit will become scarce and the carbon credit prices will go up.

Business Drivers

In the modern-day business environment, assisted by high-speed internet connections and high-powered computers, many companies are now embarking on internet speed business, mass customisation and customer value addition. Competition for market share and business survival means that companies are constantly finding and implementing world-class manufacturing processes, alternative methods and adapting to constant change in a business environment.

Prices for commodity products are determined by the balance between supply and demand. Globalisation and fluctuations in market demands coupled with less reliable production asset performance and margin erosion from reducing market prices have and will continue to push investors towards demanding higher shareholder value. It is paramount to deal with these high expectations. This may require actions such as:

- Reducing manufacturing costs.
- Reducing losses and wastage.
- Improving productivity.

- Improving cost accounting.
- Increasing plant flexibility etc.

Managers very frequently ask 'Why do I need to reduce energy?' Energy consumption has an impact on business performance. A better question would be 'What is the value to me and my business if my total operational cost for energy is 10 per cent to 30 per cent lower than my competitor's?'

An inefficient and ineffective utility plant operation will cause the plant to operate at a high cost. It also has an impact on the performance of the entire business entity, ranging from operating margins, earnings per share, premium pricing and economies of scale. Figure 1.1 shows a range of business impacts from an inefficiently operated boiler.

Energy savings opportunities may come from:

- Reduced expenditure on energy – e.g., by reducing consumption, changing tariff or fuel type;
- Reduced maintenance cost – e.g., following improved utilisation of plant and optimisation in operation;
- Savings in other costs – e.g., water charges, water treatment costs where demand is reduced;

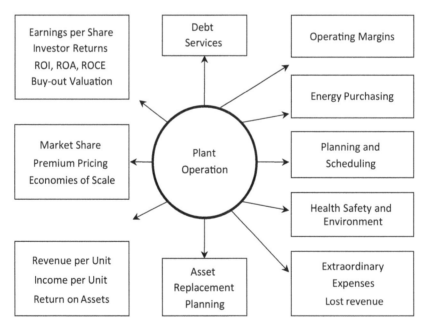

Figure 1.1   Impacts of an inefficient plant operation to businesses

- Reduced capital expenditure – e.g., where increased efficiency avoids the need for additional plant or capacity or makes possible the sizing of any replacement plant;
- More productive use of labour where staff are released for other duties – e.g., automated control systems;
- Increased productivity where working conditions are improved – e.g., improved temperature levels, airflow etc.

Case Study 1.1 shows an example of an energy reduction project having other non-energy benefits for the business.

CASE STUDY 1.1   ENERGY AND NON-ENERGY BENEFITS FROM IMPROVING STEAM BOILER

A manufacturing plant has two boilers. Each boiler is of similar capacity and is operated in modulating mode. Both boilers have variable speed drives (VSDs) modulating the combustion air requirements according to the steam demand. However, the equipment used to send signals to the VSD for modulating the combustion air fan is the original 'Cam and Link'* controls for natural gas and air. Although the boiler plants have energy efficient equipment installed, the overall system, and hence its efficiency, is still governed by the old control systems.

The simultaneous modulation of both boilers coupled with the inability of both boilers to perfectly meet the steam requirement led to a boiler control

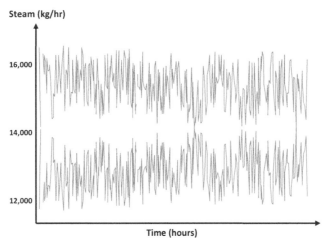

Figure 1.2   Boiler 1 and boiler 2 steam outputs

---

*   'Cam and Link' is a mechanical control system frequently installed on older boilers. This control system is only capable of responding in step changes in response to steam demand. It does not allow seemless matching of steam demand.

'hysteresis' – i.e., these controls caused both boilers to ramp up and down even when there was no change in real plant steam demand. This is shown in Figure 1.2. Over the period of monitoring, there is no change in average steam demand on the site. However, each boiler is modulating up and down as a mirror image of each other.

This continuous control conflict increases the wear and tear on the boiler control systems. It also causes extra thermal stress on the boiler shell and tube due to the constant intermittent introduction of 'cold' water into the boiler and the resultant water carry over. Historically, the boilers have had several tubes replaced over a three-year period.

The control systems were subsequently replaced with new and purposely-designed VSD controls. A 5 per cent or £72,500 energy savings was realised. In addition to energy savings, there is a reduction maintenance cost, water treatment chemicals giving rise to a total saving of £116,500 per year. With a capital cost of £84,000, the whole project was paid back in 0.72 years.

Operations Management

Most people equate energy saving with fuel bill savings. Moving beyond a cost-cutting approach to gain maximum value and profitability from production and manufacturing requires a change in traditional mindset. One available mindset is from the point of view of the operations management in search of:

- Low manufacturing cost per unit production.
- Maximum profit margin.
- Economic lifetime of equipment.
- High return on investment.

Employee redundancy is often among the first cost reduction path chosen by management. Unless there are external forces or legal requirements, energy cost and its management is probably the last to be considered.

Energy cost reduction can achieve operational goals. An efficiently designed and operated plant not only consumes less energy, but is also more reliable. This ensures that availability and the quality of utilities to support the process is high, contributing towards higher yield and lower cost per unit product.

Recalling Case Study 1.1, due to the continuous conflict in control systems on the boiler, the boiler operates at a lower water level than would normally be expected. Small fluctuations in the boiler water level would trip the boiler due to low-level alarm and trips. Both boilers have an average availability of 83 per cent. Historical records show an average unavailability pattern of 45 minutes boiler downtime every two weeks with a peak of 17 stoppages in a day.

Every time the boiler trips, there is a lot of energy lost in the trip, purging and start-up. It also has an impact on the plant production – the full plant would be generating waste and takes 30 minutes to regain production. This has a significant impact on the manufacturing plant availability and first time right portion of the overall equipment effectiveness (OEE) calculation.

After the improvements on the boiler controls were carried out, the availability of the boiler increased to 99 per cent, with many months at 100 per cent. With minimal start-ups and shutdowns, in addition to the energy and maintenance savings mentioned earlier the production plant is able to generate 10 per cent extra production. This has been quoted in the company financial report as additional sales of £1.4 million. To reap the benefits from energy savings, the concept that energy waste and inefficiencies are valueless must be rejected and replaced with the fact that they are money and profit waiting to be made.

Another important benefit of energy efficiency is the ability to improve energy cost accounting, improve forecasting and reduce budget variation. Depending on the accounting method used, raw materials and energy are usually classed as a direct cost. Proper and accurate budgeting and production decisions are important for the declaration of operating profits and taxes, and for capital budget allocations.

Managers need the ability to measure, monitor, validate and continuously reduce the energy consumed by the manufacturing plant. While there may be price variations beyond the control of managers, the quantum of energy use is within the control of managers. Consuming less energy minimises the impact of energy prices.

A less tangible and not uncommon bonus is that energy efficiency does not have to involve significant change in employment conditions, thus avoiding any human relations (HR) issues and civil actions.

Environmental Protection

Of all the rational reasons for improving energy efficiency, the environmental impact of using energy is the most publicised topic. With the exception of nuclear, hydroelectric, tidal and solar power, conversion of all other kinds of energy creates carbon dioxide (CO_2). This rise in CO_2 has been reported since the Industrial Revolution and will continue to rise with the GDP of all countries. As more and more countries become developed, energy consumption – and hence man-made CO_2 – will increase.

Climate change is among the hottest topics now discussed and published in the media.[1] The exact nature/cause of climatic change is a new form of science and is still undergoing research and development. The direct impacts, according to the majority of climate change scientists, governments and non-governmental organisations (NGOs) are:

1. Drought.
2. Floods.
3. Photochemical smog.
4. Ozone layer depletion and the creation of low-level ozone.
5. Melting ice caps and glaciers.
6. Unpredictable weather.

As a consequence of these direct impacts, the majority of climate change scientists also predict that the following may happen:

- Mass migration of people from lowlands.
- Cities become crowded.
- Availability of food and other basic human needs are stretched.
- Crime and civil disturbance may result.

NGO and public pressure to improve environmental longevity, along with constant media coverage, has resulted in many mechanisms being developed by the various government bodies and institutions to promote energy savings under the banner of climate change:

1. Climate change taxes.
2. Environmental taxes.
3. Climate change and energy efficiency regulations.
4. Legally binding CO_2 emission limits.
5. Carbon footprint awareness.
6. Carbon offsetting and carbon neutral.
7. CO_2 emissions trading.

Some countries, such as those in the European Union (EU), have voluntarily increased their CO_2 emission reduction targets and are working towards a 'green culture'. At the other extreme, there is also another group of climate change scientists who predict a 'business as usual' scenario. Here, they have

---

1   For a non-technical review of climate change, see MacKay, 2009.

predicted that earth's climate is constantly changing and that man-made CO_2 has little effect on a global scheme. This group of scientists frequently state that the other group of scientists is misguided and that the science backing the other group's conclusion is incomplete.

However, both groups of climate change scientists do prescribe to a need to use energy efficiently and strive towards using less. Regardless of whether or not to subscribe to climate change or conservation of a scarce natural resource – fossil fuel – a responsible manager would still want to save energy.

Reducing energy consumption not only saves money, it also reduces company taxes, guards against energy price fluctuations and protects the environment. This is a win-win situation for the individual as a global citizen, for companies and the environment.

Competitive Advantage

Being successful in reducing energy consumption is part of being sustainable. To many companies it means increasing operational efficiency, reducing waste, complying with regulatory requirements and minimising risk to the business. Implementing energy reduction programmes for economic, business driver, operations management and environmental protection reasons are merely operational efficiency reasons.

In addition to the cost reduction due to a reduction in energy consumption, some businesses participate in emissions trading to sell reductions in CO_2 emissions, realising extra business income. Other companies may choose to participate in carbon offsetting and carbon neutral schemes.

Competitors, for the same reasons, can implement similar programmes. Any temporary advantage gained will be eroded over time. Sustainability can be a source of competitive advantage for the business. Using sustainability for competitive advantage moves energy reduction from operational effectiveness reasons to a strategic business issue.

Creating a competitive advantage requires senior managers to review the results from energy reduction, business forces, business model and value chains that drive the business and consciously plan and carry out activities that lead to better business performance relative to the competition.

Michael Porter's frameworks such, as five forces analysis (Figure 1.3) and value chain analysis, are two such tools that enable a study of competition and strategy analysis.[2]

---

2   For additional reading on understanding competition and competitive advantage, see Magretta, 2012.

Figure 1.3   Five forces of industry

To carry out a five forces analysis and to create new competitive advantages requires the business to re-examine the existing business models, business plans and to explore questions such as:

- How could I better compete with the existing rival companies?
- How could I differentiate the company from its rivals?
- Should I expand my capacity to gain market share?
- Could I generate better links with the local communities, suppliers and buyers that ensure long-term business relationships?

MIT Sloan Management Review and Boston Consulting Group have been collaborating to study companies who use their sustainability leadership and community bond as a source of competitive advantage.[3] Advantages range from increasing the value for clients, gearing up the entire value chain for lower cost proposition, attracting top talent and investors, lowering the cost of capital, using

---

3   MIT Sloan Business Review and Boston Consulting Group have conducted surveys and published many reports spanning several years on companies that generate competitive advantage from sustainability. These reports can be found on the MIT Sloan Management Review and Boston Consulting Group websites.

energy efficiency brand reputation to gain market share and profit, increase staff motivation and/or having larger tolerance for business risk.[4]

To give a quantitative indication on the potential for competitive advantage, Willard (2004) recommends the following estimates: 1 per cent reduction in recruitment costs, 2 per cent lower cost of attrition, 5 per cent reduction in risk of capital, 10.5 per cent increase in employee motivation and productivity and 5 per cent increase market share.

---

4   For additional information on applying Michael Porter's concept in environmental sustainability, see Orsato, 2006.

2

The Measure of Efficiency

All physical material and energy in this world is governed by and conforms to two natural laws of physics. The concept of efficiency is derived from these fundamental laws by comparing any utility consumption in excess of the theoretical minimum. Scientists and engineers use the theoretical predictions with measured data to highlight inefficiencies and drive improvement actions.

This chapter provides a basic understanding of the two laws of conservation. The key takeaway message is that no production processes and energy utility processes are 100 per cent efficient. The more times energy has to be handled (heat is converted or transferred from one medium to another), the less efficient it becomes.

Conservation of Mass

The first law is the conservation of matter. It states that no matter can be created or destroyed. However, it can be converted from one form to another. From a process and/or manufacturing point of view all raw materials going into a process, such as a reactor, must equal the product coming out of the process. This is depicted in Figure 2.1(A) and the following equation:

Raw Material Input = Product Output + Raw Material in Output + Losses

When scientists and engineers carry out a so-called 'mass balance' or 'material balance' they are carrying out an assessment such that the right-hand side of the equation is equal to the left-hand side of the equation.

Scientists and engineers use the concept of 'yield' as a measure of efficient use of raw material to make a product.

$$\text{Yield} = \frac{\text{Raw Material Input} - \text{Raw Material Output}}{\text{Raw Material Input}} \times 100$$

$$= \frac{\text{Product Output}}{\text{Raw Material Input}} \times 100$$

In an ideal world, there would be no raw material left in the product and no accumulated raw material and product inside the process. The yield of the process will be 100 per cent. In practice, no processes can be 100 per cent efficient due to:

- The nature of the reaction process;
- Poor mixing of all molecules in the raw material and product;
- Turbulence in the flow of raw material inside pipes and vessels;
- Leaks in the system;
- Limitation in processing conditions such as temperature, pressure etc.;
- Limitations in the material used to construct the machinery;

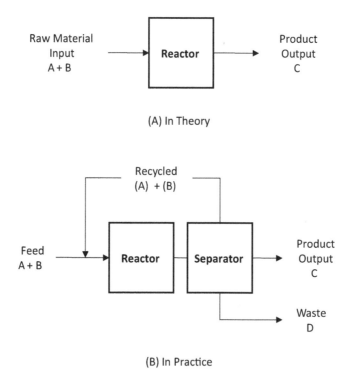

(A) In Theory

(B) In Practice

Figure 2.1   Conservation of matter in theory and in practice

- Accumulation of raw materials and products in stagnant zones inside the machinery;
- Inaccuracy of measurement, etc.

All of the above causes inefficiency in using raw material. As such, the yield will always be less than 100 per cent and forms the basis of improvement. Scientists and engineers have developed and continually seek new ways to approach this theoretical yield of 100 per cent.

Separation and recycling systems – Figure 2.1(B) – are used to improve the overall yield of the process. With the advent of modern computers and computer modelling techniques, scientists and engineers are continually working on minimising stagnant zones inside the reactor, using modern control systems etc. to improve the yield.

Conservation of Energy

The second law is the conservation of energy, commonly known by the scientific and engineering community as the law of thermodynamics. In similar fashion to the first law, the second law states that energy cannot be created or destroyed. It can, however, be converted from one form to another. Every time energy is converted, some energy is lost.

To many, energy is commonly referred to as the fuel, electricity and heat we purchase. This is a valid interpretation of energy. To further understand energy and its efficiency we need also to understand it from a scientific perspective. Very loosely, energy can be exhibited by any matter in four different forms:

1. Chemical energy.
2. Mechanical energy.
3. Potential energy.
4. Electrical energy.

Chemical energy is energy that bonds the atoms, molecules and ions together at a microscopic level to form materials we can touch and feel. Using the example developed in Figure 2.1, raw material A and B each has its own chemical energy. When they are fed into the reactor to make product C and waste D they too have their own chemical energy.

If the reaction generates heat, the reactions is said to be exothermic. This heat would be removed from the process by means of cooling water or chilled water to allow a constant and optimal environment for the reactor. A good example of an exothermic process is the combustion of fuels. We burn fuels to generate steam in power plants for electricity production and in industry for heat sources. At home, we burn fuel to generate hot water for heating, cleaning and washing. At the opposite end, if the reaction absorbs heat the reaction is said to be endothermic. Heat would need to be supplied for the reaction to take place.

Mechanical energy is energy exhibited by any matter in motion. It is also known as kinetic energy. It is proportional to the velocity of the matter. Again, using the example developed in Figure 2.1 we may need to pump or blow the raw material A and B through pipes into the reactor. Raw material A and B, when inside the pipe work are said have mechanical energy. The faster A and B flow in the pipe, the more mechanical energy they possess.

Potential energy is the energy possessed by any matter stored at height. Of the four categories of energy, potential energy is perhaps the most difficult to grasp. Any matter stored at height exerts energy in terms of pressure when it is transferred from this height. This concept is clearly demonstrated in houses where the water tank supplying water in each house is stored in the attic. When there is a need for water, it flows to the tap from the tank without the aid of a pump. On an industrial scale, the pump pressure required to pump a fluid stored at height would be the discharge pressure required for the application minus the potential energy.

Electrical energy is the easiest and most common form of energy. Electrical energy is the flow of electrons within an electrical conductor. In the case of electricity used in the house and in industry, the conductor is copper.

Figure 2.2 shows how conservation of mass and energy works in tandem. Again, similar to the first law:

$$\text{Energy Input} + \text{Energy Generated} = \text{Useful Energy} + \text{Waste Energy}$$

Similar to the mass balance, when scientists and engineers carry out a so-called 'energy balance' they are carrying out an assessment such that the right-hand side of the equation is equal to the left-hand side of the equation.

Efficiency is defined by:

$$\text{Efficiency} = \frac{\text{Total Energy Input} - \text{Unused Energy}}{\text{Total Energy Input}} \times 100$$

$$= \frac{\text{Total Energy Used}}{\text{Total Energy Input}} \times 100$$

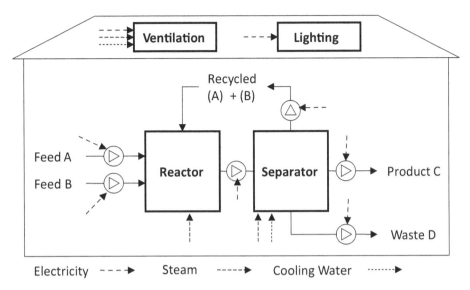

Figure 2.2   Conservation of matter and energy

Despite many attempts at breaking these laws, to this day they remain inviolate. Both laws of conservation can sometimes be expressed in common language as:

- You cannot win.
- You cannot break even.
- You cannot get out of the game.

The concept of yield and efficiency is a useful measure of performance as it measures changes in performance of a manufacturing plant, product performance and services rendered. It also allows comparison between different processes or items of equipment in terms of energy, how efficient are utilities generated, how efficient they are distributed to the end user and how effective they are used.

CASE STUDY 2.1   BOILER REPAIR VS. BUYING NEW

On a manufacturing site, two steam boilers were installed in the 1970s. Over the years they have been poorly operated and maintained, and various energy efficiency improvement projects were retrofitted poorly. Some retrofits have failed and were left in situ. Over the same period, the steam demand has increased, leading to the boilers being operated close to their design capacity. To continue operating efficiently, 10 improvements to the boilers are required.

They are:

1. Replace the existing boiler feed water valves and boiler blow down valves.
2. Install a dual fuel ready burner so that the boiler can be switched to fuel oil in case of natural gas disruption.
3. Replace the boiler level control as the existing one constantly trips the boiler even when there are no genuine health, safety or operability issues.
4. Upgrade the existing burner to comply with environmental emissions regulations.
5. Upgrade the existing boiler control system to include a troubleshooting system.
6. Install VSD combustion air fans.
7. Install a larger cold water tank to replace the several smaller tanks which are badly corroded and too small to meet existing water demand.
8. Install a boiler blow down heat recovery system.
9. Install a new hot water tank supplying water to the boiler due to heavy corrosion (the tank has been repaired seven times in the last three years).
10. Replace the economisers that have ruptured due to poor design and installation.

The management team engaged a consultant to assess the economic choice between repairing and improving the existing site boilers or purchasing new boilers complete with all the required improvements to the boiler house. Building a new boiler house also has two additional advantages: (1) several booster pumps installed over the years can be removed and (2) higher energy efficiency could be attained from newer technologies. The economics of the two options is shown in Table 2.1.

Table 2.1   Economics of repairing a boiler and replacing a boiler plant

Description	Cost Savings	Capital Cost	Simple Payback (years)
Option 1 – Repair and upgrade existing boiler.	£149,000	£234,000	1.42
Option 2 – Decommission the existing boiler house and build new.	£299,000	£299,000	1.03
Incremental comparison between Option 2 and Option 1.	£150,000	£65,000	0.50

Based on the analysis above, if capital is available for investment, Option 2 yields the best returns on investment. If capital is constrained, Option 1 provides a lower cost and lower benefit choice.

Energy Efficiency Terms Used in Industry

Although the concept of energy efficiency is a simple concept, there are many different definitions of efficiency used in the industry and tailored to specific systems or equipment items. Manufacturers, and even governments, come up with many different terminologies and different ways to calculate energy efficiency. Sometimes, the definition of efficiency could be the same but the formulation to arrive at the efficiency figure is different.

Managers and engineers must be careful when using and/or being quoted energy efficiency figures. This section explores the most common definitions of energy efficiency used in the market:

1. gross efficiency and net efficiency
2. primary efficiency and delivered efficiency
3. instantaneous efficiency and average efficiency
4. technical efficiency and cost efficiency
5. composite efficiency ratings.

GROSS EFFICIENCY VS. NET EFFICIENCY

Gross efficiency and net efficiency are primarily associated with energy systems involving the burning of fuels. Examples of such systems are boilers, furnaces, incinerators, crackers, reformers, direct-fired turbine drives, gas engines and gas turbines.

All fuels – gaseous, liquid, coal or waste-derived – contain carbon and hydrogen atoms in different ratios. In the most simplistic form, during any combustion process the carbon combines with oxygen in air to form carbon dioxide and oxygen combines with hydrogen to form water. In the combustion process, water is normally found in a vapour form.

$$C + O_2 \rightarrow CO_2$$
$$2H_2 + O_2 \rightarrow 2H_2O$$

During combustion, the chemical energy stored in the fuel is released as heat. Scientists and engineers quantify the amount of heat released from various fuels in a calorimeter. The results are tabulated as gross or net calorific values (also known is some countries as higher or lower heating values).

Gross calorific value is the amount of energy released when all the water vapour is condensed. This represents the maximum energy that can be extracted from the fuel – a theoretical heating energy. Net calorific value is the amount of energy released when the water vapour is still in the vapour form.

The majority of industrial and domestic processes do not condense the water from the combustion process for the following reasons.

- Many fuels contain sulphur or chlorine. When burned, these elements form acids. If these are condensed together with the water vapour, these acids would corrode the plant machinery.
- In a work environment, combustion processes rarely take place in the open due to the health and safety reasons associated with the build-up of carbon dioxide and hot ashes and their exposure to employees. Combustion processes nearly always happen in enclosed environments, and carbon dioxide is extracted from the process and vented to the atmosphere at height through a stack. Energy is required to vent the combustion products through the stack and is supplied by the hot gases. As a result, less useful energy is available for the manufacturing process.

The efficiency figure calculated based on gross calorific value is known as the gross efficiency. By the same logic, net efficiency is calculated from net calorific value.

When calculating the efficiency of burning the same fuel, gross efficiency figures are always lower than the net efficiency values. As shown in Table 2.2, depending on the type of fuel burned, the difference between the gross and net calorific value, and hence its efficiency, can be up to 16 per cent.

Table 2.2   Gross and net calorific value of some common fuels

Type of fuel	Gross calorific value (MJ/kg)	Net calorific value (MJ/kg)	Difference
Hydrogen	143.0	121.0	15%
Natural gas	55.6	50.1	10%
Gas oil	45.6	42.8	6%
Light fuel oil	43.5	41.1	6%
Heavy fuel oil	42.9	40.5	6%
Coal (lignite)	21.5	20.2	6%
Coal (bituminous)	23.8	22.6	5%
Wood chip	11.9	10.0	16%
Poultry litter	8.8	7.4	16%
Municipal waste	9.5	8.7	8%

PRIMARY EFFICIENCY VS. DELIVERED EFFICIENCY

Primary energy is the fossil-based fuels used directly in a unit operation, e.g., gas, oil and coal. The energy content is usually released by combustion. Very frequently, it is inconvenient to use primary energy directly in a process. It is converted into different forms and transported to the plant where it is being consumed. Common forms of delivered energy are electricity, steam, compressed air, chilled water, refrigeration, hot oil and industrial gases such as nitrogen and hydrogen.

If we remember the conservation of energy described earlier, every time energy is converted from one form to another there is a loss in its energy content. Let us use electricity generated by a conventional power plant as an example: the typical efficiency of a gas turbine is approximately 38 per cent. Referring to the definition of energy efficiency described earlier, this means that for every 100 units of electricity exported from the power plant to the electricity distribution it would have to put in 277 units of fuel. Depending on the geography and sources of electricity, the difference between primary energy efficiency and delivered energy efficiency can be as much as four times.

Modern-day power plants use a combined cycle technique and have a typical efficiency of 55–60 per cent. There is also a technique called combined heat and power (CHP), where the plant generates heat (steam and/or hot water) and electricity. Such plants have efficiency typically in the region of 80 per cent. These techniques will increase the primary energy efficiency.

INSTANTANEOUS EFFICIENCY VS. AVERAGE EFFICIENCY

Many manufacturers and equipment suppliers define the energy efficiency of equipment or processes at a specified set of conditions. Examples of such conditions are sea level elevation, temperature, pressure, humidity, running the equipment at full load etc. Trade associations, international and national standards provide a set of standard 'conditions' for use by equipment suppliers. These conditions allow similar equipment and plant machinery to be compared and benchmarked. These standards also allow product differentiation, research and development.

While it is beneficial to be able to compare the performance of equipment and plant machinery on an apple-to-apple basis, in reality a significant number of plant equipment operates at conditions other than those specified. The efficiencies under these conditions can be very different from the quoted efficiencies from the manufacturer.

It is important to obtain and check the energy efficiency data to ensure that energy efficiency is calculated according to the actual plant operating conditions.

Many good and reputable manufacturers and equipment suppliers can, and frequently do, provide efficiency curves at different loads and corrections curves to correct for different conditions. Examples of energy efficiency curves for a range of steam boilers at various loads are shown in Figure 2.3:

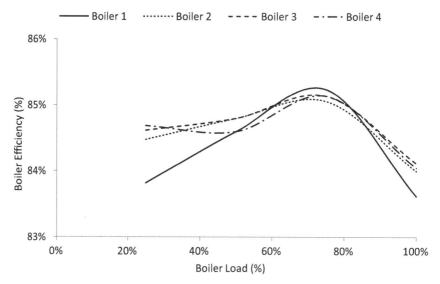

Figure 2.3   Typical boiler efficiency curves at various loads

TECHNICAL EFFICIENCY VS. COST EFFICIENCY

Another very common energy efficiency term used by consultants and contractors is energy efficiency based on economic value. These units of energy efficiency can be measured and quoted in either the absolute energy consumed to produce the product or services; energy consumed per unit of product; or, in some cases, energy consumed per unit of raw materials fed into the process.

These types of units are very commonly used by licensed processes, proprietary machinery manufacturers and specialised management consultants. These benchmark figures are useful to compare month-to-month within the same plant and between similar plants. However, the usability of such data is meaningless when comparing products that are made from different process technology or raw materials.

When utilising readily available benchmark figures in comparing more common plant machinery such as boilers, chillers, pumps and motors, energy efficiency based on economic values will not be directly comparable without additional measurements and data analysis. As an example, a heat pump typically has a coefficient of performance (COP) of 4. This is the technical efficiency of a heat pump where it generates four units of heat using one unit of electricity (see Case Study 2.2). If this heat pump is to be used in a business for heating and if the electricity is five times more expensive than natural gas, this heat pump is more costly to operate than the existing means of heating using natural gas. If the electricity costs four times that of natural gas, investing in the heat pump becomes cost neutral.

CASE STUDY 2.2   CHILLER REPLACEMENT OPTIONS

A large hospital building uses a duty-standby 3 MWt medium-temperature hot water (MTHW) absorption chiller to provide cooling for the building. Heat is rejected via a duty-standby water-cooled cooling tower. The current absorption chillers are more than 15 years old and are beyond economic repair. The cooling towers have been recently refurbished.

The Engineering Manager has received a quotation to replace the existing absorption chiller with a like-for-like replacement. To satisfy the hospital's policy for energy efficiency at design, he commissioned a study aimed at identifying the proposal as the most efficient option available.

With a COP ranging from 1.12 to 1.17 over its entire operating range, it is among the higher COP machines available on the market. Assuming an average COP of 1.15, this absorption chiller provides 3 MWt of cooling using 2.6 MWt of hot water, and rejects 5.6 MWt at the cooling tower.*

However, when comparing the proposal with alternative technologies, i.e., mechanical chillers, the proposal becomes inefficient. A state-of-the-art mechanical chiller, when properly designed, can have a COP ranging from 4 to 7 over its operating range.**

For comparison, assuming an average COP of 5 for the mechanical chiller, it provides 3 MWt of cooling with an input of 0.6 MWt and rejects 3.6 MWt at the cooling tower. In this case study, a mechanical chiller is more energy efficient because it:

1.   Consumes 0.6 MWt vs. 2.6 MWt.
2.   Rejects 3.6 MWt vs. 5.6 MWt.

The footprint of a mechanical chiller is also smaller and it is cheaper to purchase.

---

*   A COP of 1.12 means that that the chiller provides 1.12 kWt of cooling with an input energy of 1 kW. In this case, the input energy is in terms of hot water.

**   Care should be taken to ensure that the chiller and its associated systems are designed to match the maximum COP. A poorly designed system using the most efficient mechanical chiller could make the chiller inefficient.

COMPOSITE EFFICIENCY RATINGS

In recent years the terms 'seasonal efficiency' and 'integrated part load efficiency' have been introduced by several governments and equipment manufacturers. These figures use a composite of 20 years' average weather, taking into consideration the changes in temperature throughout the year and its impact on equipment loadings to compute the energy efficiency rating of energy consuming equipment. Care should be taken when using these figures for the following reasons:

- A composite efficiency rating uses a reference location to calculate efficiency. The weather records of, say, London will be drastically different from, say, Malaysia. If a rating is calculated in the USA, a rating generated for New York will be different for Atlanta because both cities have different weather profiles.
- The ratings also assume a desired operating point. For example, the seasonal efficiency rating for an air conditioning unit could be calculated to heat a room to 19°C. However, all air conditioners provide a temperature controller, allowing the user to set a temperature. If the user selects a temperature set point which is different from the figure used to calculate the seasonal efficiency, the real efficiency may be different.

When assessing energy efficiency as applied to an existing business and its potential for improvement, it is vital that the correct and appropriate definition for efficiency is selected and requested from the various suppliers.

Other Confusing Terminologies Used

So far, the concept of energy conservation, energy cost and energy efficiency have been defined. Here is a longer list of confusing terminologies used in the industry.

- *Coefficient of Performance (COP)* – the efficiency of chillers and heat pumps are normally quoted as COP. This is the inverse of efficiency, defined as follows:

$$COP = \frac{\text{Useful Chilling Energy}}{\text{Energy Input to Chiller Machine}}$$

- *Coefficient of System Performance (COsP)* – is used to indicate the COP of the chilling system as a whole. It includes all energy consuming units connected to the chilling system, e.g., pumps and heat rejection units such as air-cooled or water-cooled cooling towers. This, therefore, gives the overall efficiency of a chiller system installed in the business.
- *Energy Baseline* – a quantitative relationship that describes how energy consumption varies with the economic activities of the business. The energy baseline can also be used to measure energy reduction achieved from implementing energy reduction projects. This concept is developed later in Part 4.
- *Energy Performance Indicator* – a qualitative or quantitative key performance indicator to measure energy performance. It can be expressed as a ratio, e.g., energy efficiency, or as an energy baseline.
- *Renewable Energy* – non-fossil fuel energy sources, e.g., biomass, wood, waste, solar, wind, tidal etc.[1]
- *Carbon Zero/Carbon Neutral* – A business is said to be carbon zero or carbon neutral if it does not consume any fossil-based fuels (i.e., it consumes only renewably sourced energy) in its business activities or offsets its fossil fuel based CO_2 emissions by participating in schemes to grow renewably sourced energy crops (e.g., planting trees in certified plantations).
- *Demand-Side Management/Load Shedding* – are activities to move the peak (or maximum) energy demand by 'shedding' the peaks. This could be achieved in one of two ways: (1) scheduling and managing the start-up of machines such that not all of the major plant and machines operate at the same time; (2) storing the energy (e.g., thermal storage systems) during off-peak periods to be used during peak times.

---

1   The original renewable energy sources were from hydro power, geothermal heat and power, and from biomass such as municipal waste and food crops. These were termed 1st generation renewable energy. Newer renewable energy sources have moved away from food crops and include wind, solar, tidal and non-food crop based biomass and algae.

3

Energy Efficient Operations

How do Energy Inefficiencies Arise?

As a rule of thumb, only about 40 per cent of the inefficiency and poor use of energy is as the direct result of poor design. Figure 3.1 shows the breakdown of inefficiencies classification. This leaves roughly 60 per cent of the inefficiencies and ineffectiveness that can be controlled, managed and minimised.

All capital expenditure is approved and implemented with a specific benefit to the business. Senior management has high expectations of all the plant and machinery purchased and installed. Poorly designed and installed plant and machinery consume more energy. These inefficiencies are frequently not identified and rectified prior to signing off the project as complete. At other times, the plant and machinery are signed off in a hurry in order to be put into immediate productive use.

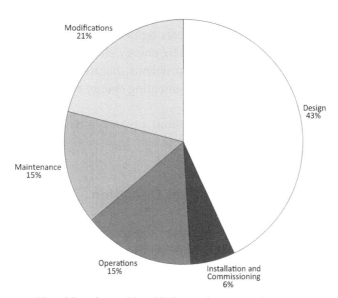

Figure 3.1   Classification of inefficiency in operations

Insufficient or poorly organised training for operations and maintenance may lead the plant and machinery to fail prematurely or more often. The overall result is high levels of apathy and even resignations among business owners and senior managers, plus the associated costs to repair the plant machinery. If this is not done well, performance spirals, generating more apathy and even higher costs.

In order to break free from the spiral of poor energy efficiency, it is important to recognise and take effective action to improve efficiency and cost savings. When improving existing and/or installing new plant and machines, it is important to apply good engineering standards: lessons learned from past experience need to be incorporated. The root cause of failures needs to be identified and avoided in the new equipment, otherwise the same failure modes will reoccur.

Improvements may come from changes in design, operation or operating procedure, maintenance practices, modifications and/or from installation and commissioning practices. Many tools and techniques are available in the market place to assist and support the implementation of energy management and efficiency improvement programmes. Use of new technologies, new approaches and new control methods is constantly marketed by various companies. All of these techniques and technologies have a novel intent and form a vision of the end results.

A good training and education regime must be provided and regularly audited to ensure that the machinery is operated and maintained according to the intended use and specifications. Adequate and appropriate monitoring and controls such as statistical process control (SPC) and preventive maintenance should be used to track and continuously tighten control variables to improve efficiency. However, when implementing energy efficiency at work, managers are faced with ongoing operational problems, failures and their resolution. Reconciling these issues and still implementing energy reduction programmes may be a challenge.

As a gentle reminder, a vision without a plan is a wish. A plan without a timetable is a wish list.

Working Towards Energy Efficient Operation

Armed with the need for energy reduction and knowledge of how inefficiencies may arise, we now focus on strategic issues: how do we implement an energy reduction programme, or where do we start or what strategy do we use?

Before embarking on an energy reduction programme, a manager needs to know where energy is used in the business, and must prioritise, define and adhere to the objectives of the energy reduction programme and its performance measures. Setting an achievable policy, objectives and target is covered in Chapter 19. This can be in the form of health and safety, reliability, efficiency, cost per unit product and speed of change.

You may ask how health and safety and plant integrity integrate with energy reduction. A holistic view and approach is essential to avoid the three common pitfalls in energy reduction:

1. Wasting time and effort improving the wrong processes or part of the process.
2. Optimising a unit operation or process to produce savings that are of no economic value.
3. Implementing a savings project that has a knock-on effect elsewhere that has not been assessed.

An ideal vision for a holistic approach would mean zero safety incidents or no near-misses; good occupational health management; good and sustainable environmental stewardship; reliable assets with high availability; and first time right throughput. Superior performance assets described in this chapter, Chapter 4 and in Chapter 11, provide a platform to build up opportunities for raw material savings, energy savings and business life cycle cost savings.

Once the strategy, policy, objectives and targets are agreed, managers should implement the strategy. This will always involve some level of risk because it is not possible to know with 100 per cent certainty and 100 per cent accuracy how the energy reduction projects will turn out. This may be due to uncertainty about the existing equipment performance, raw material input, customer demand, production or service output, unpredictable competition, and changing technology (or a combination thereof).

Energy Efficiency in New Businesses

With the exception of a limited example of manufacturing plants, the design of virtually all processes follow what engineers call the 'onion' model of process design, as shown in Figure 3.2 on the following page. It begins with the reactor or any primary equipment generating the product, albeit in unrefined form. For simplicity of explanation, we call this the reactor.

The reactor is supported by a series of separation and recycling systems to treat and refine the product into a marketable form. The reactors, separation and recycle streams will inevitably involve the exchange of heat in heat exchangers (depending on application, these may also known as condensers, evaporators

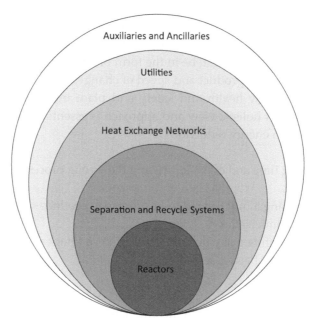

Figure 3.2   Onion model of process design

and reboilers). These heat exchangers are the next stage of the design process, followed by the transformers, switchgears, boilers, cooling towers, chillers, compressors etc. supplying the process. Finally, all of these systems need to be controlled at a certain rate to achieve optimal manufacturing conditions. The instrumentation systems, control systems and display systems are finally designed.

The design of a commercial building follows a similar onion model. The concept and unique features of the building is defined; then the ventilation system is designed followed by the heating, cooling and power systems. The monitoring and control systems can then be designed and specified.

In addition to the above, the onion would also have to fit into:

- Business requirements (economic constraints, raw material availability and economies of scale).
- Existing and known health, safety and environmental regulations
- Governmental controls.
- Local economies.
- Social responsibilities.
- Conformance to the relevant standards, codes and industrial best practices.

In the description of the onion model there exist at least seven locations where two or more parts of the process meet and where energy reduction opportunities can be found:

1. Raw material into reactor.
2. Reactor to separation and recycle system.
3. Reactor, separation and recycle system to heat exchanger.
4. Heat exchange networks to utilities.
5. All of the above to controls and instrumentation system.
6. Controls and instrumentation systems to operators.
7. Operators to management.

From the number of areas where energy savings can be found and realised, if a new plant were to be built it would be best to factor in energy efficiency at the business case, concept design and feasibility design stages of the project – it may be very costly and/or too late to do so once the plant is in operation.

Designing a new plant will benefit from incorporating the following into the design and avoid the need to spend additional capital to replace equipment or to make expansive alterations at a later stage:

- Operating history and operating experience.
- Root cause of previous failures.
- New and improved materials and/or technique of construction.
- New and improved process technology.
- Use of modern and advance design technique.
- Use of modern control techniques.
- Use of modern energy and utilities systems.

Energy Efficiency in Existing Sites

The strategy to save energy in existing businesses is similar to new businesses. Figure 3.3 represents a typical manufacturing energy consumption profile against some constraints, e.g., minimum energy consumption or acceptable quality of production. A starting point towards improving energy efficiency is to set a realistic target and/or baseline for measurement. Four basic types of energy baselines are used and commonly found in companies to measure the success of their energy reduction programme:

- Baseline at the top.
- Baseline at the middle.

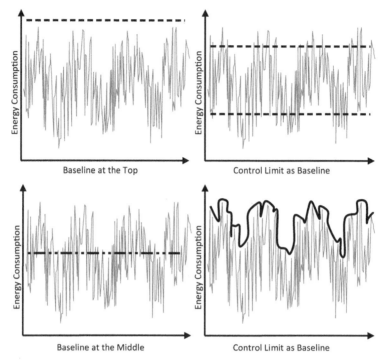

Figure 3.3   Setting baselines for improvements

- Variable baseline.
- Control limits.

Setting a baseline at the top would mean that the plant is already consuming less than expected and that no effort is required to improve energy efficiency for the plant. This baseline defeats the purpose of implementing an energy reduction programme.

As can be seen from Figure 3.3, the energy consumption is a range of values. This range can be expressed statistically as capability. Setting a baseline at the middle would at first seem an ideal target for improvement, but in practice it means that 50 per cent of the time the plant would already be efficient. If the plant is efficient for 50 per cent of the time, why is it not the other 50 per cent of the time? It also does not provide evidence that setting the baseline at the mean value would mean that the plant's actual mean energy consumption is at 50 per cent levels.

Increasingly, some consultants and contractors are recommending variable baselines. It can be proven that such techniques, when implemented, can bring about 3–5 per cent energy savings. This technique would normally require investment in a high-powered computer and advance process controls. The costs of implementing such systems are high and proportional to the number of control points.

Utilising control limits as baselines defines the upper and lower limits for energy consumption over a specific range of production. The reduction in energy consumed may centre on the mean of the energy data. It may also converge above or below the mean. This is because many combinations of factors may directly and indirectly affect the energy consumption and the efficiency of plant equipment.

A good energy management programme will identify and remove this 'background noise' such that energy consumption is directly proportional to the volume of products produced. By implementing various energy efficiency techniques over time, this range can be tightened, reducing the variation on energy consumption. The convergence of energy between a control limit has three benefits:

1. It increases the confidence of the energy baseline when evaluating energy reduction projects.
2. It increases the accuracy of predicting future energy consumption.
3. It can be used to identify energy deviation and equipment upsets, and to apply corrective actions before failure actually occurs.

Depending on the state of the plant machinery and the projects implemented, the energy saving range is 10–30 per cent or more.

This method has proven to be successful and sustainable over a long period and would represent the highest possible return on investment by the company. Many examples have been reported by the UK Office of Energy Efficiency Deployment (EEDO) and the Sustainable Energy Authority of Ireland (SEAI). At this point, if the management decides to implement advance technologies, additional energy savings can be generated.

Energy Efficiency and Plant Life Cycle

Figure 3.4 shows the typical life cycle of a manufacturing plant. Very frequently, managers and engineers only start to consider energy reduction and energy efficiency at the operations and maintenance stage.

As demonstrated previously, energy efficiency can and should be considered as early as when the business case is being developed. A sample of factors influencing energy throughout four stages in a life cycle is listed in Table 3.1, and illustrated in Case Study 3.1.

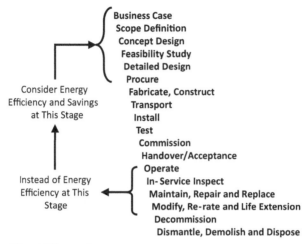

Figure 3.4   Plant life cycle

Table 3.1 Energy efficiency at four stages in a life cycle

Concept Stage	Design Stage	Operational Stage	Maintenance Stage
• Avoid using energy • Minimise energy where necessary	• Specify efficient prime movers and generators • Heat integration • Reliability and long in-service time • System efficiency • Minimise the need for reprocessing	• Operating procedures • Operating conditions · • Unit operating and machinery efficiency • Fuel and energy mix • Managing utility systems • Managing import and export streams	• Cleaning of machinery • Insulation of equipment • Prevention of leaks • Maintenance of energy and utilities systems • Service schedules • Prioritisation of maintenance systems

CASE STUDY 3.1 INCORPORATING ENERGY EFFICIENCY DURING DESIGN

In a speciality chemical manufacturing plant, a capital project has been requested by the production team. The project requires a 'sump and pump' to pump 60 m^3/hr of acid to the neutralisation plant, a distance of 250 m away, at a height of 3 m. The acid is at 50°C and contains 10 per cent abrasive and insoluble solids. This acid liberates fume at this temperature, which is a health and safety concern – plus a nuisance to operate and maintain the plant machinery. The team have also identified that the most appropriate routing of the pipeline requires 12 × 90° bends.

The design information available is depicted pictorially in Figure 3.5. In a classic design department there is sufficient information to begin the design process. However, to incorporate energy efficiency into the design, the designer would incorporate a VSD for the pump and the design would be considered to be energy efficient.

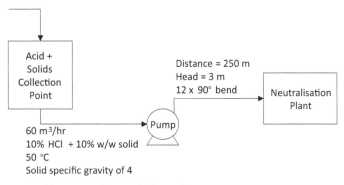

Figure 3.5   Request for capital project

To maximise the potential for energy efficiency and to reduce the capital cost for the new plant requires a fundamental thought process on each of the parameters provided. They are listed graphically in Figure 3.6.

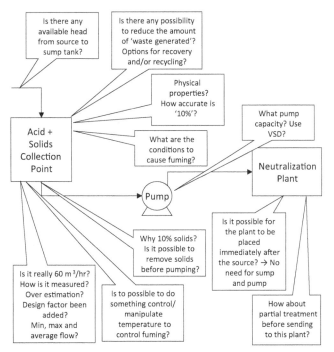

Figure 3.6   Capital project including energy efficiency

This information is more difficult for the design team to obtain. However, answers to this information not only influences the design parameters for the project, it also ensures that the new plant will be fit for purpose – minimising the design margins, energy consumed and the capital required for the new plant.

The design options with an impact on energy efficiency are as follows.

- Is it really 60 m³/hr? How is it measured? How accurate is the information? What is the minimum, average and maximum flow? Has any design factor been included?
- Is it possible to minimise the generation of 'waste'? How about recovering it or recycling it for use in another area?
- Why 50°C? What are the conditions to cause it to fume?
- Why does it generate 10 per cent solids? Can the solids be removed before pumping?
- Is it possible to have a pre-treatment before sending to neutralisation of the plant?
- Is there any available head pressure from the source area? Possibilities for VSD and feed forward and feedback controls?

To summarise the key strategic points:

1. Know where energy is used in the business.
2. Where possible, avoid using energy.
3. Limit the demand of energy. Apply measures to reduce, reuse and recycle energy.
4. Always relate it to the profitability of the company. A simple method would be to express this as a reduction in energy cost. An alternative and equally successful method would be to express it as additional capacity and/or production 'available' for sale.

4

Framework for Sustainable Energy Reduction

With a good strategy in place, it needs to be implemented to reduce energy consumed. There are many choices for tools, techniques and technology available in the market to reduce energy use.

There are many articles, advertisements and leaflets marketing 'new and improved' techniques and technologies promoting better or higher energy efficiencies. Each technique has been developed based on its own set of assumptions. Each has its own advantages, strengths and a fair share of failures. How do we choose? Which techniques will guarantee success?

To borrow a phrase from Michael Porter, 'execution [of a plan] is about carrying out strategic choices made [by the management]'. 'Practices that work well in one company may [and may also not] have the same effect in another company' (Rosenzweig, 2007: 170, 174).

Figure 4.1 shows a model for energy efficiency maturity. It is similar to the waste management hierarchy model. As the company moves upwards towards each step, an increase in knowledge of the specific energy systems, trust and accountability and capital expenditure is required in order to specify and implement these improvement projects. The energy reduction potential will also be correspondingly larger. This framework is developed to identify and prioritise actions to reduce and eliminate the background noise described in Chapter 3 and to generate the biggest energy reduction with the lowest capital cost.

Energy savings can come from all plant machinery within a business. It is not limited to any specific piece of equipment. In the market, there are many consultants and suppliers that specialise in specific areas of energy savings in utility systems: steam, compressed air, cooling water, chilled water, motors and drives, and power quality. This is purely due to utilities being the most common denominator in many businesses. The best practices to each of these systems would be similar from one industry to another. There is a lot of literature on best practices published in the market and online.

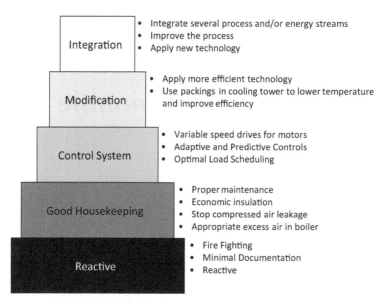

Figure 4.1   Energy efficiency maturity model

There are also some consultants and suppliers who specialise in less common areas such as reliability, furnaces, and distillation and separation systems, while others specialise in pushing the envelope of modern technology: advance process control, dynamic simulation, computational dynamics. There are also some consultants and suppliers whose capabilities are process or machine specific.

To implement a successful energy reduction programme, managers and engineers must recognise the fact that each consultant and supplier has their strengths and limitations. The key is to implement projects while not losing sight of the overall objective and the effect of each project on the other plant machinery.

Improving energy efficiency and reducing energy cost is also not just about implementing best practices. Implementing best practices requires a certain mindset involving shared company goals, company culture and proven results. Lack of best practices is often not the only reason for poor plant performance or high energy cost.

Commitment from the management to allocate resources and to take action toward improving efficiency is required. A team can be formed to assist and support the management by understanding the quantity of energy used in the plant; the strength and weaknesses of implementing and sustaining an energy reduction programme; the needs of the business, and by anticipating any likely barriers to implementation.

When this is complete, the management can work with and via the team to develop an energy management policy statement, set objectives and targets and prepare detailed action plans for their implementation. Roles and responsibilities should be allocated to prioritise improvement actions and investment requirements. Barriers to implementation need to be resolved.

Once improvement programmes are implemented, they need to be continually monitored and controlled. A progress review needs to be put in place for continual feedback, and continuously improved. Frequently, all of the projects will not be implemented as a one-off investment and/or achieve full savings in one step. The team will need to reassess the energy requirements and repeat the improvement cycle as illustrated in Figure 4.2. The concept of management systems is developed in Chapter 16.

A well-designed energy management and energy reduction programme can save significant amounts of capital expenditure. The team's challenge would be to select a pathway forward for maximum effectiveness and efficiency. This will involve selecting the right task and performing the task well. The easiest

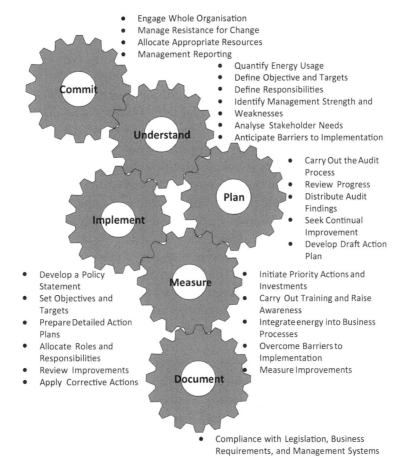

Figure 4.2   Plan-Do-Check-Act cycle

and most obvious would be to start with the cheapest and most cost effective opportunities, i.e., the 'low-hanging fruit'.

For many manufacturing plants and commercial buildings, good housekeeping is a starting point to bring large energy variation under control. Energy reduction projects should be aimed at identifying and reducing the observed energy variation as shown in Figure 3.3.

Energy reduction opportunities classified as housekeeping include the reduction in wastage, leaks, machinery idle time, production rate losses, untended taps and hoses. It also applies to using simple and readily available best practices such as implementing better cleaning methods, using sprays in place of 'fill and drain', and using a vacuum cleaner instead of a compressed air blower. Investment in employee education and training to increase awareness of and the need for energy efficiency should be complemented by the adoption of a zero tolerance policy for inefficiencies and ineffective use of utilities.

The rewards for good housekeeping in a business are widely recognised but rarely practiced. The advantages include best return on expenditure, low (or on some cases no) capital investment and less apparent energy wastage. There is no threat to operations or processes as the risks involved are minimal. However, it requires a constant effort to maintain high standards. In practice, money-saving housekeeping has a habit of disappearing over time. A good baseline for management control is essential and should be based on consistency and the smallest energy variation in energy data. There is little point looking for other energy savings unless housekeeping is under control.

The next category of energy saving measure is classified as control systems. Energy reduction projects in this category further reduce the energy variations seen during the housekeeping phase by introducing better operating conditions for existing energy users and utilities. A thorough examination of energy and utilities efficiency, system half-life etc. is introduced at this stage. The aim will be to tighten the controls of existing processes and utilities, requiring them to operate closer to the control limits. This will maximise efficiency, reduce excess usage, increase cycles of concentration, reduce blow down. Better control and measurement systems may be commissioned at this stage to facilitate accurate readings and track improvements. High efficiency motors, soft starts and VSD are also included at this phase.

There will be a higher investment required at this phase. The corresponding rewards for tighter operating control systems are reduced energy and utilities usage and higher process efficiency. However, as the energy reduction opportunities now involve process and manufacturing operations, they may cause other problems that affect product quality. For a well-designed and implemented energy reduction programme, the impact of these problems is small, identified early in its implementation and can be rectified. It requires more supervision and management of these projects and the associated measurement and monitoring system than the housekeeping phase.

Good housekeeping and control systems are typically implemented at a unit operations level, i.e., boilers, compressor trains, distillation trains etc. The relative energy savings potential and its cost of implementation are shown in Figure 4.3.

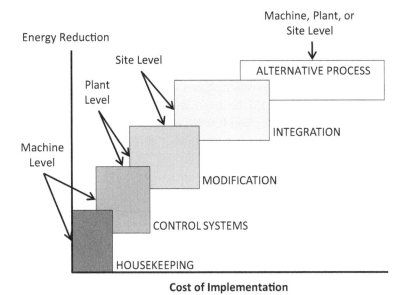

Figure 4.3   Energy saving measures and their cost of implementation

When managers and employees are successful in instilling good housekeeping and implement control systems, the business will be ready to exploit higher energy reduction opportunities from performing simple process modification to the existing facility. This will include: the reuse and recycling of thermal energy, ideally locally; direct use without the need for tanks, pipe work and pumps; waste heat recovery boilers, pre-heaters and economisers; redesign to use less energy, e.g., close the open condensate systems, use of new packing in separation columns.

These energy reduction opportunities can bring about further reduction in energy consumption, product and raw material recovery. With the modifications and recycling of energy there may be a better chance to transfer the risk of contamination from the producing process to the receiving process, resulting in poorer product quality, contamination with trace materials, scaling, fouling, corrosion or microbiological growth in the system. It may also make the plant and machines more complicated to troubleshoot. There will be a need for better control and monitoring for all the same problems as identified in the previous phase, but they are greatly enhanced and become much more apparent and at a faster pace.

Control systems and process modification are typically, and more commonly, implemented at the plant level. Further integration of processes and utilities at site level is the next natural progression for higher energy reduction. Potential areas for process integration include thermal pinch analysis, process intensification, optimisation and enhancement, plant de-bottlenecking and uprating.

The advantage of successful process integration projects can be measured in the value of energy recovered and also in product and raw material savings. With less energy being consumed, less energy will be wasted. However, it would inevitably cost more than the other phases described earlier, more equipment may go wrong and it would be even more complicated to troubleshoot. Therefore, it would require a good level of management supervision to design a successful energy reduction programme at this phase and to avoid over integration of the process.

The highest available form of energy efficiency would be from a step change perspective by commissioning an alternative and more modern process. This could range from installing and operating a combined heat and power (CHP) system, using evaporative cooling, evaporative humidifiers, using renewably sourced energy, refitting an existing steam reformer with the latest designs and improvements, to applying dynamic simulation and predictive controls and a complete change of process technology.

Before applying new technology for a step change in performance, it is essential to understand where energy should and should not be used. Cost, practicality, management and risk need to be weighed carefully before sanctioning such an option. The specific alternative process may not be 'off the shelf' and would require vision, investigation, research and many months of plant trials.

The rewards for using an alternative process are numerous. While the financial reward may be negative in the short and medium term, it may give rise to improved operability, reduced health and safety risk, less waste water, smaller and simpler waste treatment – and may even have a simpler measurement and control requirement.

One of the risks associated with an alternative process is that it may eventually change one problem area for another in the process. Poorly considered and planned alternatives may also be less efficient and/or environmentally poor. As such, this phase may be best suited for new plants and green developments rather than in old plants where capital has already been invested.

The exact energy reduction for each business and location will depend heavily on where they are in the energy efficiency maturity model, where they want to be and how fast the business wants to close the gap.

5

Barriers to Implementing and Sustaining Energy Reduction Programmes

Up to this point, we have covered why we need to save energy, how inefficiencies arise, a holistic strategy towards energy reduction, and a common sense approach to implementing energy reduction. To conclude Part 1 we will explore the barriers to implementing and sustaining corporate energy reduction programmes. What are the principal stumbling blocks of failed programmes?

Many managers and engineers assume that implementing a long-term energy reduction programme is simply about addressing the above issues. It should be a seamless process – each company having their best and most useful methodologies to do so.

The reality is that each organisation (and to a large extent departments within the same organisation) consist of 'islands', with major gaps between departmental function, methods, technologies and communication that restrict effective management of energy.

Some of the most common reasons why many projects fail are:

- There is no measurement data.
- Wrong measurement is being used.
- Instead of making improvements, measurements are being manipulated to make people or things look better.
- There is no execution of agreed plans.
- There is excessive need for very accurate measurement data.

Management will only get what they are prepared to walk past. A successful and sustainable energy reduction programme must foster a common understanding between the employees and the management. Both accept that each has their own targets and success measures, and work together towards achieving this target.

A good and sustainable energy reduction programme must promote greater understanding within the company by recognising the contributions of each department in a coordinated manner. The challenges an organisation will face in implementing a sustainable programme are as follows:

- Organisational requirements.
- Human resources.
- Equipment design.
- Operational losses.
- Project limitations.
- Wrong expectations.
- Stuck in a perpetual cycle of perfectionism.

Organisational Requirements

Although sharing a common interest and shared values among all stakeholders is an essential component in managing energy, real organisations have to face constant trade-offs, negotiation and interdependences between business owner, manager, designer, operator, maintainer, customer and regulator.

1. *Business owner*: realising maximum productivity of capital; integrating differing interests towards company interests.
2. *Manager*: balances the efficiency and effectiveness of business inputs (raw materials, human resources etc.), outputs (products/services, waste etc.) with the constraints of business (finance, regulatory, legal, clients etc.).
3. *Designer*: designing the production process (by means of adaptation of equipment) in a continually changing environment.
4. *Operator*: actual making of products, using the equipment that is placed at the user's disposal.
5. *Maintainer*: maintaining equipment, sustaining the process to produce products that conform to business needs and actual plant design parameters.
6. *Customer*: purchasing consistently good-quality products and/or services at good value.
7. *Regulator*: compliance with the rules and regulations of the land.

Each of the above has differing focuses and interests within the business. Their vocabulary used in daily communication may also be different. When they are not aligned, each of the seven groups pulls the business in a different direction.

Continuous conflicting interests can result in cyclic patterns of energy cost to the business and management efforts in reducing energy consumption and cost. It is important to engage with all groups of people constantly in a language every group can relate to and appreciate.

To meet the needs of all seven groups of people, it is common for new plants and machinery to be designed and installed based on allocated budget and time and space constraints instead of energy efficiency and engineering best practice.

Human Resources

When investments are made to train employees in developing and implementing energy reduction programmes, frequently it is the senior management that is selected for detailed training. However, senior managers have the least time to learn as they have highly pressing areas of concern – to keep the company up and running. New employees, on the other hand, have the highest propensity for learning but are least likely to be selected for training. An appropriate balance needs to be achieved between selecting the right training for the right level of employees, and with the right accountabilities.

During the implementation of energy reduction projects from each of the efficiency categories described in Chapter 4, personal interest and time spent to ensure a good job is performed is inversely proportional to the technical challenges. This is shown in Figure 5.1 on the next page. Matching the responsibilities and accountabilities to the right level of employee is very important.

For some organisations, there is a lack of human resources to focus on management of energy consumption and improve its efficiency of consumption. These companies devote maximum resources to the essential task: production and projects to increase production. As such, there is a lack of skills and experience in the implementation of energy efficiency initiatives.

Equipment Design

Latest developments in technology generally have led to more energy efficient equipment being manufactured and sold on the market. However, these devices may not be perfect and are not without faults or side-effects on plant operations, and therefore need careful consideration and selection. An example would be a poorly specified VSD that may cause more harmonics in the electrical system.

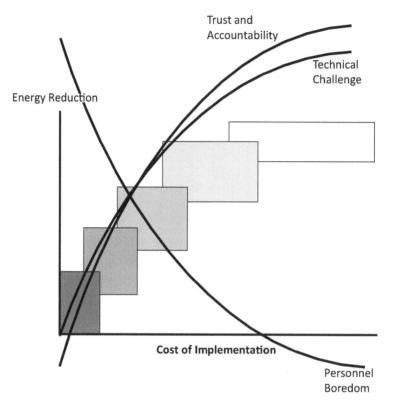

Figure 5.1   Corporate interest superimposed on the implementation plan

One of the factors commonly overlooked is the overdesign factors used when designing a plant and during specifying equipment and plant machinery. From plant conception to commissioning, many levels of overdesign factors and safety factors are applied in the design and selection of unit operations and equipments. Installing and operating these processes and equipment results in inefficient use of energy as more energy is supplied than required per unit product produced.

Consider a pump with a process power requirement of 20 kW: 10 per cent is typically added for head and flow by the designer; another 10 per cent is added by the design checker to ensure that the pump will work when installed. This specification is forwarded to the purchasing department, which will purchase the next available frame size. In the actual design and manufacture of the pump, an internal safety margin of 10–20 per cent is normally added. This pump, when installed, could end up with a 30–40 kW motor to drive 20 kW of actual load.

This pump would be more expensive to purchase, its utilisation would be low and have a high reactive power during operation. If the electricity tariff for the business contains a reactive power charge, there would be a penalty charge plus additional capital cost to purchase and operate power quality correction equipment.

Many consultants, contractors and equipment suppliers prefer to sell energy reduction projects by implementing 'black box' technologies. Very often, such projects can lead to contractual difficulties at a later stage, especially in baseline disputes and savings disputes. Disputes normally arise in five areas:

1. Claiming a saving in a particular area but there is no observable savings and/or the overall energy bill for the customer is increasing. For example, the industrial best practice for installing a boiler economiser would indicate an energy reduction of between 3 per cent and 7 per cent. However, when a company installed an economiser, the hotwell tank temperature had to be kept lower to avoid tripping out the boiler; there was an increase in energy consumption; and the economisers failed within six months of operation.

2. Claiming an energy reduction but other costs within the same area or in other area have gone up. For example, energy cost in compressors has gone down but compressor maintenance cost has gone up; or there is now insufficient air pressure to control the pneumatic valves, causing poor production quality, etc.

3. Claiming a saving by installing a 'black box' that eventually proved inappropriate for the operation of the company.

4. Little or no buy-in and/or participation of the management and employees to meet the high maintenance requirements of the 'black box'.

5. Claiming that the equipment is very efficient under laboratory conditions that are not representative of actual environmental conditions. For example, a heat pump typically has a coefficient of performance (COP) of 4. If the ambient temperature falls below 7°C, the condensers section of the heat pump ice up and stop working. To counter this, the machine operates in reverse until the condenser is defrosted. During this period, all energy used is to defrost the condenser and there is no useful energy output. In effect, the COP in cold weather is only half of the claimed COP. The COP of a heat pump can fall below 1 under extreme conditions (Strong, 2009).

Operational Losses

Operational losses are usually not easily visible, in spite of their size. Conventional cost management systems rarely capture all real costs attributable to the condition of assets and to maintenance practices. While costs of breakdowns and unavailability are captured, speed or flow rate reductions, off-spec productions, waste of fuels, utilities etc. are rarely recorded. As such, the maintenance of a reliable process operation is of importance and impacts the efficient and effective operability and efficient use of energy.

It is interesting to note that the asset management model and the safety management model (Figure 5.2) are also similar to the energy efficiency maturity model, both in terms of construction and make-up. Very frequently, assessing the maturity of a business in each model will yield the same result.

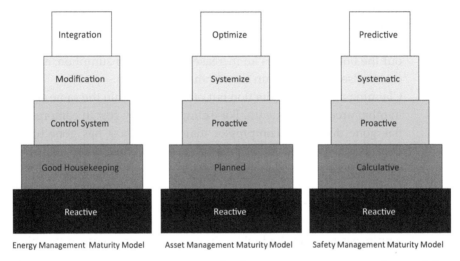

Figure 5.2   Asset management and safety management maturity models

Overall equipment effectiveness (OEE) has impacts on the energy consumption and hence its efficiency. Idle times and production rate reduction are sources of energy loss and inefficiency which are rarely considered and recorded. The ability to reduce downtime and the ability to schedule downtimes will significantly impact energy reduction and business profits.

Project Limitations

Another very common reason for failures in energy reduction projects is the fragmented approach to improvements being implemented. This can be most commonly found in:

- Forgetting to manage the behavioural and managerial aspects.

- Poorly defined project scope.
- Poorly assessed impacts on other parts of the business.
- Modification of parts of the plant being considered in isolation of other equipment.
- Root causes of historical failures were wrongly or inadequately assessed.

When assessing energy reduction opportunities, to a large extent many additional advantages are not quantifiable until they are implemented and measured. Reduction in quality losses, reduced maintenance, spares inventory, and de-bottlenecking and increasing the rated outputs are just some of the 'difficult to quantify' items.

Frequently, they can be estimated by managers and engineers based on operating experience and historical information. Also on the list are factors used in evaluating the viability of the projects: fuel and energy price fluctuations, production fluctuations, customs hold-ups, logistics, scheduling, spares, and training aspects of the project etc.

The development of energy reduction projects often involves various parties. In a typical project there may be contracts for construction, building, project management, independent consultants, fuel supply, operating and maintenance etc. Guarantee of performances and liabilities forms limitations on energy reduction project.

All these need to be identified and their risk managed early on during the project evaluation stage. Analysing the project to be implemented in relation to the whole system helps to define and pin down many of the above uncertainties.

Wrong Expectations

Not another consultant!!! There is no point in hiring consultants. Whatever they do, as soon as they leave, eventually everything goes back to normal.

Many companies have experienced or have used similar phrases themselves at one time or another. A company is made up of the (1) mood, (2) competency, (3) commitment and (4) intention of the people in it. When these come together, they create an organisational culture. Figure 5.3 shows a traditional coaching model for success. For a company to achieve sustainable energy efficiency operation, the company first and foremost needs to 'be' efficient: i.e., have an environment for promoting and encouraging energy efficiency; think about and reinforce ideas of energy efficiency in everything they do; be competent

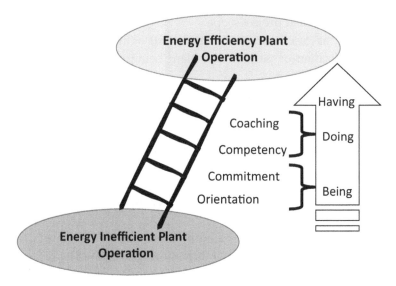

Figure 5.3   Relationship between organisational readiness and efficient
operations

and committed to creating an energy efficient workplace. Then the company
needs to 'do' efficient practices (behavioural, change the ways of working and
applying new technology) in order to 'have' an energy efficient operation. This
is called the 'Be-Do-Have' coaching model. This model is also known as the
'ABC' model as an acronym for 'Attitude-Behaviour-Consequence'.

Any other way around (Have-Be-Do, Do-Have-Be etc.) will have short-term
and unsustainable effects. Any reduction on energy cost would be temporary.
However, there are many consultants and many books published on 'having'
energy efficiency by doing this, this and this. It is very common to neglect the
management and human factors in energy reduction efforts by ploughing
straight into the technicalities. This is principally 'do-have' without the 'be'
component and would only be a quick fix – and would most probably find that
the issue will resurface sometime later.

For a majority of businesses with long chain of communication, top
management intentions for energy reduction and allocated resources is
lost during the communication process, leading to disconnection between
management and the employee.

Very often, employees tasked with implementing energy reduction are, in
their mind, conflicting with their existing job description and work objectives.
One such example is that a production worker's main job is to produce products.
Energy reduction does not produce products for sale.

Stuck in a Perpetual Cycle of Perfectionism

Many business managers will be aware that sometimes corporate initiatives can be stuck in a cycle where employees are too focused on getting every single detail of the energy reduction programme perfect. This need for perfectionism has led to:

- Programmes or projects not being introduced or significantly delayed.
- Businesses spending a lot of time and effort to quantify the quantum of reduction and costs that can be covered by a reasonable contingency budget; and/or
- A lot of time spent fine tuning projects that do not result in economically significant improvement over those already achieved.

Ronald Howard, at Stanford University, recounted his experience with organisations and recalled that they often spend more than 10 times the economic worth of the information that they are analysing (Savage, 2009). Managers and engineers need to constantly remind themselves of the question: 'What is the economic value of what I'm trying to achieve?' This time and cost could have been better spent on focusing on other improvement projects.

Case Study 5.1 shows several barriers occurring simultaneously.

CASE STUDY 5.1   BARRIERS TO IMPLEMENTING ENERGY EFFICIENCY

In a large commercial building, the senior management is considering installing a combined heat and power (CHP) system to supply part of its electricity and hot water demand. The complex uses 9.7 million kWh per year of natural gas, which costs £160,000. Approximately 20 per cent of the gas is used in the restaurant kitchen. The annual electricity consumption is 18.9 million kWh and costs £1.5 million.

The proposal for CHP will consume an additional 4.4 million kWh of natural gas (£71,000 per annum) to meets the building's heating needs and reduce the electricity purchased by 3.2 million kWh (£250,000 per annum). With a capital cost of £1.26 million, it has a simple payback of 6.5 years.

In addition to the proposal for a CHP plant, they have also shortlisted 12 other potential energy reduction projects. These 12 projects are independent of each other and there is no technical interaction between one another. All 12 projects, if implemented, will reduce the electricity and natural gas consumed by the business. It is estimated that implementing all 12 projects will reduce the electricity consumption by 27 per cent and natural gas consumption by 8 per cent, with a combined saving of £448,000 per annum. With a capital investment of £693,000, these projects have a simple payback of 1.55 years.

Implementing a CHP after the completion of the 12 projects will result in a CHP two sizes smaller. With a capital cost of the smaller CHP at £1.24 million, it also has a simple payback of 6.5 years. However, the total energy saved becomes £638,000 per annum vs. £193,000 per annum by implementing CHP alone. The total portfolio of energy savings projects costs £1.9 million and has a simple payback of 3.0 years.

With careful planning, the CHP project can be staggered into the future. The energy savings from the 12 projects (£0.7 million) can be used to offset the capital allocation required for the new CHP.

All of these barriers to implementation need to be considered and planned out for a successful energy management programme. They have an almost direct impact on the success of the programme and affect the production schedules, OEE, cost of operations and opportunities for future improvements.

PART 2
Tools and Techniques

The need for energy efficiency and a strategy for its implementation have been established in the previous chapters. The various barriers to implementation have also been described. Chapter 2 succinctly put the basic terminologies of yield and efficiency in place. In reality, energy use, and hence energy efficiency calculation in, say, a manufacturing plant, is far less easily separated into an idealised and simplified box of processes shown in Figure 2.1 and Figure 2.2. Figure PT2.1 shows a typical relationship between energy users and its source.

The process may consist of a series of energy users. Each of the 'users' is supplied with the quantities and different mix of energy. This energy mix may consist of electricity, steam, hot water, water, cooling water, chilled water, compressed air, process gasses. Additional energy is used to provide a healthy,

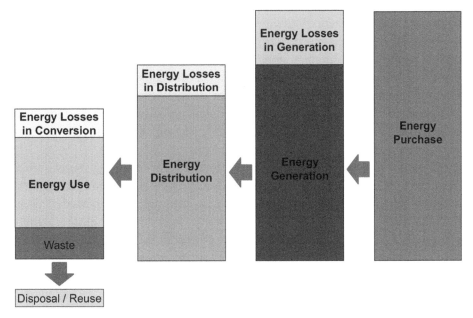

Figure PT2.1 Energy use in a manufacturing business

safe and productive working environment. These additional energy users could be in terms of air ventilation along with the associated heating, cooling and air conditioning systems, lighting, canteen, wash rooms, other welfare.

With the exception of a limited number of businesses, the majority of companies will buy electricity from the power network and generate its own energy mix required to operate the business. The generated energy is then distributed to each end user via a distribution network.

As described in Chapter 2, no processes are 100 per cent efficient. In a manufacturing environment, these inefficiencies result in by-products, products not meeting the product specification and waste. Some businesses reprocess the waste. Other businesses dispose of these by-products and waste. For the majority of manufacturing processes, manufacturing quality products and graded products consumes the same raw materials and energy. The more graded products and waste a business generates, the more energy is required to make up for the 'losses'.

It is very common for businesses to assume that all of the energy purchased is used by the end users. This is not the case, as conversion of energy from one form to another will never be 100 per cent efficient. These losses are collectively known as efficiency losses. It follows that the bigger the losses, more energy is consumed to meet the demand of the business.

Sometimes, the generation plants could be very efficient but the losses occur elsewhere, i.e., on the end user or distribution system. One of the most apparent reasons is energy loss due to leaks. Take compressed air for example: the bigger the leak, the more energy will be used by the compressor to make up the losses until someone stops the leak. The reason behind this is that compressors operate to a set pressure. When a user consumes compressed air, the air pressure in the distribution system drops, signalling the compressor to operate and make up air pressure inside the distribution system. The compressor and its control system could not differentiate between a reduction in pressure due to legitimate use or due to leaks.

Similar logic could be applied to the majority of energy systems. Other frequently overlooked energy systems are failed valves and steam traps. When a valve or steam trap fails closed, it is easily detected and replaced. This is because valves that have failed in a closed position or are blocked exhibit symptoms that inhibit the normal running of energy systems, translating into observable issues. Failed open valves and steam traps result in wastage of energy which is more difficult to detect. However, it is not an impossible task.

For small and/or simple energy systems, issues with deteriorating energy performance can be identified and isolated easily. As the business grows larger and more complex, for example a highly integrated processing unit in the same facility, the ability to account for and troubleshoot deteriorating energy performance becomes more complex.

Understanding where and how energy is used within the business is the first step to successful reduction in energy costs. Among the very first steps in implementing a sustainable energy management and energy reduction programme is to conduct an energy 'audit'. An energy audit evaluates the efficiency of all process systems that use energy.

This next part presents a systematic approach to assess and compare the energy consumed within a business. Consultants and contractors use this information to identify and scale the cost benefit of applying various energy reduction techniques. When the analysis is completed, a report is normally generated. This report documents the use of energy and the condition of the plant machinery and systems. It recommends ways to reduce energy consumption via various improvements, ranging from operation and maintenance to installation of energy efficient equipment.

The benefits of such an exercise are well documented. Many industries not only experience energy cost reduction, but also productivity improvements. This part will explore the following questions.

- What is an energy audit?
- Why are there so many tools and techniques used?
- When do we bring in 'common sense' and 'reality checks' when ranking options for projects?

6

Common Tools and Techniques Used

Effective management of energy-consuming systems can lead to significant cost and energy savings, as well as increased comfort, lower maintenance costs and extended equipment life. A successful energy reduction programme begins with a thorough energy audit.

The term 'energy audit' is very loosely defined and among the most misunderstood terminology used by many business, consultants and contractors. To many people energy audit conjures up the image of experts coming into the business, finding faults in how the business uses energy, highlighting failures in using energy efficiently and effectively, and identifying opportunities for energy reduction and engaging managers and engineers to take action.

The service offering of consultants and contractors is also frequently called a review, study, survey, assessment, diagnostic. This adds to the confusion in the market. However, when analysing and comparing the business models of many consultants and contractors across many countries, many standard approaches and work methods can be found. Each consultant's or contractor's scope of work and methodology varies slightly to differentiate them and to win business.

Consultants and contractors generally use the term energy audit to mean one or a combination of the following five tools and techniques:

- Energy accounting.
- Energy balance.
- Energy monitoring and targeting.
- Energy benchmarking.
- Energy opportunity finding.

These are a loose set of guidelines and procedures to organise the work process and to minimise the possibilities of jumping to conclusions from established facts, figures and opinions.

Energy Accounting

Similar to year-end accounts auditing, energy accounting is merely an exercise to:

1.   Assess the effectiveness of an energy management system via its policies, plans and practices;
2.   Determine how a business entity accounts for energy it consumes, means of reporting and controls in place; and
3.   High-level checks and balances, reconciliations, energy balances, variance investigations where energy reduction projects are identified, prioritised and implemented.

Energy accounting can only be carried out on auditable systems. Many countries have prescribed guidelines for an energy management system. They are inevitably the standard against which energy accounting measures compliance.

   Instead of carrying out full energy management accounting, it is sometimes easier or more beneficial to carry out a gap analysis on the energy maturity introduced in Chapter 4. The assessment collects supporting soft data that defines the appropriateness and readiness of a business for energy reduction in terms of:

-   Strategy.
-   Management systems.
-   Operational readiness.
-   Organisational behaviour.
-   Implementation.
-   Monitoring and targeting.

Some consultants present the data in the form of matrices, while others prefer to present the data as a chart. Very frequently, the energy maturity models use the rankings of 'one', 'two', 'three', 'four' and 'five'. A score of five does not mean 'world-class' and a score of 'zero' does not mean 'worst in class'. Some consultants and contractors use 'zero' to 'four', while others use a rank from 0 per cent to 100 per cent, or the letters A to G for their matrices.

   These are merely a means of qualitative data representation by positioning business practices on a matrix. Some aspects of energy management within a company may be better than others, in which case the energy reduction programme becomes imbalanced: the improvements will not be sustainable.

This should be used as a prompt to determine underlying deficiencies in practices and to address these deficiencies.

Details on the various elements assessed vary with each consultant and contractor. Examples of energy maturity matrices can be found in BRESCU (1995, 2001) and NIFES Consulting Group (2002).

Energy Balance

Very frequently, analysis of energy and utility bills enables cost savings to be achieved with no capital outlay. Mistakes can and do occur from utility metering and it is worthwhile checking the accuracy of meters and to reclaim any excess payments based on incorrect invoices. This can also be used to compare energy supply contracts. However, the primary purpose of energy balance is to quantify all energy flows inside the boundary of the business. The sum of all energy use should equal the quantity of the purchased energy.

Consultants and contractors collect and review the immediate past 12–36 months worth of utility energy data for all fuels, including electricity, natural gas, fuel oil and any other delivered fuels. Other data required is listed below but is not limited to the following:

- existing plant descriptions and specifications;
- simple plant layout and process flow diagram;
- outlook of the future plant expansions and/or capacity addition plans;
- material and energy flow diagram;
- production rates to match energy data;
- utility consumption profiles (electricity, water, steam, fuel, compressed air and cooling).

A computer spreadsheet is very useful to input, calculate and to plot utility information. Relationships between energy use and those factors that drive energy use can be determined by analysing the data. Some of these factors include major equipment, occupancy, sales volume, floor area and either fixed or seasonal loads.

Figure 6.1 shows a sample selection of the typical outputs from analysing natural gas and electricity bills for a manufacturing company.

It may also be useful to draw the energy consumption in a Sankey diagram – a tool for visualising energy flow by distinguishing between energy use and losses and their relative magnitudes. This provides a visual method to identify areas likely to generate quick wins. However, this does not quantify losses associated with process unreliability. Figure 6.2 shows a typical Sankey diagram.

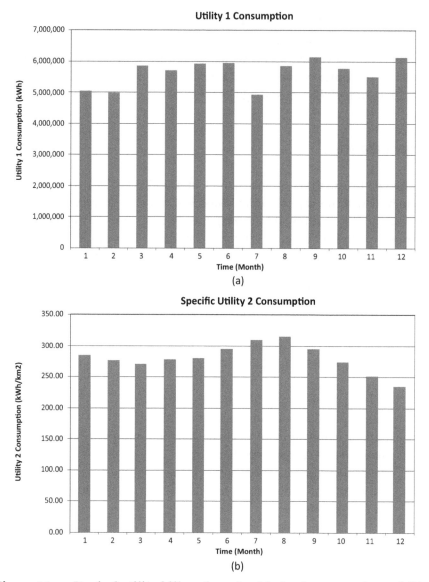

Figure 6.1 Typical utility bill analyses by (a) absolute quantity and (b)
specific energy

Apart from the desktop study, consultants and contractors very frequently
meet with several key personnel within a business to obtain a better overview
of the company and its intricate relationships between each business function.
A sample of key personnel to be interviewed is listed below:

• Site/plant manager.

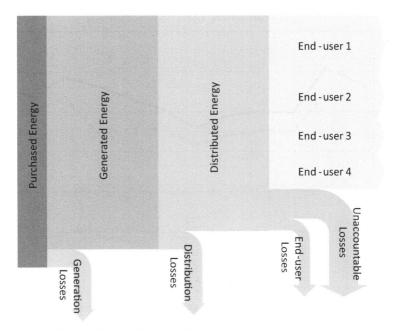

Figure 6.2   Example of a Sankey diagram

- Finance manager.
- Energy manager.
- Production manager.
- Maintenance manager.
- Operations technology/technical service manager.

An energy balance forms the starting point for implementing any energy reduction programmes. The data from this stage can be further used with other tools and techniques described. When used appropriately, it can:

- Show the proportionate use of each energy source and waste.
- Analyse the best energy tariff..
- Provide a Pareto analysis of the major energy consuming areas.
- Detect discrepancies and errors in billing and losses.
- Trend past and present energy consumption.
- Project future energy demand.

Figure 6.3 shows the analysis of energy data as a means to track and validate invoiced utility.

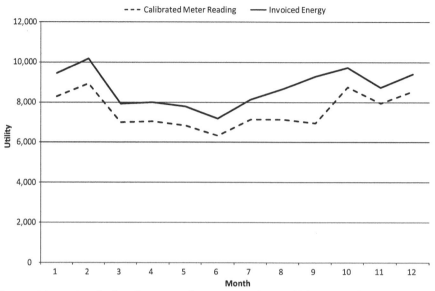

Figure 6.3   Analysis of energy data as a tool to validate purchased utility

Energy Monitoring and Targeting

One of the most important keys to a successful energy reduction programme is to base the energy reduction project on real and irrefutable data. Energy consumption and energy efficiency data can be highly variable. The noise in the energy consumption data is very frequently related to production pattern. It can also be influenced by weather and seasonal variations. This tool is used principally to create a baseline to enable predictability and control of energy consumption.

The theory and principle is based on applying statistical analysis. In companies where the energy price is fixed, the energy cost will be proportional to the energy consumption. This methodology consists of eight simple steps:

1.   Identify the energy users and consumption within the business.
2.   Determine the energy attributable to the weather.
3.   Examine energy used in transportation.
4.   Evaluate the heating and space requirements.
5.   Estimate the efficiency of generating utilities.
6.   Examine how the process uses energy.
7.   Evaluate the process of energy efficiency.
8.   Set up an energy monitoring system.

Consultants and contractors use statistical tools to determine if weather, transportation, heating, cooling and ventilation related energy consumption exists in a business. If so, it is necessary to remove these components from the total energy consumption to arrive at an estimate of the manufacturing only energy consumption.

Once all non-production related energy consumption is separated, a conceptual model to predict the energy consumed in a production process becomes available to compare the actual energy consumed. This model can be developed from a theoretical understanding of how much energy is required to manufacture the product, i.e., applying the laws of conserving mass and energy. It can also be developed empirically via further statistical tools.

In many countries, degree-day data is published by the meteorological office and by some selected universities. The use of degree-day data is described in Chapter 18. A simple plot of the energy consumed vs. the degree-day data reveals the existence of any weather-related relationships in the business. Figure 6.4 shows an example of manufacturing energy consumption vs. degree day data.

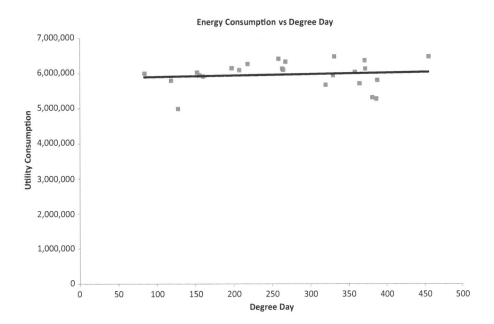

Figure 6.4   Manufacturing energy consumption vs. degree day data

The model can be improved by incorporating more variables. For a business that has several value streams or product streams, this could be achieved by splitting the energy consumption by product or business unit. A sample selection of the types of monitoring system used by various companies is shown in Figure 6.5a–j.

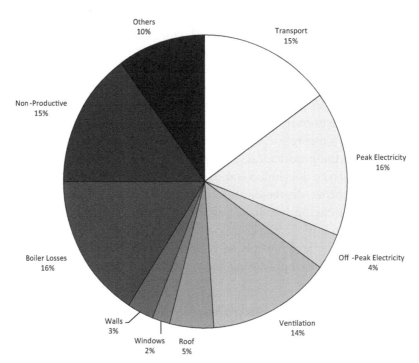

Figure 6.5a   Selection of monitoring and targeting – pie chart

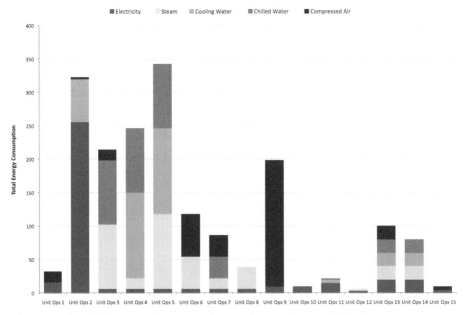

Figure 6.5b   Selection of monitoring and targeting – stick chart

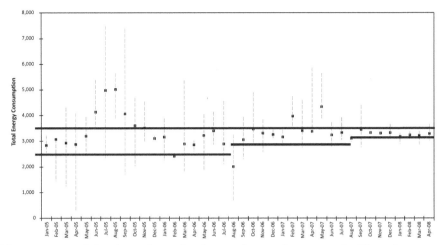

Figure 6.5c   Selection of monitoring and targeting – stacked bar chart

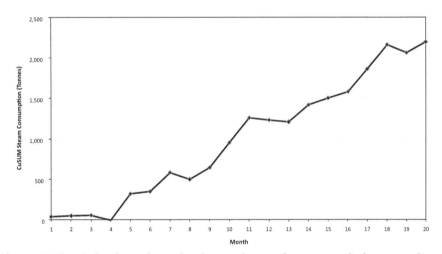

Figure 6.5d   Selection of monitoring and targeting – cumulative sum chart

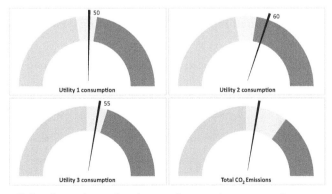

Figure 6.5e   Selection of monitoring and targeting – speedometer chart

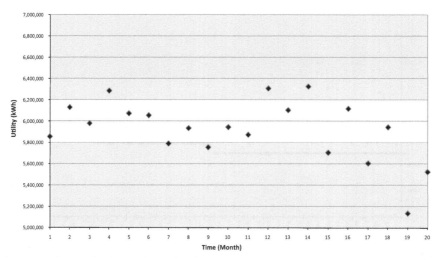

Figure 6.5f   Selection of monitoring and targeting – statistical control chart

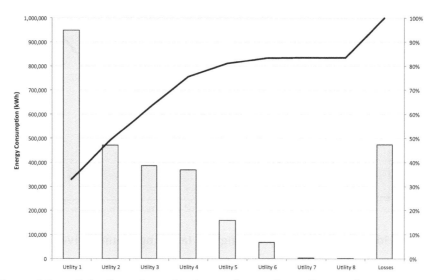

Figure 6.5g   Selection of monitoring and targeting – Pareto chart

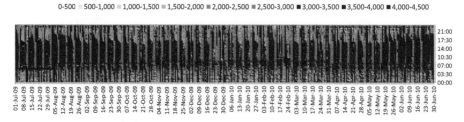

Figure 6.5h   Selection of monitoring and targeting – surface area chart

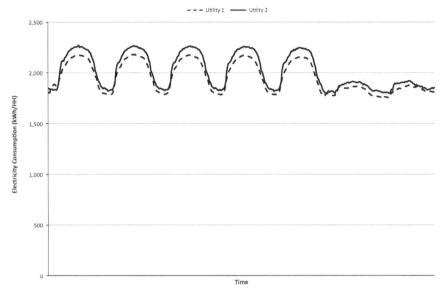

Figure 6.5i   Selection of monitoring and targeting – trend chart

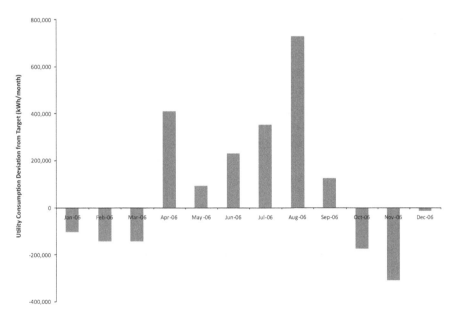

Figure 6.5j   Selection of monitoring and targeting – difference from target

Making energy consumption predictable is a user friendly and powerful tool to track deviations from expected energy consumption patterns, and highlights the need for closer management control. It is also a tool to indicate, at an early stage, where energy reduction opportunities can be found or areas to focus efforts. However, the latter use of this tool depends heavily on the skills and experience of the managers, engineers, consultants and contractors.

Managers achieve this by allocating the energy use to the various departments where it can determine any deviation from the model to detect any deviation, determine its root causes, take corrective action, account for these deviations, and/or to set up energy cost centres.

However, this tool lacks the ability to describe in full the total energy reduction opportunities to generate proposals for capital sanction. It also lacks the ability to identify the speed of improvement required to be able to effectively compete and excel in the market. Consultants and contractors use other tools, described below, to further define the energy reduction projects.

Energy Benchmarking

Once energy consumption and energy cost can be accounted and predicted, consultants and contractors then compare the energy consumption and energy cost information with other businesses. They use this comparative information to make a judgement and to determine important factors to meet and exceed the competitor's business performance.

This systematic comparison is called benchmarking. Benchmarking is a structured process of continuously measuring and comparing energy processes and performance against comparable processes in leading organisations to obtain information that will help a business identify and implement improvements. It asks the following questions:

1. How does the energy performance compare with other similar business?
2. How big are the improvement opportunities?
3. How far are we behind best-in-class performers?
4. How quickly can we close the performance gap?
5. What will be the financial impact of closing the gap?
6. How appropriate are our levels of spending to achieve the goals?

A benchmarking exercise can be done for specific processes within an organisation (internal); specific processes across a broad range of organisations (external); or with similar processes across a broad range of organisations.

While benchmarking provides a mechanism or process for comparing energy performance, it does have several common pitfalls:

- Wasting time and effort optimising or enhancing the wrong process or part of the process.
- Optimising a unit operation or process to produce savings which have no economic value.
- Allocating resources to solving problems of lower economic value at the expense of higher value problems.
- Seeing solutions from a purely functional point of view.

When conducting energy benchmarking, many consultants and contractors go straight into comparing parameters related to energy. A good benchmarking exercise assesses the whole business value chain from production throughput, downtime, quality, yield, rate, variability, fixed cost, maintenance, utilities and labour cost.

Figure 6.6 shows the scope of a good benchmarking study. Apart from the energy cost components, a direct cost to the business, almost all other parameters are indirectly linked to energy. Generic descriptions of these are:

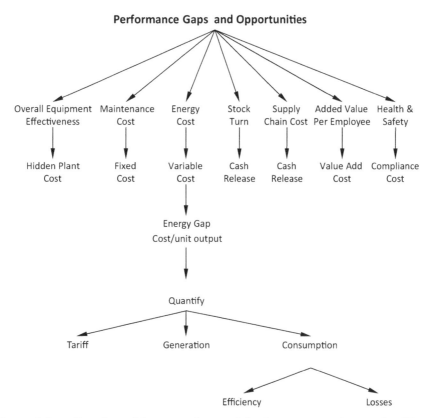

Figure 6.6   Benchmarking as a signpost for improvement opportunities

- *Overall equipment effectiveness (OEE)* – energy consumption when the plant is idle; energy consumption associated with producing and reprocessing non-saleable goods.
- *Maintenance* – capability to reduce idle time, and hence energy lost due to idle time.
- *Stock turn* – warehouse and intermediate inventory energy consumption.
- *Supply chain* – energy due to transport.
- *Added value/employee* – non-production based energy consumption.

Detailed assessment of production, manufacturing processes, maintenance and other supporting facilities along with the identification of energy reduction opportunities are not assessed during a benchmarking study. They are carried out using other tools.

Once this information has been calculated, the consultants and contractors then compare key performance indicators (KPIs) with a single source or multiple sources of benchmarks. Sample KPIs used in industry are shown in Table 6.1.

Table 6.1   Common key performance indicators (KPIs)

Manufacturing Value Add	Manufacturing added value per employee Ratio of total employees to value adding employee
Customer Service	On-Time In-Full (OTIF) Inventory record accuracy (%) Customer complaints (% of orders) Adherence to production schedule (%) Finished goods days of cover
Quality	Right first time (%) Quality rate (%) Process capability C_{pk}
Supplier Performance	Supplier OTIF (%) Raw materials days of cover Supplier C_{pk}
Manufacturing	Product rate (%) Maximum proven rate Availability (%) OEE (%) Capacity used for changeover (%) Manufacturing velocity (%) Work in progress (WIP) stock turn/days of cover Maintenance spend (% of replacement value) Spares days of cover

Table 6.1   Continued

Reliability	Own maintenance labour cost
	Contractor labour cost
	Maintenance material usage
	Maintenance spare turnover
	Backlog (days)
	Reactive maintenance (%)
	Preventive maintenance (%)
	Predictive maintenance (%)
	Turnaround/overhaul (%)
	Special projects (%)
	Overtime
Energy	Useful energy extracted per unit of fuel consumption, e.g., kWh of steam used per kWh of natural gas used in boiler, etc.
	Energy consumed per unit production, e.g., GJ/m^3 of product, MWh of total energy consumed per kg of raw material etc.
	Energy cost per unit energy of utility, e.g., £/tonne of steam, £/m^3 of compressed air etc.
People	Absenteeism (%)
	Training days per employee
Lost Time Events	Safety performance
	Environmental performance

Typical sources of benchmarking data are:

- historical data;
- published data but limited to generic systems such as boilers, compressed air etc.;
- industry specific surveys, consultant databases providing work in similar industries;
- market research for best-in-class business – not necessarily in the same business sector;
- internal benchmarks such as sister companies, comparison between shifts, competitors etc.

When comparing different plants, a representative value is needed to eliminate the effect of weather and to reflect 'true' operation. Using weekly or daily data instead of monthly or yearly data may be beneficial. Care is required when comparing benchmarks.

The difference between the 'calculated KPI value' and the 'benchmark KPI value' is the improvement gap. The business then needs to decide on the required speed of change to 'close the gap'. The consultants' and contractors' experience in implementing similar systems can act as a guide to the achievable time frame and the practical aspects to implement the energy reduction projects.

It is important to note that any benchmarking exercise, and following the results of a benchmarking exercise, is only valid at the time the benchmark results are reported. Technology is being improved by continual research and development –new products are continually being introduced in the market that pushes the boundaries of energy technologies.

Some operational excellence techniques – such as lean manufacturing, total productive maintenance – while they are also applicable to energy systems and work for some businesses, the application of specific techniques to other businesses can vary and differ from those suggested by the benchmark, as in Case Study 6.1.

CASE STUDY 6.1   BENCHMARKING BETWEEN TWO COMPANIES

Two companies manufacture a specialist intermediary product. Both companies have a combined market share of approximately 80 per cent and control the market price of the product. Both companies use similar process technologies and have similar utility requirements for their process. For simplicity, the companies are denoted Company A and Company B.

In a benchmarking exercise, the energy performance of both companies was obtained and compared. Figure 6.7 shows the energy performance of Company A (solid line) and Company B (dotted line). Company A has the higher (almost double) specific energy consumption. There is a clear gap in energy performance between the two companies.

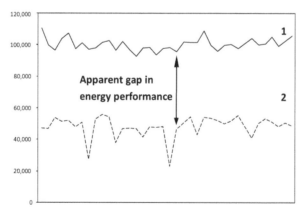

Figure 6.7   Energy benchmarking for Company A and Company B
               (before)

If Company A carried out an assessment to find opportunities to reduce its energy consumption, it would be able to close the gap between the two companies.

Reducing Company A's energy consumption would reduce energy costs and increase Company A's profit margin.

At the point identified as '2', Company B implemented several energy efficiency improvement opportunities. These resulted in a reduction of energy consumption, drawn as a different dotted line to point '3'. In this scenario, the gap for Company A has become larger. Assuming that Company B's sale price remains the same, the cost reduction will result in an increase in profitability.

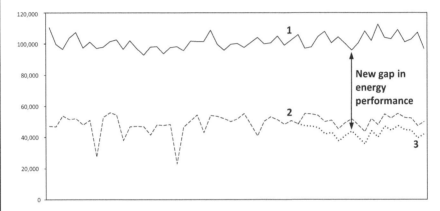

Figure 6.8   Energy benchmarking for Company A and Company B (after)

As a duopoly, depending on Company B's business strategy and capacity to increase output, Company B could also choose to reduce its price. In this manner, it could potentially capture Company A's market share and eliminate Company A from the market. A thorough analysis of the strategic actions that Company A and Company B could take can be analysed using game theory.*

---

*   There are many good books on game theory, which is a tool used in business and in social science to predict the actions or reactions of other parties. As a general and easy to understand introduction on game theory, see Courtney (2000) and Courtney, Horn and Jayanti (2009).

Energy Opportunity Finding

This tool is concerned with identifying potential areas for energy reduction and quantifying the extent of energy reduction and the cost of implementation to arrive at a list of economically viable projects for the business. Figure 6.9 shows a typical workflow in an energy opportunity finding exercise.

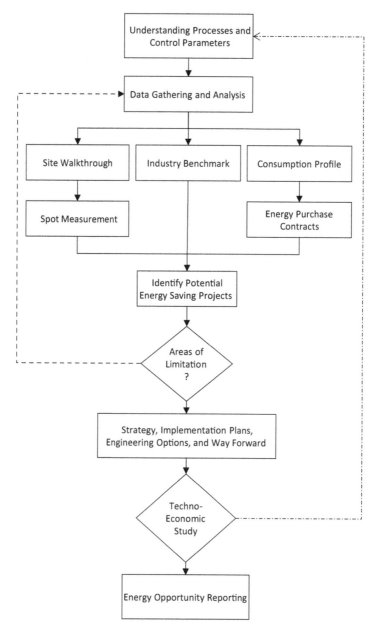

Figure 6.9   General work flow of an energy opportunity scoping study

Energy opportunity finding is the most frequently used tool in energy audits. This tool also has the highest degree of procedural innovation, patents, and naming conventions. There are also many standards and guidelines available to carry out this study. Gradually, the various standards and guidelines are converging into a regional and global harmonised methodology.[1]

Ideally, an initial guided tour of a plant allows the consultant and contractor to become familiar with the process flow and identify the major operational and equipment features of the plant. A plant walkthrough is beneficial for:

- Observing the actual operating conditions.
- Identification of energy inefficiency and wastage.
- Identification of energy intensive areas and equipment.
- Identification of potential problems and limitation.
- Plant/facility familiarisation.

Consultants and contractors who specialise in specific equipment will have more sophisticated tools to assess energy reduction opportunities. Boiler and furnace experts regularly use combustion analysers and computer software to tune the process. Compressor experts utilise power meters, data loggers and original equipment manufacturer (OEM) supplied software etc.

One of the most common problems in finding and quantifying energy reduction opportunities is in the quality of the information available and/or provided. Poor-quality information and data will result in wrong quantification of energy reduction. Sources of poor-quality data may include, but are not limited to, the following:

- Wrong information.
- Limited available data.
- Plant fluctuations.
- Random measurement errors.
- Systematic measurement errors.
- Systematic operating errors.
- Unknown statistical distribution.

Good and experienced consultants and contractors may be able to identify discrepancies and inconsistencies in the data provided. They may also be able to advise on the steps and/or alternative measures needed to arrive at a better quality of information in order to firm up the energy reduction projects. These may include:

---

1   In Europe, this tool has been developed by the European Committee for Standardization (CEM) and European Committee for Electrotechnical Standardization (CENELEC) as EN 16247 energy audits, to meet the requirements of European Directives. It is a four-part standard covering general requirements, buildings, processes and transport. The International Organization for Standardization (ISO) equivalent is currently under development.

- Calculating the amount of raw materials, products, by-products and waste from the manufacturing process.
- Reviewing the purchasing records, production records, sales and stocktaking.
- Information from main meters, sub-meters and the use of portable meters.
- Analysis of emissions data.
- Estimation from authorisation, discharge consent.
- Timed trials.
- Bucket and stopwatch.
- Samples for lab analysis.
- Original equipment manufacturer manuals.

Opportunities for energy reduction are identified by assessing each energy user within the business. These opportunities have an energy reduction component and may include other benefits such as new/redefined work plans and sub-routines, new/redefined procedures, modification of operating framework and assumptions, and installation of additional or more efficient equipment. This will be developed later in Chapter 11.

7

Types of Energy Saving Packages on the Market

As shown in Chapter 6, there are many tools, techniques and approaches available in the market with different names and different variations on the approach to find energy reduction opportunities. Each offering has a broadly similar outcome and is connected to its management style, scope of work, thoroughness, auditing procedure, cost, time, phasing and reporting characteristics. On a broad-brush basis, the majority of the energy audit approaches can be classified into four categories:

1. Bottom-up approach.
2. Unit operation approach.
3. Top-down approach.
4. Hybrid approach.

A bottom-up approach typically starts by assessing and identifying individual machinery and/or processing steps such as pumps, motors, steam traps and applying insulation. It then works its way up the plant and groups the individual techniques together to form a business case. This approach is normally time and resource intensive but is favoured by equipment manufacturers and specialist contractors.

In engineering, many seemingly different chemical, physical and biological processes can be broken down into a series of separate and distinct processing steps. A 'unit operation' is a basic step in a manufacturing plant. Sometimes, the word 'system' is used. Examples of unit operations and/or systems are:

*   Heating and the associated piping.
*   Cooling and the associated piping.
*   Refrigeration and the associated piping.
*   Ventilation and the associated ducting.
*   Mixing.

- Heat exchange
- Boiling
- Evaporation
- Condensation
- Drying
- Distilling
- Absorption
- Membrane separation
- Liquid–liquid extraction
- Adsorption
- Ion exchange
- Liquid–solid leaching
- Crystallisation
- Mechanical–physical separation.

A manufacturing plant may have many unit operations connected to create the overall process to manufacture a desired product. Each unit operation follows the same conservation laws and limitations. For example, a ventilation system will consist of air aupply and extract fans, heating and cooling units to make up the full system. A unit operation approach assesses each individual component within the unit operation and its interaction between systems in the business as a whole. Examples of unit operations assessments are shown in Table 7.1.

Table 7.1   Examples of unit operations and their components

Unit Operation	Components of Unit Operation	Relationship to Other Machinery
Boiler	Fans, pumps, motors, furnace, (big) heat exchanger, water treatment system, controllers, insulation, etc.	Supplies steam and/or hot water at a certain flow rate, temperature, and pressure to the process.
Distillation	Pumps, motors, heat exchangers (reboilers, and condensers), control systems, insulation, etc.	Separate impurities from products or separate two or more components in a mixture into various processing streams.

A top-down approach applies statistical and benchmark figures to arrive at the achievable energy savings. This method is prone to under- and over-estimate energy reduction but serves as a quick guide to the achievable energy reduction. This method is generally favoured by management and technical consultants when performing a study to identify and prioritise areas for improvement. Detailed analysis will be required to quantify the achievable savings at a later stage.

A hybrid energy audit approach combines the best of bottom-up, unit operation and top-down approaches to identify energy reduction opportunities, technical feasibility and economic viability to implement specific energy reduction opportunities. This can be loosely grouped into three levels of service, in order of increasing complexity, time and cost:

- *Energy Conservation Review* – screening study or high-level opportunity scoping;
- *Plant Walkthrough Survey* – analysis to a level where opportunities can be generated into a portfolio of projects or target areas;
- *Investment Grade Study* – detailed study of large or complex energy reduction opportunities before capital sanction.

A company may decide on any single level of audit, or start with an energy conservation review, and use the results to decide whether to progress to one of the other levels. Figure 7.1 shows the degree of thoroughness of each level, and how its accuracy and confidence of the cost and savings figures will be different at the different levels.

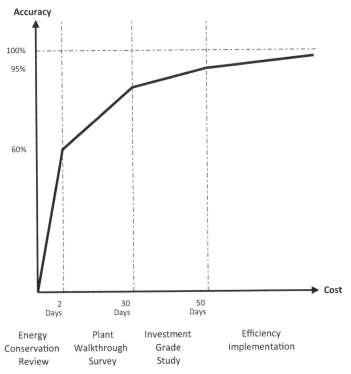

Figure 7.1   Accuracy of energy audit and its cost

Energy Conservation Review

An energy conservation review is a quick and inexpensive initial assessment carried out to identify potential energy reduction opportunities. It is typically conducted over half or one day to establish the basic information – how much energy is consumed, how it is used, the potential for further reduction – and to avoid wasting time and effort studying the wrong process in later audits. The typical scope of an energy conservation review is to:

- Carry out an audit of energy management practices, benchmarking of energy performance and site energy usage;
- Identify key areas of potential energy reduction;
- Provide an estimate of potential annual energy cost reduction;
- Identify methods to achieve, maintain, and recognise further potential opportunities;
- Highlight easy energy reduction opportunities with no cost/low cost to be implemented immediately;
- Prioritise an action list for implementation;
- Generate a business case for energy reduction programmes.

Plant Walkthrough Survey

This audit usually ranges from four to five days for small sites to over one month for large sites. It gives an outlook of the energy consumption profile and the projection of energy consumption in line with any future development plans. This survey will also highlight opportunities for energy reduction along with savings potential and preliminary project costing. The scope of work during this stage includes:

- On-site preliminary data acquisition and documentation review to establish the energy demands of the various energy users;
- Review of existing facilities, modification history and utility infrastructure;
- Overall heat and mass balance (as far as possible);
- highlighting data inconsistencies/metering errors;
- benchmarking the plant energy consumption against available benchmarks;
- defining the baseline for energy saving
- identifying and evaluating energy reduction opportunities;
- formulating possible reduction projects and economics;

- providing recommendations for further actions;
- the production of an audit report.

Investment Grade Study

The two previous phases of energy studies are superficial by nature. They work to identify the ultimate potential for energy reduction, quick wins and highlight the major improvement projects to allow the business to home in and focus on relevant energy reduction opportunities. For simple and low cost projects, the two studies are sufficient for implementation.

An investment grade study is a major exercise used to firm up capital intensive and high business risk projects. This study will take all the necessary measurements, energy engineering analyses, and technical-economics analyses. Finally, this study will recommend optimised opportunities along with the investment budget and return on investment. The scope of an investment grade study includes, but is not limited to:

- Identification of opportunities based on previously identified opportunity or based on engineering drawings aided by the use of a specially designed methodology.
- Detailed assessment with measurements and performance modelling.
- Front-end design and calculations of energy reduction opportunity.
- Conducting techno-economic evaluation and life cycle cost modelling.
- Consideration of existing issues:
    - hard issues: operational conditions and effects on overall site energy efficiency;
    - soft issues: operating philosophies, actual practices and perceived constraints;
    - maintenance issues: reliability, integrity, plant maintenance policies;
    - commercial issues: commercial arrangements for energy and utility;
    - health, safety and environmental issues;
    - compliance with statutory regulations.
- Project schedule based on equipment supply lead times, testing and commissioning times, and plant operations.
- Providing the final 'Go – No Go' recommendations for the energy reduction projects.

As can be seen from the three generic energy audits described above, they are a combination of different tools, techniques and approaches.

Top-down activities are predominantly used in energy conservation reviews and plant walkthrough surveys in the form of benchmarking and broad overviews. They provide large and readily quantifiable savings and improvement opportunities. They use a specific methodology and generate relatively few projects.

Bottom-up activities are principally used in investment grade studies in the form of detailed scrutiny of plant and equipment efficiency. Although bottom-up approaches are the most accurate, they are also technically more time-consuming and costly. Because of this, they are normally carried out to firm up large investment projects only.

An energy study should not be considered a one-off exercise. To be effective, it should become an integral part of an ongoing improvement process with the goal of keeping abreast of the ever evolving techniques and technology for reducing energy consumption.

Recently, the energy reduction market has introduced two new services loosely based on the same tools and techniques. At the present moment, they are used by multinational and multisite businesses as well as independent consultants and contractors to:

- Review major energy reduction investment proposals for maximum energy reduction for the business.
- Carry out due diligence on their existing energy service company (ESCO) to ensure that all contractual terms are fulfilled and all energy reduction opportunities are identified and fully exploited.

8

Energy Reduction Opportunities

Quick Wins

Some quick win opportunities would have been identified in the various levels of energy studies described in Chapter 6 and Chapter 7. Quick wins are relatively simple and straightforward to identify and form no cost, and/or low cost, opportunities to start an energy reduction programme, and generate cost benefits for the bottom line, internal marketing and promotion on energy management work. Some examples of quick wins are:

- turn off any equipment that is not in use
- isolate energy supplied to dead ends
- repair leakage (steam, water, compressed air etc.)
- repair and/or replace faulty control systems
- insulate steam/hot water and/or chilled water pipes
- reduce temperature and/or pressure set-points
- root cause analysis for equipment failures
- specifying high efficiency motors, variable speed drives (VSDs) and soft starts
- turn down excessive air flow
- stop simultaneous heating and cooling
- clean heat exchangers
- reduce distillation reflux/reboil ratios
- optimise feed rates and/or batch sizes
- ensure equipment runs at maximum efficiency
- better production scheduling to minimise energy consumption.

Savings generated from quick wins can be utilised as a tool to gain trust and accountability. It is also an excellent source of generating money to fund further investments in energy reduction within the company. Quick wins will be explored further in Part 3.

Non-Energy Based Benefits

Moving beyond quick wins, many energy reduction opportunities identified may also have non-energy related business benefits, be technically more complex, or incur higher business risks (higher capital cost or operational risks). A detailed assessment is normally commissioned to study any opportunity in greater detail. This may also include the interaction between the energy systems and other systems, or may involve more sophisticated computing techniques (e.g., thermal integration).

Very frequently, the quantum of energy reduction such as steam, natural gas, electricity, chilled water, etc. is relatively straightforward to determine. A common failure during the financial appraisal is omitting other benefits and costs associated with the energy reduction opportunity. Apart from energy reduction, consultants and contractors can offer very little quantitative input on other business benefits and business risks. It is the responsibility of the business to take charge and define these benefits and cost savings.

Many of the newer technologies, when properly sized and installed, will reduce the need for maintenance. The direct benefits of reduced maintenance can be evaluated in terms of longer time to failure, reduced inspection, reduced manpower, materials and spares. There may also be other benefits, which are usually reflected in increased output and quality; improved production scheduling and reduced waste, reduced labour requirements and hence overtime; improved working conditions and savings in floor space (see Case Study 8.1).

CASE STUDY 8.1   NON-ENERGY RELATED BENEFITS FROM AN ENERGY REDUCTION PROJECT

A vacuum is used in a manufacturing plant to extract any remaining moisture from the upstream processes before being processed into the final product. The vacuum, generated by steam ejectors, uses approximately 4.2 million kWh and costs £83,000 per annum.

A mechanical vacuum pump can be used to generate a similar vacuum requirement. For the same vacuum requirement, the mechanical pump would consume 230,000 kWh with an electricity cost of £11,000 per annum. With a capital cost of £360,000, it gives a return on investment (ROI) of five years. This is outside the investment criteria for the plant.

Detailed discussion between the energy manager and production, maintenance and sales teams indicates that additional savings could be made from the energy reduction opportunity.

> The flow of steam through the ejector erodes the orifice inside, enlarging the orifice and causing a drop in steam pressure. This leads to a drop in vacuum levels and in turn generates defective products. Therefore, using a mechanical vacuum pump generates additional savings from (1) raw material savings, (2) avoided waste processing, and (3) avoided annual cost to replace steam ejectors and associated parts.
>
> The additional and frequently hidden savings were quantified and reduce the ROI to less than four years, and meet the investment criteria for the plant.

For example, VSDs – also known as variable frequency drives (VFDs) – are normally used to match a pump's or a fan's electrical consumption with the actual end-user requirement. When VSDs are implemented correctly, they have a lower start-up current, which in turn means lower maximum demand and electrical demand charge for the business. From a maintenance point of view, this means lower wear and tear on the electrical components, mechanical components, all valves and fittings and control instruments connected with the pump or fan.

Depending on the nature of the business, an improvement in quality could translate to lower reject. Quality improvement to an established product is a useful vehicle for introducing a price increase – a proportion of any price increase resulting from a project could also be counted as part of the financial benefit.

Assuming that the additional throughput can be accommodated in subsequent manufacturing stages and that there is a market for the increased throughput, the improvement will result in extra production and sales.

A full evaluation may be difficult because of inadequate information, but the unknown should not simply be ignored. Nonetheless, these less tangible benefits have an intrinsic value at a business level. Many of these benefits are virtually impossible to quantify using scientific and engineering data. However, senior management can take a view on these benefits or, perhaps, assign a value to them.

9

Selecting and Prioritising Energy Reduction Projects

Once the financial benefits of energy savings projects are quantified, a quick and reliable process of screening the projects is required to prioritise and select projects for improvement. The screening procedure should eliminate opportunities that are not feasible, not economic or that present significant business risk.

Complexity of site operations, availability of cash, business priorities, the economic health of sector and the remnant asset life will inevitably mean that not all opportunities can be implemented in one stage.

An investment appraisal is merely a rational method of making choices. It is a tool assisting senior management in determining which investment makes the best use of the company's money, ensures optimum benefits from each of these investments and minimises risk to the company.

A number of methods are available to provide a consistent method of comparing and selecting projects. The least complicated of these methods is simple payback (SPB), which is calculated by dividing the cost of the project by the cost savings. The result is the number of years the project will take to pay for itself. Those projects with the shortest paybacks are assumed to be the most cost effective. Other analysis techniques are available to assess the financial viability of energy reduction projects, including:[1]

- Net present value (NPV).
- Discounted cash flow (DSF).
- Internal rate of return (IRR).
- Life cycle assessment (LCA).
- Return on equity (RoE).

The exact financial tool to use may be prescribed by the business. However, these tools have their own drawbacks. Two of the most common reasons cited

---

1   For a review of project valuation, see Luehrman, 1997.

are that these tools rely on a fixed discount factor, called weighted average cost of capital (WACC), and that the assumptions used in the calculation are also fixed. In reality, legislation, costs and project cost (if the implementation is phased over several years) change over time. In large multinational companies, real options[2] and flexible design valuation[3] are used.

All financial analysis is at best only a 'snapshot' of cost benefit for each investment opportunity at the time the analysis was carried out. The actual energy reduction depends on the future demand and utilisation of the energy reduction project. If demand for the machinery fell by 50 per cent, it would take twice as long to pay back the investment.

The accuracy of capital costs used in the financial analysis depends heavily on the type of financial estimate obtained and needs to be moderated by manages and engineers. Types of estimate are:

- *Order of magnitude* ('ballpark' or 'guesstimate') – very crude estimate derived from intelligent guesses;
- *Study* ('evaluation' or 'pre-design') – approximately quantifies the cost of the major components, rule of thumb calculations and using blanket figures for other works;
- *Authorisation* ('sanction' or 'funding') – most of the costs are known to a sufficient level of accuracy for the project to be submitted for approval;
- *Definitive* ('control') – all project execution costs identified;
- *Detailed* ('tender' or 'contracting').

Some managers and engineers carry out very detailed financial analysis for every energy reduction opportunity identified. Moderation is a good practice. For simple or low-cost opportunities, an order of magnitude or study estimate should be sufficient. Detailed estimates should be limited for high-cost, high-risk investments.

Many technically oriented staff assume that if an opportunity has good financial return the business will find the capital resources to implement it. While this is generally true, seeking funds and marketing energy reduction projects are two of the key stages in making the project work and realising the savings. In general, they are also among the most difficult hurdles for engineers, scientist, consultants and contractors. This is because business management, finance and marketing are not normally the forte of engineers and scientist.

On the part of consultants and contractors, they may not have sufficient knowledge to fully identify and quantify any business risk associated with the

---

2   For an introduction to real options, see Savage, 2009.
3   For further details on flexible design valuation, see Neufville and Scholtes, 2011.

energy reduction project and compute the 'real' cost and benefit to the business of implementing the identified projects.

Although each company has different preferred methods for screening projects, whatever method is used, understanding the minds of senior management and where funds can be made available is essential to ensure a higher chance of success in seeking funds for energy reduction projects. Senior management need answers to the following questions in order to evaluate the capital request and to allocate funds efficiently:

- How will the management approach and achieve the vision for energy reduction?
- Is it the right vision for the business?
- What is the opportunity cost for choosing one energy reduction opportunity over another opportunity?
- Is it financially viable?
- Does the energy consumption have enough leverage to significantly impact the bottom line?
- What is the value of energy efficiency vs. the risk to production and profit lost?
- What will be the consequences if it is not implemented?
- In what order should these programmes be implemented?
- Can the chosen option be implemented in a reasonable time without disrupting day-to-day operations?
- Does the option chosen have a good track record? If not, is there convincing evidence that the option will be successful?
- Will new technology and techniques prevent future failures? Will they have any impact on other processes?
- Will future business requirements restrict the choices and options for energy efficient techniques?
- Does the chosen technique limit or hedge future business and climate changes?

Charles Handy and Michael Porter, two world-renowned management thinkers, define the purpose of a business as being to provide its customer with products or services in a manner that exceeds the economic performance of its competition.[4] Very frequently, the word 'exceed' is defined by a combination of 'faster than the competition' and 'better than the competition'.

---

4   Both Charles Handy and Michael Porter emphasise the need for long-term business performance, the sustainability of the environment, coexistence and a symbiotic relationship between business and society. These ideas are frequently ignored by choosing to focus purely on short to medium returns for the shareholders returns.

The management team steers the business into profitability by ensuring a good public image; compliance with national health, safety and environmental regulations; high sales volume; high machinery availability and utilisation; assured long-term asset life; low product variability; low inventory; and operating the plant on (or below) budget. All these items are planned and incorporated into the objectives and targets of each individual management team. In order to fulfil these requirements, the business operates within a management system of practices to supply labour (own and/or contract), raw materials, engineering materials, machinery, tools, spare parts and utilities. This is shown in Figure 9.1:

Figure 9.1   Simple operating plant management model

A company's income and expenditure relate directly to quantities recorded on the profit and loss statements, balance sheets and cash flow statements. These form the evidence by which the performance of the business can be quantified. To assess business performance, a senior manager simply examines all the expenditures and revenues.

An energy reduction projects does not create an 'income' that appears on profit and loss statements. It also does not appear as a line item in the balance sheet or cash flow statement. The value of an energy reduction project can be assessed in three ways:

1.   Continue the same level of performance with less cost;
2.   More production with the same cost; or
3.   Both.

The vocabulary of the management team, hence the success of seeking authorisation and funding, is to describe the project in terms of the business goals and targets. Reasons to fund any proposals for energy reduction projects could include:

- Generating business revenue – boosting revenue from improved plant capacity and capability via faster processing speeds, flexibility in product specification and consistent product quality.
- Reducing operational cost and variation against budget – lowering raw materials, waste, idle time and energy costs by applying the right amount of materials and energy resources at the right time.
- Reducing operational risks – breakdowns, corrective maintenance, preventive maintenance, predictive maintenance, asset replacement, asset renewal, inventory investment and avoidance of capital expenditure.
- Corporate sustainability – better detection and correction of plant operations, resulting in lower safety and health issues, lower environmental emissions and brand image.

Managers and engineers who make time to understand the purpose and principles of business management can use this knowledge to gain attention from senior management and the appropriate investment priority within the organisation.

Sometimes, having assessed all of the benefits, some energy reduction projects could not, individually, meet the return on investment criteria. Depending on company policy, it may be possible to group several energy reduction projects into a portfolio that, as a whole, meets the investment criteria.

10

Implementing Energy Reduction Projects

Financing Energy Savings

The general financing options available to finance energy reduction projects are:

1. Cash purchase.
2. Loan.
3. Capital or operating lease.
4. Performance contracts.
5. Pay as you go contracts.

Cash purchase is the simplest method of financing energy improvements. When the business has cash reserves and a strong balance sheet, a cash purchase makes sense. The advantage of cash purchase is that all cost savings from the improvement are immediately available. For some investments, government incentives are available to fully depreciate the cost of the project within a year. However, the disadvantage of cash purchase is the lost capital for other investments.

Besides cash purchase, the conventional alternative is to apply for a loan. Obtaining a loan may require a significant down payment by the business and the owners (or senior managers) will have to identify business assets as collateral to secure the loan. Some governmental departments, local councils and local development agencies provide interest-free unsecured loans or grants for energy reduction projects.

Leasing is a financing option that allows the payment for the energy reduction project to be spread out over a longer term and often with lower payments. A capital lease is an instalment purchase of equipment. Little or no initial capital outlay is required. The business eventually owns the equipment and may take tax deductions for depreciation and for the interest portion of payments. A capital asset and associated liability will be recorded on the balance sheet.

Under an operating lease, the leasing company owns the equipment. The leasing company, rather than the facility owner, claims any tax benefits associated with the depreciation of the equipment. At the end of the contract term, the facility owner could have an option to purchase the equipment at fair market value or at a predetermined price, to renegotiate the lease or to have the equipment removed. The facility owner deducts lease payments as an ordinary expense and the equipment does not affect the owner's balance sheet.

A performance contract is a service provided by an energy services company (ESCO) where they will identify, implement and fund (by the ESCO or via a private financer) energy reduction projects within a facility in exchange for a share of the project's future savings. If the project does not achieve the declared energy savings, the contract normally requires the ESCO to pay the difference. The services of an ESCO may include an energy audit, design, procurement, financing, operation, maintenance, and measurement and verification of savings. The ESCO owns the equipment installed during the term of the contract. The equipment asset and debt do not appear on the facility owner's balance sheet.

Performance contracting services were originally developed in the 1970s by small departments or divisions within large power and automation manufacturers such as General Electric (GE), ABB and Siemens. The ability to accurately monitor and verify the energy reduction is a key part of an ESCO's contract and has led to a global explosion of patents and standards in energy reduction verification. One such standard is the Efficiency Valuation Organization's International Performance Monitoring and Verification Protocol (IPMVP®).[1]

At the beginning of the twenty-first century many of the original ESCOs stopped providing this service because of information asymmetry between the ESCO and the facility owners resulting in difficulty in quantifying energy reduction. However, this service concept continues to flourish in the buildings sectors.

When the original providers of performance contracting stopped that service, many of them developed a new service commonly known as a 'pay as you go' contract. This is a hybrid contract containing elements from both operational leasing and performance contracting. It is used in large power plants and in turbines for airplanes. Here, when an airline decides which turbine manufacturer to use on their aircraft, it leases the turbines from the

---

1   For further details of the standard, see International Performance Monitoring and Verification Protocol parts 1, 2, and 3. Available at: http://www.evo-world.org.

manufacturer. The manufacturer monitors and maintains the performance of the turbine leased to the airline. The airline pays the manufacturer based on the amount of thrust provided by the turbines. Similarly, a power plant operator pays the manufacturer based on the amount of energy the turbines generate.

Each financing option carries a risk and a corresponding reward to the business. The decision to choose one financing option over another requires careful analysis to ensure that all options are properly analysed.

Scheduling Energy Reduction Projects

The next and final major step in an energy reduction programme is its implementation. As the former CEO of ABB, Percy Barnevik, put it: 'Success is 10% strategy and 90% execution.' Without execution, no energy reduction can be realised.

Once the capital has been approved, the next logical questions on many managers' and engineers' minds are:

1.   In what order should we implement the various energy reduction projects?
2.   On which project shall we focus our resources?

There is no one single answer to these questions. Using the strategy and model developed in Chapter 4, the business should have implemented or be in the midst of implementing housekeeping opportunities.

Reductions in wastage, leaks, dead legs, unnecessary energy supplied to machinery, machinery idle time, production rate losses, untended taps and hoses, procedural changes to minimise energy and poor insulation are examples under the housekeeping banner. They generate immediate benefits to cash flow, are easy to monitor for progress and are great topics for initiating and engaging employee behaviour changes.

The next steps are to implement opportunities classified as simple control systems. Very frequently, these opportunities would be in the form of compressed air or electricity savings because electricity is, in general, three or four times more expensive than natural gas. However, this may not always be the case. The quantum of thermal energy used (in the form of steam, hot water, thermal heat transfer fluids) could outweigh the quantum electricity used.

If a facility has plans to install a combined heat and power (CHP) plant and/or district heating and cooling project, CHP plants and district heating and cooling plants usually have a long lead time (typically 12–18 months). Implementing good housekeeping and simple control systems involves significantly shorter timescales. As such, any change in CHP or district heating and cooling plant can be incorporated in a relatively short time and can be started at the onset of the energy reduction programme.

When scheduling the rest of the energy reduction project, it is important to point out that there are other selection criteria to consider and that they may sometimes take precedence over energy savings. Some of these are:

- business risk
- health and safety
- environmental emissions such as CO_2, NO_x and/or other emissions
- other regulatory liabilities
- reliability etc.

Regulatory and economic incentives have been excluded from the list above. This is because incentives can be changed and/or withdrawn at short notice.

Sometimes, a visual model gives a powerful representation of energy reduction projects and facilitates selecting and prioritising them. This can be achieved by using a simple to use ranking matrix based on the hybrid energy model and implementation strategy described in Chapter 4.

A ranking matrix (Figure 10.1) is a two-dimensional matrix consisting of the capital cost and complexity of each energy reduction project. To prioritise the projects, the relative position of each project on this matrix should be determined. This is a subjective evaluation based on the perception of employees and management of the business, and the knowledge and experience of consultants and contractors in the technical aspects of the projects. The evaluation is carried out in three stages.

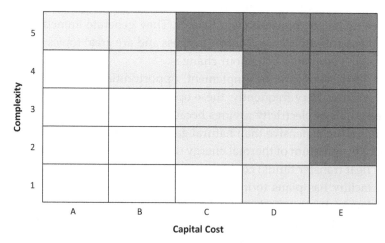

Figure 10.1   Ranking matrix

Stage 1 – determine the category of improvement, without regard to investment costs:

1.   housekeeping
2.   control
3.   modifications
4.   integration
5.   alternatives.

Stage 2 – determine the classification for investment costs:

1.   no (additional) cost measures
2.   low cost measures (< 1 year return)
3.   medium cost measures (< 4 years return)
4.   high cost measures (> 4 years return)
5.   very high cost measures (> 8 years return).

Stage 3 – determine a timescale for implementation:

1.   Immediate – actions should be implemented as soon as possible
2.   Moderate – implement at next convenient time, planned shutdown, etc.
3.   Implement when best solution is determined.

Once the categories have been defined, a project can generally be sorted very quickly, with its speed of implementation identified as shown in Figure 10.2.

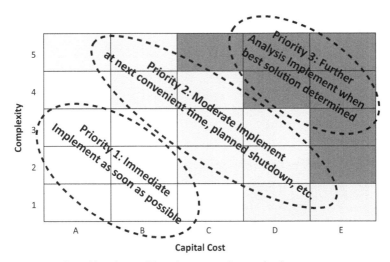

Figure 10.2   Visualisation of implementation priority

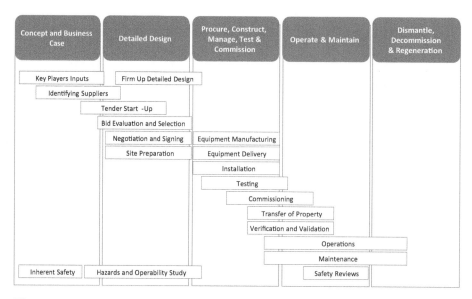

Figure 10.3   Stages of project management

Depending on the size of the project, the size of the project team and resources allocated will vary. However, all of the activities required to deliver and realise the energy projects are in line with normal project management activities. A summary of good project management activities is shown in Figure 10.3.

In Part 2, many tools and techniques of finding energy reduction opportunities and methods of bringing them to realisation have been described. Some of the common reasons why an energy reduction project could fail have been indirectly described. If the energy reduction programme is to be successful, lines of responsibility must be identified, made clear and fairly distributed among all employees.

PART 3
Avoidable Energy Losses

In Chapter 8, the concept of quick wins was mentioned. This part is concerned with the concepts and ideas that generate quick wins in energy savings. Recalling the framework for energy reduction programmes introduced in Part 1, quick wins are predominantly the domain of housekeeping and simple control systems.

It is essential that managers and engineers overcome the insurmountable barriers to maximise the opportunities presented as quick wins. There are two halves to quick wins:

1. Doing the Right Things.
2. Doing the Things Right.

As easy as it seems, in practice quick wins are poorly identified and executed. It is unnecessary to get consultants and contractors to identify and quantify quick wins. Paraphrasing the above into simple, common sense and easy to remember steps:

- Know where energy is used.
- Maintain your assets according to original equipment manufacturer (OEM) recommendation.
- Turn it off – it is not possible to save more than by turning a machine off.
- Turn it down – minimise energy losses and match the machine to demand.
- After implementing all of the above, recover any excess energy.

The majority of quick wins opportunities do not require capital investment and can be funded from revenue and/or the balance sheet. Each individual opportunity generates a small saving. However, in each business there are many quick wins, giving rise to big total savings. They are also opportunities for the business to provide leadership to engage employees.

Quick wins reduce the energy consumed by the business, sizing of future energy reduction opportunities and the capital investment required for future energy reduction opportunities.

Many managers, engineers and scientists are aware of and are able to recite ideas of what constitute a quick win, the need to plug them and their effect on the business:

> *You don't have to preach to me about the benefits of a quick win; you will only be preaching to the converted.*

The ability to recite and discuss these concepts will not generate any reduction in energy consumption; it will only make you sound smart. What is important is to take action to implement all quick win opportunities. As quick wins are easy to miss, especially for employees working in the same environment every day, it is even more important to ensure that once quick wins are implemented, they do not recur in the same area or in other areas of the business.

We will first explore some fundamentals so that managers have a basic understanding of failures. Then, we will explore some ideas where quick wins can be found. Many case studies have been used to illustrate some of these quick wins.

11

Doing the Right Things: Moving from Firefighting to Energy Savings

Understanding Failures: The Maintenance Cycle

When a company purchases a new energy consuming plant or machinery for use within the business, once it is installed, tested and commissioned it is handed over to the business for normal operation. During its life it will operate until it develops some symptoms of failure. Until this happens, many companies choose either to operate the machines until these symptoms occur or choose to have the machines inspected and serviced at regular intervals. Other maintenance options are to swap operations to a standby unit; inspect the equipment to find potential signs of failures; continuously monitor the conditions; and carry out tests to detect hidden failures.

When equipment begins to exhibit symptoms of failure, it could be overhauled (online or offline), online settings adjusted; or the business could continue to operate it to failure, increase monitoring activities and/or operate it under conditions that are within the capabilities of the equipment. If the equipment were allowed to deteriorate further, the maintenance options would be significantly reduced to continue to operate to failure, overhaul, adjust online settings or change the equipment.

If and when the equipment fails catastrophically, the only options are to remove and repair the equipment or to replace it. If the business has backups or spare machines, the business can continue to operate the backup while the equipment is being repaired. Otherwise, the business will have to stop until the repair is complete. Very frequently, the equipment is replaced like-for-like. The description above constitutes a cycle known as the maintenance life cycle. This is shown graphically in Figure 11.1. The earlier maintenance plans are developed and implemented in the life cycle, the more maintenance options

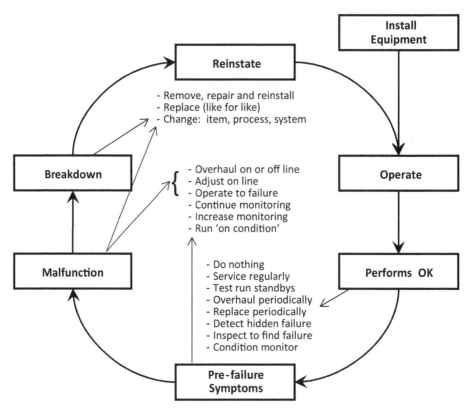

Figure 11.1   Maintenance life cycle

are available to ensure longevity and reliability, and represents the higher returns on investment on that equipment.

Most business takes a reactive approach to maintenance. An 'If it isn't broken, don't fix it' attitude may help the business in short-term cash flow but will result in long-term cash drain. This is because any maintenance work required will be put off until the next maintenance period. In the meantime the failure could begin to affect other parts of the machine, until a more severe fault develops.

A more proactive style of maintenance is to smoke out potential signs of failure. This may involve routine inspection, routine service and overhaul. It does not mean that failure would not occur. However, for the majority of failures that do occur they could have been identified early and a potential plan developed in time for the imminent failure.

An emerging form of maintenance involves predicting the failure of equipment. A simple thought process in the choice of maintenance actions is shown in Figure 11.2. Each business will need to tailor the choice of maintenance plans to their own business requirements. Ultimately, a balance between

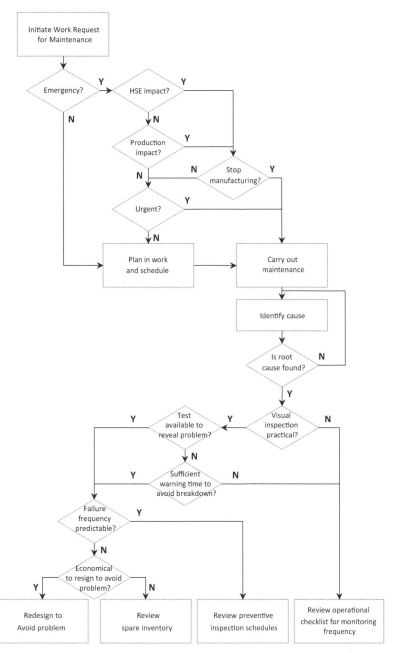

Figure 11.2   A simple maintenance plan

maintenance cost and the financial benefit of maintenance has to be achieved. An excessively far-sighted approach to maintenance will lead to an expensive maintenance regime without the associated benefits to the business.

There are many tools in the market that help to develop this balance. All of these tools are legitimate approaches and achieve similar results. Many of these tools are best applied under specific equipment conditions and situations. It is unlikely that the significant majority of companies will achieve superior and lasting performance simply by following a specific formula or a sequence of prescribed steps (Rosenzweig, 2007).

Many of the consultant and contractor services on offer will, regardless of the naming conventions and marketing languages, contain a cocktail of tools tailored to specific needs of the business. The balancing act between the choice of tool, its cost and benefits will have to be determined in collaboration between the consultants and the managers. It will vary across the industry of the business, its asset maturity (see Figure 5.2 on page 58), and to some extent the geography and capabilities of the consultants and contractors in engineering and maintenance.

From Firefighting to Energy Savings

In a business environment, energy cost is a distant second or third largest component in annual operating cost. The largest components are normally materials and labour expenses. However, energy consumption is the largest total life cycle cost in all energy using equipment and has the largest potential for significant savings.

Following closely behind energy cost is maintenance and engineering cost. During periods of financial constraints, maintenance and engineering budgets are normally the first targeted. From a business point of view, this decision makes sense. Raw materials, labour and energy are essential for the business. Without them, the business does not exist. The cost of associated maintenance and engineering increases every year. To continue making a sustainable profit, businesses have to find ways to manufacture more efficiently, to cut costs or both.

A budget reduction in maintenance and engineering results in deferred maintenance activities. Alternatively, maintenance work is carried out below the level recommended by the manufacturer. Initially, reducing maintenance expenditure could save the company some money. This is because the maintenance team may be able to carry out essential works within allocated shutdown times. This is only true up to a point: where continued expenditure reduction will lead to planned maintenance to be incomplete, equipment failure starts to increase and there is an increase in energy consumption, reduced equipment life, followed by capital expenditure to replace the equipment sometime in the future.

In practice, approximately 70 per cent of the inefficiencies and ineffectiveness in energy consuming machinery are the direct result of poor engineering and maintenance. Of these, 80 per cent of the problems manifest themselves within the first year of operation.[1] These inefficiencies can be found in:

1.   Poor cleaning;
2.   Leaks – accepting the fact that leaks are inevitable;
3.   Breakdowns – (a) breakdowns are repaired temporarily until the next available maintenance; (b) during repairs, the main process and machinery is off but the auxiliary units are kept running.
4.   Misalignment – motors and drives are misaligned, leading to additional heat due to friction and accelerated failure rate.
5.   Machines running at sub-optimal speeds – (a) energy is used due to low loadings; (b) lack of knowledge to optimise run settings.
6.   System design – design of energy systems that causes inefficiency or is inherently inefficient.
7.   Idle time – inefficient start-up sequence resulting in energy wastage.

The statistics quoted above beg the question whether companies should put more emphasis on equipment maintenance – especially when 70 per cent of problems arise from poorly executed engineering and maintenance. Case Studies 11.1–11.6 illustrate the needs for and quanta of energy reduction from maintenance and engineering related issues.

CASE STUDY 11.1   ENERGY REDUCTION FROM MAINTENANCE ISSUES – HEAT EXCHANGER

A manufacturing plant uses solvents as part of their product cleaning process. The solvent and water are mixed at different stages in the cleaning process. Traditionally, all of the solvent and water is discharged to effluent. As part of its environmental initiative to reduce environmental pollution, the plant has installed a distillation column to recover all solvents for reuse, and discharges nearly pure water to the effluent (another potential for energy reduction could be to recover and reuse the 'near' pure water). A schematic of the distillation column is shown in Figure 11.3 on the following page.

The distillation column operates at 99°C. In the column, all solvents will boil at 80°C and leave the distillation column at the top.* Here, they are condensed

---

*   If the solvent boils off at 80°C there is no need to operate the column at 99°C. Technically, any temperature above 80°C will suffice. However, changing the temperature set point could reduce the purity of recovered solvent or increase the solvent content at the bottom. This needs to be done with care.

---

1   Personal communication from Dr Rob Terrell.

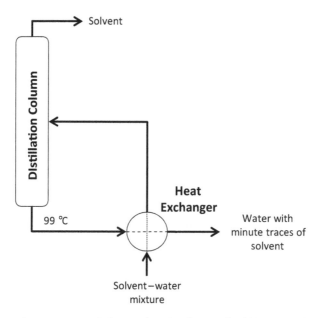

Figure 11.3   Schematic of solvent distillation column

and reused in the process. Water leaves from the bottom. Steam is used to keep the whole column at 99°C.

The mixture of solvent and water is fed through a feed/bottom heat exchanger, where it is preheated before entering the distillation column. This heat exchanger is designed to preheat the feed to the distillation column from ambient temperature to 89°C while cooling the bottom stream temperature from 99°C to 50°C.

During an energy audit it was discovered that the heat exchanger was only heating the feed to 50°C and cooling the bottom stream to 73°C. Detailed investigation was carried out to determine the cause of this deviation. The logical conclusion, supported by the evidence from maintenance records, was that the heat exchanger was blocked and needed to be cleaned.

Because of this blocked heat exchanger, additional steam was required to heat the column to 99°C. This was quantified to be an additional 135 kW or 434,000 kWh/yr of steam (costing £8,000/yr). This had also caused a violation in the effluent discharge permit. The permit states that all effluent discharge from the site should be less than 55°C.

At the next plant shutdown period the heat exchanger was cleaned and a cleaning schedule was incorporated into future shutdowns. The operating temperature from the heat exchanger returned to the normal designed parameters.

CASE STUDY 11.2   ENERGY REDUCTION FROM MAINTENANCE ISSUES – TEMPERATURE INSTRUMENT

A multi-storey commercial building is occupied by 2,000 people. Each floor, constructed using an open plan concept, is occupied for 12 hours per day five days per week. The air ventilation system supplies fresh air and extracts air from the building via four separate zones.

Operation of the ventilation system in each zone is monitored by a building management system (BMS). There is no humidity control requirement in the building. The air is cooled to a set point temperature (14°C) and reheated to room set point temperature (24°C).*

During an energy survey, it was found that the air is cooled to 10°C instead of 14°C. This was verified by a temperature measurement inside the fresh air supply duct. The temperature instruments controlling the fresh air cooling were faulty. Since the probes were installed several years ago, they had not been checked, serviced or calibrated.

Replacing the faulty temperature instruments is not a cost item for the building because it is covered by a service contract. The energy cost avoided from not cooling the air to 10°C is £8,900/yr. Additional savings can be achieved by not cooling the supply air below 24°C. This is a set point change in the BMS and does not incur any capital cost. The energy savings is £10,600/yr, giving a total saving of £19,500/yr.

---

*   As the room required 24°C air, cooling the air to 14°C and to have it reheated to 24°C is a waste of energy. Fresh air should only be cooled to 24°C. This avoids overcooling and heating.

CASE STUDY 11.3   ENERGY REDUCTION FROM MAINTENANCE ISSUES – LEAKY ROOF

A process plant consumes, on average, 700 kg/hr of steam. This figure has gradually increased over several months to read above its steam meter calibration range (more than 1,500 kg/hr). There were no apparent changes in operating schedules or maintenance requirements.

A site-wide investigation was carried out to identify the source of extra steam consumption. Many managers and engineers scoured the whole processing area but could not find any anomalies to explain the increase in steam consumption.

Several months later, after accepting that the steam consumption must be being used in the process, the site personnel experienced a continuous 'raining' effect even though it was a sunny day. The site initiated another round of investigations of the whole site, including non-processing areas and the roof. It was found that the steam supply to the heating and ventilation system, located on the roof, had a pipe fracture and was venting large quantities of steam. Repairs were immediately initiated and the steam consumption returned to 700 kg/hr levels.

CASE STUDY 11.4   ENERGY REDUCTION FROM MAINTENANCE ISSUES – HEAVY SCALING

In a commercial building, a hot water boiler is used for heating, including for domestic hot water via a calorifier. The boilers were replaced several years back. It is now an energy efficient condensing boiler.

During an energy survey it was found that the boiler supplied hot water at 90°C and returns to the boiler at 80°C. However, according to the commissioning documentation, the system is supposed to operate by supplying hot water at 75°C and returns to the boiler at 65°C.

A follow-on investigation was carried out and found the reason for boilers being operated at 90°C – to keep the domestic hot water temperature at 65°C. It was discovered that the area was supplied with hard water: the domestic calorifier contained a thick layer of calcium salts on the surface and had not been cleaned in five years.*

Because of this and the hot water generator and its associated pipe work are also poorly insulated and during peak demand there is insufficient capacity to generate domestic hot water in a short time. These reasons cause a need to raise the boiler temperature set point to meet the hot water generator requirements.

A maintenance programme was introduced for cleaning the calorifier annually. In areas where insulation was found to be deficient, the old insulation was removed and new insulation installed. This was carried out as part of a wider hot water systems upgrade.

------

*   Calcium salts in water have a tendency to deposit on hot surfaces. In areas where the water is hard, the white coating found inside is calcium salts. Overtime, calcium salts build up inside the boiler and cause it to use more energy to boil the same amount of water. Removing the calcium salts returns its efficiency to normal.

CASE STUDY 11.5   ENERGY REDUCTION FROM MAINTENANCE ISSUES – WRONG PARTS USED

A large cheese- and milk-powder plant uses coal as a fuel to generate steam. In any combustion of solid fuel, ash residue is collected at the bottom. A sample of the ash was analysed for its carbon content. The typical carbon content of residual ash from a well-operated and maintained coal-fired boiler is 3–5 per cent. The analysis showed the actual carbon content was 12 per cent. This means that approximately 8 per cent (12 − 5 = 8) is wasted and could be recovered and reused. This is equivalent to 95,258 kWh/yr.

At the next available opportunity, the boiler's burners were recalibrated and the grates where the coal is fired were replaced with the manufacturer specified model. As the replacement and service were funded from the maintenance budget, there was no capital cost incurred by the business.

CASE STUDY 11.6   ENERGY REDUCTION FROM MAINTENANCE ISSUES – ROOT CAUSE

A manufacturing business consumes 720 kg/hr of steam. After the steam is used, it is returned to the boiler house via a condensate return tank and pump set located in the basement.

During an energy audit, it was found that the condensate return pipe at the boiler house was cold. When investigating, the energy audit team found the condensate pump was operating, and the condensate tank was full and overflowing into the drain next to it. The discharge of hot condensate into the open drain in the basement made the area hot and humid. The energy audit team also found an extractor fan installed in the basement to vent the heat and humidity outside the building.

Detailed investigation led to the condensate return pump, rated to pump water at 25°C, being used to pump condensate at 95°C. It was also noted that the pump was fairly new, installed a few months earlier when the original pump failed. A mismatch of pump rating led to the following wastage:

1. The condensate tank was full and overflowing into a nearby open drain, leading to 100 per cent increase in water consumption, water treatment chemicals consumption and effluent discharge.
2. There is also an additional cost of natural gas because the boiler has an additional heating demand to heat the fresh water from 18°C to 90°C (condensate temperature) before converting it to steam.
3. Additional electricity is used by the extractor fan to remove the heat and humidity at the basement.
4. There is also an unnecessary capital expenditure to purchase and install an extractor fan.

Installing a correctly rated condensate pump gives multiple cost savings from water, water treatment, natural gas, electricity and trade effluent. This was estimated to be £10,000/yr. The cost of replacing the pump was £3,000, giving a simple payback of 0.3 years.

A good rule of thumb for estimating leaks is as follows:

- Compressed air – in a quiet room, each tiny 'hissing' sound costs approximately £500/yr; a loud hissing sound costs approximately £7,000/yr.
- For compressed air application, every 1 bar pressure reduction at the compressor reduces the energy consumed by 6 per cent. If compressed air is generated at 10 bar and the highest pressure user is 7 bar, there

is an opportunity to reduce the compressor energy consumption by 18 per cent.

- To estimate steam leak, first observe the plume from a household kettle when it is boiling. If the kettle is rated 2 kW, the plume when water is boiling is equivalent to 2 kW. Using the plume volume from the kettle, estimate how many 'kettle plumes' could fit into the actual steam leak to estimate the energy loss from steam leaks.
- In cooling and refrigeration systems, reducing the set point temperature of the supply by 1°C will save approximately 3 per cent of the electricity consumed. If the plant needs cooling using 10°C water but the refrigeration supplies cooling water at 6°C, there is an opportunity to reduce the refrigeration energy consumption by 12 per cent.
- For water, or any other liquid leak, a drop per minute is approximately 0.5 l/hr.

To break free of the cycle of reactive maintenance and begin reducing energy consumption, the following lists a comprehensive set of tasks to be carried out.

1. Become good and efficient at reactive maintenance: repair failures with good-quality parts and to the recommended specifications.
2. Get to the root cause of these wasteful practices: resolve problems at source.
3. Use data analysis and planning to optimise performance.
4. Use quick wins to create the time to tackle the remaining steps.
5. Understand and prioritise the maintenance and engineering problems.
6. Reduce and eliminate the recurring problems.
7. Involve the entire workforce in keeping equipment in tip-top condition.
8. Introduce measures that predict failures in the future.
9. If and when there is a need to replace plant and machinery, use the highest efficiency models.

An electric motor is among a range of energy consuming plant machinery that will need routine maintenance and replacement. When an electric motor has failed, there are two options to rectify the situation: rewind the motor or replace it with a new motor.

The International Electrotechnical Commission (IEC) classifies motors according to their efficiency: called simply IE1, IE2, IE3 and IE4 in Europe. In the USA and Canada they are called 'standard', 'high efficiency', 'premium' and 'super premium' efficiency motors.

The choice to rewind or replace the motor is a function of cost. Every time a motor is rewound it loses some of its efficiency because the majority of motor service workshops do not have access to the high-standard and precision equipment used to manufacture IE2, IE3 and IE4 motors.

For small motors, up to 5 kW, the cost to rewind the motor is approximately the same as to purchase a new motor. For motors between 7.5 kW and 30 kW it may be economical to rewind the motor once before replacing it with a new motor. For larger motors economics favour having several more rewinds before the efficiency reduction from the existing motor makes a new motor more economical.

When replacing an electric motor, purchasing a higher efficiency motor can be between two and three times more expensive. However, over a five-year period the electricity consumed by the motor can be up to 30 times its purchase cost. If there is an opportunity to replace a motor or install a new motor, specifying the highest efficiency motor available will pay for itself over a few months of operation.

12

Doing the Things Right: Avoiding the Common Mistakes

There are seven additional areas where energy reduction can be achieved within a short time. Together with good-quality maintenance practices described in Chapter 11, these are commonly known as quick wins. Some consultants and contractors call them 'Just Do It' (JDI) or 'Do It Now' (DIN). These additional seven ideas are:

1. Install correctly.
2. Sizing to match demand.
3. Turn off when not required.
4. Operate to match demand.
5. Start up and shut down.
6. Insulation.
7. Heat recovery.

Although each individual quick win opportunity is small, collectively these savings can become substantial. Some of these are easier or cheaper to implement when designing new plants and energy systems but more costly to retrofit. The costs involved to implement these are also relatively small (or incremental costs to incorporate when designing from new). To find and implement quick wins using in-house resources has a typical return on investment within months. Involving an external consultant and contractors to identify these opportunities will drastically increase the cost to implement these energy reduction opportunities.

Good command in finding, managing and minimising the recurrence of quick win opportunities not only saves energy, but also changes the energy baseline, the sizing and the capital required to implement other energy reduction projects. Good command in exploiting quick win shows the clients, consultants, contractors and other service providers that the company is committed to reducing energy consumption and may act as a deterrent for others to pull the wool over the company's eyes.

Install Correctly

This is crucial in energy reduction. Very often, the proposals received from consultants and contractors are logical and, on the surface, make sense. However, the actual installation may be far from the proposed scheme.

The most common error involves installing variable speed drives (VSDs). The purpose of a VSD is to vary the speed of the motor to match the demands of the pump or fan. VSDs could be installed but do not generate energy reduction. There are many reasons as to why.

- The business specifies a pump or a fan with VSD and the contractor installs a pump or fan with VSD with no means of varying the flow.
- In order to win a contract, the contractor leaves out essential parts for energy efficiency (e.g., temperature controllers, level controllers).
- During construction, the remaining capital fund is near the budget or installation time is near the handover time; the contractor completes the project without the essential parts for energy efficiency.
- There are some sales personnel who have a theoretical appreciation of energy efficient systems but do not have the technical insight and practical know-how to implement energy efficient systems.

The key questions to ask the consultant and contractor proposing a VSD are:

- How will the VSD vary its operating speed? What input tells the VSD to vary its speed? What input tells it to stop? Some installed VSDs operate at their electricity supply frequency – in the UK and in some other countries it is 50 Hz; in the USA and Canada it is 60 Hz. Some installed VSDs operate at a fixed frequency (less than the electricity supply frequency). The correct way of controlling a VSD is to modulate the flow by means of an installed instrument such as a temperature controller.
- What is the likely range for the VSDs to be modulating? If the drive is going to be operated at less than 25 Hz, the pump or fan is too large. Operating a light loaded pump or fan will result in significant reduction in power factor (an efficiency multiplier for electrical equipment). A review of the pump or fan sizing is in order. Otherwise, the electricity consumption will increase.

- If the drive is going to be operated at more than 45 Hz, the VSDs and associated pump or fan will use more electricity than that of a pump or fan without a VSD. The total electricity consumption will increase.
- From the drawing of the system where a VSD is to be installed, look for any means in the piping system that allows the pumped liquid to return to the pump without going to an end-user. This could be a bypass line, three-way valves, four-way valves, valves that are partially open (this is known as throttling) or automatic valves that are operated partially open.

The pumping system needs to be viewed as a whole system. Very often, the throttled valve or bypasses are far away from the pumps. If any of the conditions described above exists, the benefit of a VSD can be maximised by removing these issues. Case Study 12.1 demonstrates the application of VSD in a building complex where many of the concepts are present.

Other technologies commonly installed poorly are:

- Condensing boilers – the buildings described in Case Study 11.4 uses condensing boilers. According to manufacturer literature, in order to maximise the efficiency of a condensing boiler, the hot water supply temperature needs to be less than 60°C. In the case study, the supply temperature is well above 60°C, which means that the boilers are not condensing.
- Voltage reduction – voltage reduction work on lighting and small power systems. For lighting, the light fitting needs to be non-electronic ballast type. For other plant machinery, a reduction in voltage will result in an increase in electricity consumption.[1]

Many of the case studies in this book can also double up as opportunities for installing energy efficient plant machinery correctly. In Case Study 12.8, if the manufacturing process were designed to use hot water instead of steam, the company would use 40 per cent less energy.

The same energy reduction is also true for buildings. Lockwood (2006) reported that energy efficiently built buildings use more than 40 per cent less energy, 34 per cent less water, have a 15 per cent boost in employee productivity and 5 per cent less absenteeism when compared to standard buildings of comparable size.

---

1   For a short review of voltage reduction, see Vesma, 2006b.

CASE STUDY 12.1   VARIABLE FLOW HOT WATER SYSTEM

A commercial office complex consists of four separate buildings, code named Building One, Two, Three and Four respectively. An 85°C hot water boiler, generated from three energy efficient state-of-the-art condensing boilers located in Building One, provides the heating needs of all four buildings. Figure 12.1 shows a schematic of the hot water distribution.

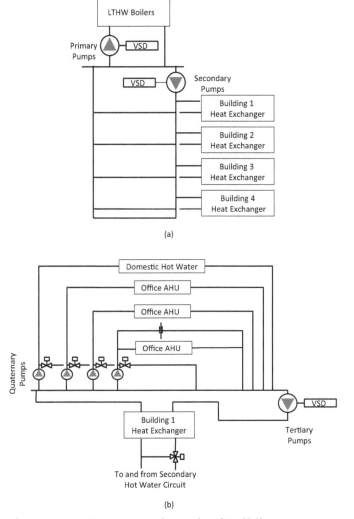

(a)

(b)

**Figure 12.1   Hot water schematic of Building 1, 2, 3
and 4**

To analyse this hot water distribution system, there are four separate and distinct circuits:

- *Primary circuit*: circulation of 85°C hot water from the boiler to a common header. From this header, the flow is returned to the boiler via a set of VSD-controlled primary pumps. These VSDs are operated at fixed speeds.
- *Secondary circuit*: hot water take-off from the header mentioned above via a set of VSD-controlled pumps through to all four buildings and back to the same header. These VSDs are operated at fixed speeds. When a building does not need hot water, 85°C hot water is returned to the secondary distribution via a three-port control valve. When the building needs hot water, 85°C water flows through the building's heat exchangers to generate lower temperature hot water.

All four buildings have identical third and fourth distribution circuits. These circuits generate 60°C hot water for use within the building:

- *Tertiary circuit*: uses a VSD controlled pump to pump water through the building's heat exchangers to a second header. Any hot water return from the building and excess hot water is returned to the inlet of the same pump. The tertiary pumps are operated at fixed speeds.
- *Quaternary circuit*: each user within the building takes off 60°C hot water from the header (described in the tertiary circuit) via its own pumps and returns cooled water to the same header. These pumps are fixed-speed pumps. If the end user does not need hot water, an automatic control valve on each quaternary circuit opens and bypasses the flow to the end user.

During an energy audit, it was found that the primary, secondary and tertiary pumps are significantly oversized and there is always flow through all headers, bypass lines and the three-port control valves. It was also noted that although the primary, secondary and tertiary pumps are controlled by VSDs, they are operated at full speed (50Hz) constantly throughout the year.

When there are no heating requirements, hot water is pumped throughout the whole system and ultimately returns to the boiler or heat exchanger. Pumping low temperature hot water (LTHW) around the circuit without any heating demand is a waste of electricity.* As there are no means of varying the flow of hot water based on demand, the pumps consume 169 kW of electricity. This is equivalent to 1.5 million kWh/yr.

Two options are available to reduce the energy consumed by the pump:

---

* All hot surfaces will lose heat to the surroundings; heat will also be dissipating from the hot water distribution. Applying insulation to hot pipes will minimise the heat loss but it does not stop this heat dissipation completely. This phenomenon is known as parasitic losses from a hot water system. For the purpose of this case study, the heat dissipation is considered to be negligible and ignored.

- *Remove the VSDs*: VSDs consume electricity. As the pumps are running at full speed, the VSDs could be removed from the primary, secondary and tertiary pumps. The electricity savings that can be achieved was calculated to be 40,000 kWh/yr or 3 per cent of electricity consumed by the pumps.
- *Maximise the potential of the VSDs:*** Making the whole hot water distribution system a variable flow system maximises the full potential of the existing VSDs and provides the largest energy reduction. This involves: (1) installing several low-cost pressure transmitters; (2) isolating all of the common headers so that there is no opportunity to pump hot water around the system when there are no users requiring heat; (3) replace all three-port control valves with two-port control valves and remove all bypass lines; (4) a simple programme change allows the VSD to start/stop and modulate the pumping speeds to meet the heating demand. The electricity savings that can be achieved was calculated to be 840,000 kWh/yr (57 per cent of electricity consumed).

The second option was chosen for implementation. With a capital cost of £57,000, it has a simple payback of 1.05 years. If these features had been incorporated during the construction phase, the additional cost would have been £16,000, with a simple payback of 0.2 years.

** There is a potential disadvantage in the second option: When heating is required, it would take slightly longer for the system to reach full operating temperature. Depending on the size of the distribution, this could range from a few minutes to a few hours. In general, for small to medium sized buildings this is acceptable. For a large building complex, the hot water system would need to be started, say, one hour before the occupants arrive for work.

Sizing to Match Demand

One of the key barriers to energy efficiency described in Chapter 5 is equipment sizing. Very frequently, equipment and plant machinery is oversized because of uncertainty in its demand. From a business perspective, in order to meet clients' demands it is better to have oversized equipment and plant machinery than undersized.

This idea revolves around having energy consuming plant and machinery that is significantly oversized, especially thermal energy systems such as heated systems (steam or hot water), cooled systems (cooling water or refrigeration), pumps and fans. Significantly oversized equipment is more expensive to purchase and install. A significantly oversized thermal and cooling system is inherently inefficient because of parasitic losses. Significantly oversized pumps and fans will have a low power factor, which will lead to higher energy cost.

This also extends to energy consuming systems that are designed for larger consumption but the site has diminished use. Some examples are:

- Steam boilers operating at 10 barg, when the highest pressure user uses very little steam at 10 barg and the rest of the users are at 3 barg.
- Air compressors operating at 9.5 barg when the highest pressure user is 6.0 barg.
- Operating the ventilation, heating and cooling system for a full office block over weekends and at night when the only user is the security office.

In the examples above, it is frequently possible to use dedicated energy systems for a specific application: in the case of air compressors, operate the compressors at 6.0 barg and use a booster compressor for the 9.5 barg user.

Another common mistake is supplying a form of energy that is not readily usable by its end-user. A good example would be supplying steam when the process needs hot water. A good example is in many food and beverage, such as milk and other dairy product, manufacturing plants. Here, the process typically needs a maximum of 80°C hot water.

Many plants generate hot water from steam. A steam system is cheaper to install because it uses smaller pipe sizes. After the steam is used (condensed), the energy remaining in the condensate is usually wasted, giving rise to heat recovery opportunities. If the plant chooses to use hot water, a hot water boiler is slightly more efficient, significantly cheaper to buy and there is no need to recover heat from condensate as it is automatically returned to the boiler. Over the lifetime of the plant, a steam system will consume more energy than a hot water system and be subjected to a more stringent insurance inspection requirement.

Another similar example would be to use refrigeration cooling to cool a UK-based office space to a comfortable working temperature. UK weather conditions allow for more than 90 per cent of the cooling to be achieved using a cooling tower. A cooling tower is also 12 times more energy efficient than a refrigeration unit, i.e., it will use 12 times less electricity than a commercial refrigeration unit. During the hottest months during summer, an evaporative cooling unit can be used to supplement the cooling requirements.

CASE STUDY 12.2   SIZING AIR COMPRESSOR TO MATCH DUTY

In an alcoholic beverage plant, low pressure compressed air is used in fermentation vessels to:

- reduce the viscosity of the fermentation broth and allow the agitator to function;
- provide oxygen to micro-organisms in the fermentation process.

Depending on the stage of the fermentation, the compressed air ranges from 2,500 Nm³/hr to 4,000 Nm³/hr. Compressed air is generated from a fixed-speed compressor rated at 7,000 Nm³/hr and has a minimum output of 4,000 Nm³/hr. As the fermentation process only needs less than 4,000 Nm³/hr, all excess compressed air generated is vented into the atmosphere.

Venting compressed air is inefficient because energy is consumed but is not put to use. A new variable-speed compressed air system was installed to meet the full range of demand. This new compressor has a simple payback of 2.8 years.

CASE STUDY 12.3   SIZING WATER SYSTEMS TO MATCH DEMAND AND BUSINESS RISK

Purified water in a pharmaceutical plant is distributed in close-loop pipe work to various end users and back to a storage tank. The distribution, operated 24 hours a day seven days a week, is controlled by a variable-speed driven pump operated at 50 Hz. When there is no use for purified water, the calculated velocity of the water distribution is 7.50 m/s, giving rise to a Reynolds Number (measure of turbulence) of 176,000.*

A survey carried out found that purified water is only required by the end users for two hours/day. When there is no water demand, the pumping requirement is 5 per cent of the rated capacity; when there is demand, the pumping requirement is 30 per cent of the rated capacity.

The operations team believed that the regulation requires a minimum flow of 1 m/s at the return pipe to the tank at all times. Upon checking the regulatory requirement, it only specifies for the return leg to be turbulent.

The most energy efficient option to supply purified water is by using a suitably sized two-speed pump or a suitably sized VSD driven pump. This reduces electricity by up to 95 per cent.

---

*   Any Reynolds number over 4,100 is considered to be turbulent.

Turn Off When Not Required

When finding opportunities to turn equipment off, managers and engineers need to challenge the normal practices and beliefs of the business – if this involves regulatory or contractual agreements, make sure to obtain the latest applicable copy of the documentation. Very frequently, there are more opportunities to turn things off than the norms would allow.

A survey of 6,000 business users by British Gas (2012) found that up to 46 per cent of electricity use occurs when office staff have left the office for the day. A common item that can be turned off is lighting. There are many myths about turning off lighting. One of the persistent myths is that at the moment of turning on a light it instantaneously uses more electricity and then falls back to the rated electricity. This is not true: turning on a light consumes no more than the maximum rated electricity printed on the light fitting. In fact, the surge of power is only significant to a fraction of a second.

Another good example of energy consuming equipment that can be turned off is the heating and cooling systems within an office environment. During cooler months, the cooling systems, e.g., cooling towers, chillers and associated pumping, can be isolated and turned off. During warmer months, the heating systems, e.g., hot water boilers and associated pumping, can be isolated and turned off. Implementing this low-cost action could reduce the energy consumption for heating and cooling by up to 10 per cent.

The energy savings from turning off heating and cooling systems come from avoiding parasitic losses. Sometimes, this is also called cycling losses. Using a refrigeration system as an example, when there is no user demand for cooling, leaving the chiller and pumps on means that the chiller and pumps continue to consume electricity. All of the electricity they consume is converted into heat. In addition, the chilled water circulation inside the pipe works absorbs heat from the surrounding environment. The result is that the chiller will need to power up and dissipate the heat gathered in the system. This phenomenon is the reverse for boilers. If the boilers and cooling towers cannot be turned off because they also supply other users, consider investigating the opportunity to separate those users from the main heating and cooling system.

Other opportunities for turning off is when the machinery is idling but not producing products, e.g., during lunch breaks, change of tooling etc.

CASE STUDY 12.4   TURNING OFF AIR EJECTORS

A life science research and development laboratory generates vacuum using compressed air ejectors. There are six dedicated vacuum ejectors, each connecting to laboratory equipment. Vacuum is generated 24 hours a day but the laboratory equipment is used nine hours per day. As the vacuum is only required for nine hours per day, it is not energy efficient to generate vacuum 24 hours per day.

Initially, the site received a proposal to replace the compressed air ejectors with a bench-scale vacuum generator. With an equipment cost of £13,300, the project has a simple payback of 1.05 years. A cheaper option was to install an isolation valve to prevent compressed air from going into the air ejector. This option has a capital cost of £2,700 and a simple payback of 0.23 year. This option was approved for implementation.

Operate to Match Demand

Following on from sizing and designing an energy system that meets the user demand, this category is concerned with matching the demand of the business or plant to the highest efficiency from the range of available equipment. For example:

- A site may have several boilers or several refrigeration units that have different capacities. Choose to operate machines that generate the right quantities of products using the least amount of energy or have the highest efficiency at the stated demand.
- Matching the ventilation requirement to the occupancy of the building.

All energy consuming equipment will have load efficiency data. This is available either in tabular form or in graphical form. An example from a steam boiler is shown in Figure 12.2. If this is not included in the equipment manual, it can be obtained by contacting the equipment supplier.

CASE STUDY 12.5   ENERGY REDUCTION DUE TO CHANGING VENTILATION REQUIREMENT

A large room was converted from a hazardous manufacturing space into an office space. Before the conversion, fresh air was supplied using a full fresh air supply and extract system. Due to the hazardous vapours, the heating, ventilation and air conditioning (HVAC) supplies and extracts were operated with an air change rate of 12.* The HVAC fans consumed 52 kW of electricity costing £33,000 per annum.

The office conversion project utilises the same HVAC systems without considering the fresh air requirements for the new office. Several years later, realising that the office HVAC is only required for 12 hours per day, instead of 24 hours, the energy manager installed a timed switch to turn off the HVAC at night. The 228,000 kWh/yr was saved and is equivalent to £16,500/yr.

When the energy manager checked the legal requirement for fresh air per occupant, it was discovered that the fresh air per person is 8 l/s and that the existing office HVAC far exceeded this requirement. Installing a suitably sized and commission VSD to control the HVAC fans resulted in an additional 220,000 kWh/yr saving (£16,000/yr).

---

*   The air change rate is the number of times the full volume of air within a room is changed in an hour.

CASE STUDY 12.6   MATCHING THE DUTY TO THE RIGHT EQUIPMENT CAPACITY

A secondary pharmaceutical site has a steam demand of between 1,500 kg/hr and 2,500 kg/hr, with an average of 1,800 kg/hr. Steam is generated from one of three boilers on the site, designated B1, B2 and B3. Each boiler has a different output capacity.

The site chose to operate the biggest boiler (B1) to meet the demand of the site on the basis that the biggest boiler would be able to cope with any foreseeable demand fluctuations. During an energy survey, boiler efficiency data was plotted for the site and is shown in Figure 12.2.

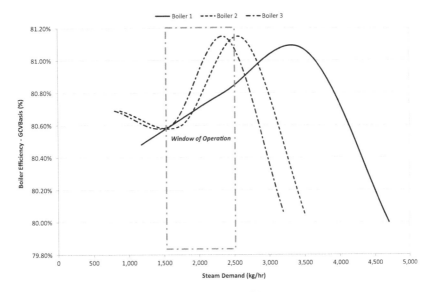

Figure 12.2   Boiler load-efficiency profile

Although B1 has the capacity to meet a wide range of steam demands, all three boilers can meet the steam demands of the site. B2 and B3 are fractionally more energy efficient in meeting the site steam demand. A simple change in the choice of boiler to operate would generate a saving with no capital outlay.

Start Up and Shut Down

The start up of energy consuming equipment is inherently inefficient. Starting up motors may cause a peak in electricity demand. The start up of other processes may incur a long start up time. Sometimes, a start up sequence is inefficient because the procedure causes it to be inefficient. At other times, start up may be efficient but there is a long idle time before the process is ready for production. All these present an opportunity to minimise energy consumption.

CASE STUDY 12.7   MATCHING THE OPERATING PARAMETER TO DUTY

Ultra pure water, used in a process plant, is generated by a multiple effect evaporator. The evaporator uses steam at 8 barg. Ultra pure water is stored and distributed from a tank.

A level controller at the tank starts the ultra pure water generator when the tank is 68 per cent full and stops the tank at 75 per cent. For business risk mitigation, it is not acceptable for the ultra pure water tank to fall below 50 per cent. At every start up, the generator undergoes a sanitisation cycle where the generator is heated up and held at the operating temperature for 15 minutes. All hot water generated during the sanitisation period is discharged to the effluent.

A week's worth of tank level data was collected to assess the energy efficiency of the ultra pure water generator. The generator starts 62 times per week. This means that 15.5 hours of steam input and water generated during this week were disposed.

During the study, it was found that the ultra pure water generator can be operated at pressures ranging from 3 barg to 8 barg. The generator is most energy efficient at 3 barg but generates water at a slower output rate (Figure 12.3).

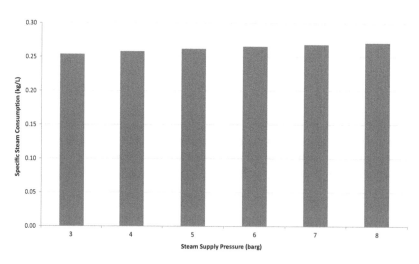

Figure 12.3   Specific steam consumption of ultra pure water generator

A model was developed to assess the energy saving scenarios for reducing the number of start ups and to reduce the operating steam pressure. An optimised model was chosen for implementation using 3 barg steam and by widening the start-stop tank levels to between 60 per cent and 80 per cent. This model predicts the number of starts as 14 per week and meets all of the business risk management requirements.

Steam savings are achieved as a result of fewer start ups and less energy consumed to generate ultra pure water. There are also water savings, water treatment costs and effluent treatment costs reduction, giving a total benefit of £19,300/yr. With an investment cost of £35,000, it has a simple payback of 1.8 years.

Insulation

The need to insulate steam, hot water and chilled water pipes is well established. Do pay attention to insulation of valves, flanges and pipe supports. In a manufacturing plant, these can contribute up to 20 per cent of the total heat loss (steam or hot water system) or heat gain (cooling water or chilled water pipes).

Mineral wool insulation degrades over time and has an average insulation life of between seven and ten years. It needs to be periodically replaced. If any insulation is found to be wet, e.g., after repairing leaks, that section of insulation will also need to be replaced. This is because wet insulation material will provide very little insulation. If a certain section of insulation needs to be routinely removed, e.g., for inspection, do consider the use of removable insulation.

Other types of insulation material are available. It is advisable to consult insulation contractors on the applicability of different insulation materials for the specific application.

Insulation typically has a simple payback of less than one year. If consultants are involved to identify and specify insulation improvements, the simple payback can increase to more than 2.5 years.

Heat Recovery

Apart from small number of applications where very high-quality energy is required to manufacture saleable product and leaves relatively 'low-grade heat' for recovery, an opportunity to recover energy is, in general, a symptom of energy waste that occurred elsewhere. By applying and taking advantage of quick wins described in this book, many heat recovery opportunities would have been removed. Case Study 12.8 is a good example.

CASE STUDY 12.8   USING HOT WATER INSTEAD OF STEAM

A malted drink manufacturer generates steam using natural gas. The boiler does not have an economiser and has a gross efficiency of 80 per cent. The plant received a proposal from an ESCO to install an economiser generating a natural gas reduction of 5 per cent with a simple payback of four years.

A mixing process, consuming 33 per cent of the site's steam consumption, uses hot water. The hot water is generated from steam via a heat exchanger. The steam is distributed via three mile long distribution pipe work before reaching the mixing area. Detailed analysis of the process showed that the process needs 528 kW of thermal energy.

Inefficiencies in the heat exchanger, energy losses in the distribution and inefficiencies in the boiler mean that an equivalent of 872 kW needs to be purchased to supply the mixing process. Using a locally operated hot water system, a thermal energy reduction of 322 kW can be achieved.

At a budgetary cost of £141,000, the simple payback for a new hot water system is 3.2 years. In addition, discussions with the operations and maintenance department revealed additional benefits from reduced temperature of the mixing process: less need for heat exchanger cleaning due to scaling every two weeks; increased availability for production, leading to increased sales.

Another example is the installation of a steam turbine (also known as turbo-expander in some countries) to reduce steam pressure before end-use. This might involve generating steam at 12 barg and allowing it to run through the turbine to generate some electricity before using it in the business at 3 barg. If steam is not necessary (or only little used) at any pressure above 3 barg, then the right thing to do is generate steam at 3 barg (and use separate steam generators for higher pressure).

A closely related application for heat recovery is to 'recover more heat from the same application' or to 'use heat more efficiently'. Utilities such as steam, hot water, cooling water and chilled water are seldom used directly in a manufacturing process or building. Heat is transferred to a different medium before it is used. Traditionally, this occurs in a 'shell and tube' type heat exchanger.

Shell and tube is a mature technology. As the name implies, it consists of a series of tubes inside a cylindrical shell. The design of a shell and tube tends to give large surfaces for heat loss from the surface; exhibits a high pressure drop necessitating a higher pump pressure; and is easier to foul up, thus reducing the mean time between maintenance. This type of heat exchanger tends to have an efficiency of around 80 per cent.

A modern and more energy efficient alternative would be to use a plate heat exchanger. With an efficiency of around 95 per cent, it transfers heat more efficiently or uses less energy to provide the same amount of heat. It also has a lower pressure drop, thus allowing the pump pressure to be turned down.

Other options are to replace either the tubes (e.g., twisted tubes or corrugated tubes) or the shell internals (e.g., rod or HELIXCHANGER®) with differently configured designs. These options, although less efficient than plate exchangers, are still significantly better than conventional shell and tube designs.

Very frequently, opportunities for recovering heat are easy to identify. The benefit of recovering heat is from using it elsewhere. Identifying a user for recovered heat tends to be less intuitive for managers and engineers, and both the heat source and the heat user need to be found before the cost and benefit can be quantified. Managers and engineers also tend to think only of opportunities inside the boundary of the business. Potential users of low-grade energy may be outside the boundary of the business. However, these projects are more complex and fall into the modification and integration categories.

CASE STUDY 12.9   USING COOLING WATER INSTEAD OF CHILLED WATER

A data centre located in the UK is cooled using a closed-loop refrigeration system. Cooling air at 18°C is supplied into the data centre and 26°C air is extracted from the room, where it is cooled by the refrigerator before being sent back to the room. This closed-loop refrigeration system uses 2.2 million kWh/yr of electricity.

Based on historical weather data over several years, for 96 per cent of the year the ambient temperature is below 18°C. This means that the data centre can be ventilated and cooled using ambient air for 96 per cent of the year.* For the remainder of the year, a cooling tower could be used to meet the cooling requirement. Using a combination of free cooling and the cooling tower, 2.1 million kWh/yr could be saved.

---

* This phenomenon is known as 'free cooling'.

13

Choosing a Consultant and Contractors for Energy Reduction

Apart from the technical skills, there are other reasons why consultants and contractors are brought into an organisation. *Harvard Business Review* research (Kauffman and Coutu, 2009) reported that business managers value the superior technical skills of consultants and contractors only 26 per cent of the time. There are other skills that managers value in consultants and contractors. These are shown in Figure 13.1.

Apart from identifying opportunities for energy reduction, managers frequently rely on consultants and contractors to support them to develop capabilities of an internal change team, facilitate a transition and act as

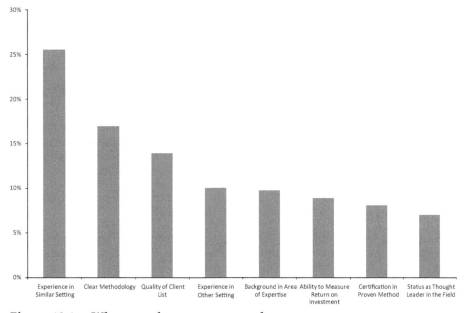

Figure 13.1   Why consultants are engaged
Source: Data for the figure drawn from Kauffman and Coutu, 2009.

sounding board on energy reduction programmes. Sometimes, consultants and contractors are used to facilitate and enhance the interaction within the business.

Therefore, there are four key aspects a business must consider when choosing energy consultants and contractors:

1.   How do the capabilities of the consultant and contractor 'fit' in with the work required by the business?
2.   What are the desired outcome and outputs required from the business?
3.   Should the business trade the specialist skills for some general skills?
4.   Should the business choose the best consultant in the market?

The most important aspect is the knowledge, skill and experience of the consultant fitting your business needs and requirements. There are many ways to assess the experience of a consultant and contractor: reputation, client list, case studies, references etc. In general, energy consultants and contractors range from those that are generalist to those that specialise in a specific technology or techniques.

There are advantages and disadvantages in choosing consultants or contractors with different degrees of fit to meet a business need. Sometime, choosing a specialist would limit the type of energy reduction technique that could be employed. Case Study 13.1 and 13.2 are examples that require 'out of the box' thinking by marrying different fields of specialism – such skills are, in general, the capabilities of generalist consultants and contractors. On other occasions, a specialist brings very specific skill sets that a generalist lacks.

CASE STUDY 13.1   ENERGY REDUCTION IN NEWSPRINT PAPER PLANT

In a recycled newsprint paper plant, waste paper sludge is incinerated in a waste fuel boiler. The sludge contains 50 per cent moisture and 50 per cent combustible waste. This waste fuel boiler supplements the other steam boilers located on site. A dryer sludge will have higher energy content than wet sludge.

The waste boiler blows down at 2,500 kg/hr.* The blow down occurs at 180°C and is cooled to 50°C before discharging to the trade effluent.

By applying lateral thinking, an improvement opportunity arises by marrying both facts: use the blow down, through a dryer, to dry the sludge; then feed the dryer sludge to the boiler. A dryer sludge generates more steam, reducing the demand from a fossil-fuel fired boiler.

---

*   Blow down is an important part of safe boiler operation.

Based on modelling and calculation, a moisture content reduction of up to 1 per cent can be achieved. This corresponds to a 1 per cent increase in heating value, or 74,900 tonnes/year of steam fired from fossil fuel could be avoided. This project had a simple payback of 2.3 years.

CASE STUDY 13.2   ENERGY REDUCTION IN LARGE DATA CENTRE

In a very large three-storey commercial building, a large data centre is located on the ground floor. The data centre is fully surrounded by open plan office spaces and the reception area.

This data centre room contains 28 rows of server cabinets with each row containing 24 cabinets. The air conditioning in this enclosed room is a closed-loop design supplied with cold air at 14°C and is extracted from the room at 30°C. This hot air is cooled and sent back into the room. Cooling is achieved by a chilled water system. Arithmetic calculation showed that the heat rejected by the chillers to the atmosphere is approximately over 1,000 kW.

Two complementary options for improvement are available:

- Utilise free air cooling during cold months, thus avoiding the need for cooling energy.
- Reuse the heat rejected by the server room by ducting it back into the building, thus avoiding the necessity for heating.

With an investment cost of £68,000, it has a simple payback of 1.6 years. Implementing this project requires careful planning in order to minimise disruptions to the IT equipment.

Many business managers forget to define the outcome or results required by the business from engaging consultants and contractors. Frequently, the details on deliverables lack clarity, leading to rework and disappointment for the business and the consultants. It is important that the work requirements are as detailed as possible, commensurate with the breadth of information available in the business processes and the technical expertise required.

International and regional energy management standards and energy audit standards are available. They are sources of information to set the scope of the energy reduction works. As an alternative, the business may choose to specify that the work required be in line with the available standards.

It is also important to engage consultants and contractors with a broad range of associated skills. A full spectrum of skills and know-how is required for timely and successful implementation of energy reduction projects with minimal capital expenditure. The detailed requirements of these skills and their relationship to energy efficiency are subjects for debate.[1]

For convenience of selecting the right consultant for the business, the key skills are:

- Health, safety and environment
- Understanding and application of material and energy balance
- Understanding and application of fluid flow
- Understanding and application of heat and mass transfer
- Understanding and application of electrical systems
- Understanding and preparation of flow diagrams
- Sampling and interpreting laboratory results
- Conceptual design, technical and economic evaluation
- Process development and intensification
- Equipment selection and specification
- Technical sales, marketing and contract negotiation
- Energy data analysis
- System boundary
- Process simulation and modelling
- Asset integrity and reliability
- Industrial utility systems
- Energy auditing
- Standard operating procedures
- Managing projects
- Operator training
- Managing people
- Advance process control
- Thermal integration
- Dynamic simulation
- Technology gate keeping
- Energy legislation and other requirements.

Lastly, in order for the business to gain any value from engaging an energy consultant and contractor, both the managers and engineers within the business need to be able to communicate with the consultant and contractor in

---

1　The issue of energy manager and energy auditor competency is currently being debated by energy management committees within the European Committee for Standardization (CEN) and the International Organization for Standardization (ISO). While there are some countries and regions that have formal qualifications for energy management and energy auditing, an education in carrying out such work is no guarantee of skills in executing such work to a level acceptable to the business.

a manner that is both fulfilling and that meets the business goals. Many skills are required from both parties. These range from the active participation by the managers and engineers from the business to listening to and discussing ideas, to authentic communication and commitment to build a good relationship. Sometimes, assuming business managers can distinguish the capabilities of a consultant,[2] they forego choosing the most competent one in preference to working with one who is congenial and likeable (Casciaro and Lobo, 2005).

Energy management and energy reduction is not a one-person responsibility. It is very easy to fall into the trap of engaging a consultant and forget about all other key players in realising the benefits of a sustainable energy reduction programme. Many a time, managers and engineers with little resources and/or experience in managing energy reduction programmes can become confused or inundated with the many choices for implementing energy reduction projects at the business. A good step forward is to engage a good, independent and carefully selected consultant or contractor.

At other times, managers, engineers and scientists are inundated with the quantity of quick wins that mask greater opportunities. Sometimes, when the quick win opportunities have been implemented and the management focus moves to other priority areas, these quick wins disappear and 'old' ways of working reappear. There is a way to retain these quick wins permanently. This will be covered in Part 4.

---

2   Very often, it is difficult to decipher the level of competency of a consultant and contractor. This is especially true when the manager does not have the same skills as the consultant and contractor. No matter how objective the consultant and contractor selection, their likeability comes into play (de Rond, 2011).

PART 4
Management

Energy reduction has a direct link with business profitability and competitiveness. We have explored a holistic strategy for energy reduction programmes and seen the tools and techniques used by consultants and contractors, and the importance of avoiding energy wastage.

A joint survey by Cranfield Business School and Oracle (Neely, Yaghi and Youell, 2008) revealed that more than 40 per cent of top executives do not think that their performance measurements are based on good-quality data. In many organisations, there is a willingness to do something about saving energy. However, poor visibility of factual energy data can and will lead senior management to make wrong decisions.

Moreover, many companies implement energy reduction programmes on an adhoc basis. Some businesses rely on one or two employees orchestrating and facilitating energy reduction in the company without embedding energy efficient behaviours. Others focus solely on implementing technology or have contracted the responsibilities for energy reduction to consultants and contractors – both of which ignore the management aspects. Very few businesses put together a comprehensive plan involving technical, people and management aspects to drive long-term and sustainable energy reduction.

This part explores this most important, least understood, appreciated and practised topic by pulling together many topics from management science and social psychology: the management aspects – specifically, 'management activities' – that lead to long-term and sustainable energy reduction. Without these, energy reduction initiatives will not be sustainable, giving rise to the common phrase, 'when the consultants leave, everything returns to normal'.

This part focuses on:

1. Selecting (and developing) the right energy manager.
2. Engaging the organisation to participate in the programme.
3. Monitoring and targeting energy performance.
4. Framing long-term and sustainable energy policy.
5. Developing realistic and achievable goals, objectives and targets.

14

Gaining Commitment from Senior Management

To achieve lasting energy management initiatives, the first step is to gain commitment from the senior management. An unyielding and consistent commitment from senior management communicates the company's intention to seek energy efficiency and to drive energy reduction. An energy policy documents senior management's intentions and sets a series of objectives, goals and targets to drive the company towards lower energy consumption. It facilitates allocation of roles and responsibilities, and identifies the appropriate resources to support the management efforts.

Many managers and engineers become puzzled as to how to ask for endorsement and support from senior management. Some managers and engineers constantly look for a proven or universal 'formula' to get senior management buy in. The issues faced by senior management vary from each business, industry and cluster. As such, there is no one fixed answer or fixed solution to achieve senior management commitment.

Regulatory, economic and general public sentiments on climate change along with the frequent media coverage have made significant headway in this area. The creation of an international standard on energy management (ISO50001) has elevated the status of energy to be on par with quality (ISO9001), environmental (ISO14001), safety (OHSAS 18001) and sustainability (ISO22000).

The easiest and simplest way to gain senior management commitment is to request, in simple terms, their support to:

1. Identify and overcome barriers towards energy reduction.
2. Make energy a topic at management meetings.
3. Appoint an energy manager.
4. Allocate sufficient funds for energy reduction programmes.
5. Engage the organisation in energy reduction by assigning roles and responsibilities and by allocating the appropriate resources to support the responsibilities.

6.   be visible in saving energy as part of their daily and routine work;
7.   (if necessary) ring fence a pool of funds for energy reduction projects;
8.   (if desired) certify the company to ISO50001.

Before asking for support, setting aside some time to plan and collate potential questions from senior management can pay off. Using intuition, insider knowledge of the organisation and the way members of the senior management asks questions can uncover their issues and concerns. Having potential solutions ready shows that these issues have been thought through and minimises their reservations.

The availability of a sponsor from the senior management team would be beneficial. They can provide useful input and insights into the business; advocate future projects and advise on options in line with the business; remove any technically complex wording used during meetings; provide guidance in developing a concise and convincing business case to demonstrate a good return on investment and develop a realistic plan for implementation. Senior management is likely to be interested in planned and sustain the energy reduction efforts.

The majority of the information necessary to gain the trust and commitment of senior management is easily available. It can be found in the activities described in the previous chapters and summarised in Table 14.1:

Table 14.1   Sources of information

Requirements	Information Sources
Business case	Data analysis Energy balance Energy benchmarking
Return on investment	Opportunity finding Financing options Quick wins and non-energy related benefits
Action plan	Accounting – organisational maturity Prioritised list of actions and improvements
Sustaining	Engaging the organisation – management, communication and behaviours Monitoring and targeting

Another key step in continued support from senior management is to build and publish successes. Following the strategy described in Chapter 4, pursuing no-cost or low-cost projects generates quick success and adds credibility to future and higher-cost projects.

15

Myth of a Perfect Energy Manager

There is a lot of confusion as to the function of an energy manager. Since the Kyoto Protocol in 1997, there has been a surge in energy management publications, training and qualifications in the market. Almost 100 per cent of these offerings are based on technical and engineering competency. This gives the impression that energy management is a technical skill. While scientists and engineers have the benefit of understanding the detailed operation of plant machinery, it is not necessary to be proficient in this topic to be an effective energy manager.

Energy management, as the name implies, is first and foremost a management function. The subject or 'thing' being managed is the energy consumed by the business. Similarly, a business manager is in a management position, the context of management being the 'business' activities. The same analogy can be applied to 'engineering', 'production', 'quality', 'environment' and so on. Adapting Henry Mintzberg's (2009) concept of managing, energy management is about:

1. *Controlling and budgeting the energy consumed by the business.* It involves understanding how the business uses energy, how a change in key processes affects the quantum of energy consumed and how to budget future energy consumption. This could be in terms of energy cost, in energy units or both. In some businesses, managing the cost of energy is the remit of accounting or purchasing departments.

2. *Being the nerve centre for providing energy data* to government agencies and any other agencies the business has to report energy consumption to. The manager must first identify the key and critical information according to the business needs. Then, it involves having the appropriate meters installed in the right locations, having the meters calibrated and collating the information into a usable format for dissemination. An energy manager could also be the spokesperson in communicating all matters relevant to energy consumption to the media.

3. *Monitoring the patterns of energy consumption* and communicating any deviation to the relevant departments for corrective actions. Energy managers also assess the performance of each key critical business process; analyse the quantity of energy used and identify options for improvement; analyse the cost and benefits of improvement opportunities; recognise fallacies; avoid common errors; handle ambiguity; and market the opportunity for improvement. In a busy organisation, energy managers rely on consultants and contractors to identify and propose energy reduction opportunities.

4. Managing people networks within the business to *energise and promote engagement from all personnel* in controlling and reducing the energy consumed. In a large organisation this may involve building teams, changing business culture and creating a network of energy change teams. It also involves providing education to the business on the needs and means to reduce energy consumption. A key success factor in this area would be the buy-in and participation of the whole organisation in reducing energy consumption. In some organisations, energy managers also mediate in disagreements between departments and provide energy consumption input such that an overall business cost is established.

5. In small improvement projects or in small organisations, the energy manager may be *managing all improvement projects*, liaising with all parties to bring the project to successful implementation.

As can be seen, the functions required and expected from an energy manager are not technical functions. They are a combination of analytical skills, hands-on experience and the art of being a manager, using the appropriate tools to achieve the end goals.

Mintzberg went on to list key competency descriptors for being a manager. Table 15.1 shows adapted competency descriptors for an effective energy manager. The skills required from an energy manager go beyond technical engineering – all of the tasks and skills described involve working with and via different groups of people.

Table 15.1   Key competencies for managing energy

Skills Area	Competencies
Personal management	Managing self (internally) for energy efficient behaviours. Managing self (externally) for energy efficient use of energy. Scheduling, prioritising and juggling personal actions, agenda setting, time and other resources.

Table 15.1   Continued

Skills Area	Competencies
Interpersonal management	Leading individuals via teaching, mentoring and coaching. Inspiring others to take action. Dealing with consultants and contractors. Team building, resolving conflicts, facilitating meetings etc. Building an energy efficient culture. Organising resources, delegating and authorising tasks, setting business goals and performance appraisals. Creating and managing networks within the organisation that result in reducing energy consumption, creating collaboration between departments, promoting energy efficient techniques etc.
Information management	Listening, interviewing, speaking, presenting, briefing, writing, gathering and disseminating energy consumption information using clear and accessible language. Seeing and sensing business processes and extracting non-verbal information critical for the success of energy reduction programmes. Energy data processing, modelling, measuring and evaluation.
Taking action	Planning and creating visions for improvements. Commercial awareness to identify the risks and opportunities presented by an energy reduction opportunity. Mobilising tools and resources to reduce energy consumption; this could also include actions such as quick wins, project management, negotiation, managing resistance to change and managing organisational politics. Empowering others to take action.

Source: Adapted from Mintzberg, 2009 and Ipsos MORI, 2010.

Frequently, top management believes that a perfect or ideal energy manager exists in the market place. Senior management seeks to employ this 'super human' for their miraculous capabilities to manage energy and reduce energy consumption. When the appointed 'super human' does not deliver to their expectations, they are quick to criticise and blame the energy manager for not able to live up to these expectations.

Energy managers will not be able to deliver any energy reduction on their own. Energy managers do not possess all of the skills to implement energy reduction projects. They also cannot feasibly be present in every location within the company to enforce energy efficient behaviours. Energy managers need to work alongside and through others to collectively manage and reduce energy consumption.

It is not possible to 'learn' management: functional knowledge of management may be learned at university, but the act of managing comes from consolidation, reflection and experience fitting the business needs (Barker, 2010). Therefore, the degree to which an energy manager is seen as competent to manage energy is based purely on the fit of their knowledge and skills within the business culture. Each individual brings together different sets of skills and competencies. No one individual can excel in all of the skills listed.

If an energy manager is disliked or socially inept, they are strongly disliked by employees irrespective of their competency (Casciaro and Lobo, 2005). A trade-off between technical competence and social intelligence of an energy manager is therefore required. This can be a challenging and difficult choice for the business.

Sometimes, hiring an 'outsider' can bring a temporary technical competency in applying specific skills to specific applications (Bower, 2011). However, in the short and medium term, they lack 'insider' knowledge of the business and are therefore unable to maximise energy efficiency for the whole business.

An alternative option for the business is to identify a person competent in management and respected within the company, and to appoint this person as an energy manager. If this person is not from an engineering background, the first development plan would be for them to learn the basics of energy and utilities operation. This enables the energy manager to understand and engage in technical discussions with consultants and contractors.

This is the rationale behind why energy management training is based on technical skills. Managers who are technically competent but lack people skills would require people skills training not covered in energy management courses.

16

Integrating Energy into Management

Most managers and engineers go about energy reduction by installing new technology, meters to make sure that the new technology saves energy – and applying fancy data analysis tools to budget energy consumption and track energy reduction. In the market, there is an ocean of technologies and techniques available. However sophisticated the new technology and exact the energy information, many managers and engineers soon find that:

1. Energy reduction falls short of the intended target and/or loses its momentum, resulting in little or no energy savings.
2. Energy reduction is on target but could not be sustained over the medium and long term.

For some businesses, energy reduction projects are not implemented because managers and engineers try to quantify all energy reduction opportunities to the minute detail. In this instance, managers and engineers are spending a lot of time and money trying to measure parameters that may be too complex or too difficult to quantify. Some use multiple models to quantify the measurement to multiple decimals of accuracy.

Chapter 5 introduced seven areas where a business can face difficulties when implementing an energy reduction programme. A study by Mankins and Steele (2005) reported that only 63 per cent of companies are successful in realising their intended strategy. A careful examination of the reasons for barriers to achieving energy efficiency shows the root cause in management. These issues arise from a combination of the following:

• Reduction targets are set too low or too high; employees do not buy into the programme.

- Spending too much time trying to quantify all areas of the energy reduction, leading to the time spent exceeding the value of the energy savings to be achieved.
- Organisational barriers impede progress as people begin to question the need for energy reduction or the value it can bring.
- Keeping a sense of direction can be difficult as other issues compete for the attention and resources of the management and employees.
- For other businesses, employees are faced with an overload of business initiatives driven by management that has insufficient skills as change leaders.
- Management expects energy reduction to occur and be sustained without active management.

These are further compounded by two very frequently found organisational issues.

- The wrong people are appointed to reduce energy consumption without being provided with or authorised to use appropriate tools and resources. A survey by BMG Research (Vesma, 2010) showed that approximately one-third of so-called energy managers are administrators, clerical and junior employees within a company. Another third are business owners and the remaining third are managers and engineers. Of those who are managers and engineers, more than 90 per cent claim to spend more than 75 per cent of their time on other business priorities.
- The significant number of layers within the organisation and 'chain of command' slows down and distorts the communication from top management. A survey by the Economist Intelligence Unit (2011) shows that up to 80 per cent of C-level executives report that there are more than three levels between the boardroom and the front line (see Figure 16.1) This provides more than three opportunities for all communications to be delayed and distorted between the boardroom and the front line, and vice versa.

All of the mentioned issues could be easily avoided by a good management system. Chapter 4 introduced the concept of a management system used to drive and sustain long-term energy reduction. This chapter describes the features necessary to make a management system work within a business.

In business education, management students are taught about business management based on W. Edwards Deming's cycle. It consists of planning, doing, checking and acting. This cycle is also known as the Deming circle or

Deming wheel, the Shewhart cycle, the control circle/cycle or the Plan-Do-Check-Act (PDCA) cycle. Figure 16.2 shows a generic PDCA cycle.

Robert Kaplan and David Norton (2008) define a management system as 'an integrated set of processes and tools that a company uses to develop its strategy,

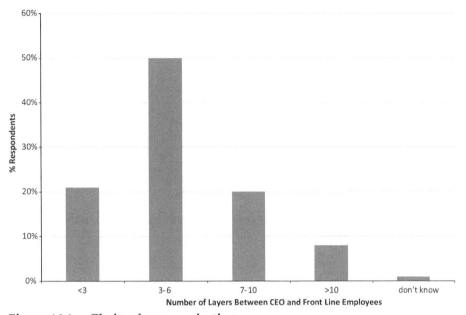

Figure 16.1 Chain of communication
Source: Data for figure drawn from Economist Intelligence Unit, 2011.

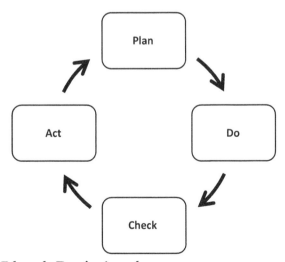

Figure 16.2 Edwards Deming's cycle

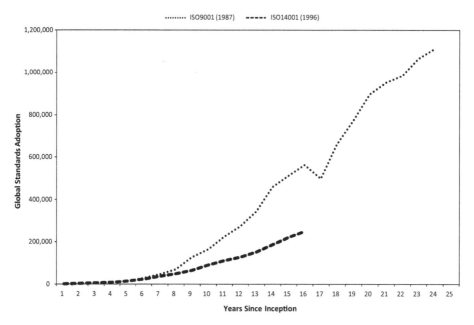

Figure 16.3   Global adoptions of quality and environmental management
               systems

translate it to operational actions, and monitor and improve the effectiveness
of both'. In essence, a business management system forms the link between a
chosen business strategy and the measurable business performance. The same
model has been applied to business continuity, information technology, health
and safety, quality, environment, sustainability and energy.

ISO9001 and ISO14001 were originally developed in the UK as BS5750 in
1979 and BS7750 in 1992. The number of companies that have adopted ISO9001
and ISO14001 has grown exponentially[1] since their publication (Figure 16.3):
65 per cent of businesses using a management system reported a cost saving;
77 per cent reported an improvement in company reputation; and 62 per cent
reported a boost in employee morale (Bell, 2011).

Features of a Good Energy Management System

Chances are that when you mention ISO9001, ISO14001 or ISO50001 many
employees will automatically think about the boring meetings, thick
documentation and the large company resources (time and money) diverted

---

1   This data comes from tracking the annual ISO survey results over many years.

away from their core business – to produce good-quality products or services and to generate a profit.

This is a general misconception. Implementing a management system does not have to be long-winded. It does not have to be resource intensive. Development of a management system can be a company-wide learning exercise. Employee involvement in learning about energy is highly motivating and can be used to energise the workforce to save energy from the start.

The international standard on energy management (ISO50001) is one of the available closed-loop management systems, written and approved by the international community. It supersedes the European Standard for Energy Management EN16001.

Each business is unique to its industry, industry sector and its geography. As such, there are no set rules, strategies and templates to achieve a useful, successful and sustainable energy management system. However, there are eight features of a successful management system which are key drivers to ensure sustainability and long-term energy reduction. They are:

1. Use a set of consistent terminologies.
2. Allocate responsibilities and resources early.
3. Involve the whole company.
4. Challenge established assumptions.
5. Integrate into daily operations.
6. Utilise appropriate performance measurement.
7. Integrate into whole life cycle.
8. Continual improvement.

A thorough understanding of these requirements and how they apply to each individual will help ensure that such goals are achieved. It is also recommended that the list be extended by two further features not specified in any management system standard when designing a management system for the company:

1. Set stretched but achievable objectives and targets.
2. Generate opportunities for quick wins.

USE A SET OF CONSISTENT TERMINOLOGIES

As demonstrated by the closed-loop management system described earlier, many of the terminologies are common in business, quality, environment and many other management systems. These terminologies are short, concise, to the point and are understandable to the whole organisation, not just a few

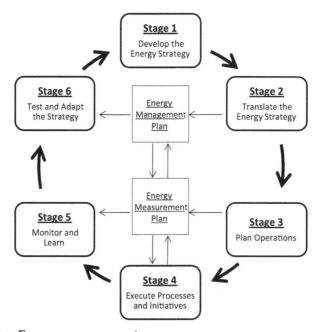

Figure 16.4   Energy management processes

Source: Flow chart for the figure drawn from Kaplan and Norton, 2008 and ISO, 2011.

employees within each business. Figure 16.4 shows the process flows of an energy management process.

Using these ready-made terminologies allows unambiguous setting of objectives, targets and action plans. It also allows all communication between the management team, employees and stakeholders to be 'executed' in a consistent manner.

ALLOCATE RESPONSIBILITIES AND RESOURCES EARLY

A management system facilitates fast and easy assignment of roles and allocation of resources to the appropriate employees. These employees then have the correct tools and authority to carry out the assigned functions, manage departmental conflicts and to track and apply any corrections during its implementation.

Roles and responsibilities are sometimes assigned without communicating with the personnel involved and/or to his peers. At other times, it could be assigned based on a broad brush understanding of the roles and responsibilities without any details on the specific work output required. These can lead to misunderstanding and generate friction between various people within the company, especially when people interpret the role and work requirements differently.

Its closed-loop nature combats the 'smart talk, no action' syndrome. Other common phrases of this syndrome are 'talk only, no action' and 'many-employee, many-meeting company'. Smart talk (Pfeffer and Sutton, 1999) is a product of education where children and students learn to project confidence and be articulate, having interesting information and ideas.

The key to success is through taking consistent and effective action. This smart talk syndrome is counteracted in a management system by the following means:

1. Using simple and consistent terminologies.
2. Colleagues following up on assigned action.
3. If external consultants and contractors are part of the plan, they would follow up on the actions.
4. If there is no action, the issue could be escalated up to management level.
5. If there is still no action, the issue may be picked up by the company's internal auditor.
6. If the issue is still not acted upon, this issue will be picked up by the external auditor (either during a certification audit or during surveillance audits).

INVOLVE THE WHOLE COMPANY

In many companies, senior management draws up an energy reduction strategy, objectives and targets, and allocates resources. Very often, this is guided by services offered by an external consultant and contractor or is arbitrarily chosen with insight from the day-to-day operations. There is an explosion of businesses that publicly announce their desire to reduce energy consumption by a fixed figure within a certain time frame. Although noble by nature, this action solicits a completely different response from the employees within the business.

Such an approach limits the energy reduction that can be achieved. The majority of the employees will choose the biggest opportunity (or a portfolio of opportunities) that will deliver the management declared reduction within the time frame. Once these projects have been successfully implemented, no further opportunities will be actively pursued. Many other opportunities for improvements are ignored and remain untapped.

On the other hand, in order to meet the requirements from the publically announced targets, the people within the organisation could be frantically looking for opportunities to reduce energy consumption and lose focus on the purpose of the business: generate a profit by providing goods and services to the customers.

Henry Mintzberg (1994) said that: 'The notion that [energy management] strategy is something that should happen way up there, far removed from the details of running an organisation on a daily basis, is one of the greatest fallacies of conventional strategic management'.

Energy reduction can be achieved from all areas within the business. A good closed-loop management system requires the business to review all opportunities from all areas of business operations: from the shop floor upwards and involving the whole company.

CHALLENGE ESTABLISHED ASSUMPTIONS

Many businesses are legally, contractually or socially bound by a set of operational requirements. These may be a group of regulations with implications for energy consumption. Other examples are industry specific regulations, validation requirements, contractual agreements, standards, codes of practice, product specifications, operating procedures, scheduling, choice of raw materials etc.

These requirements are often defined and integrated over a long period of time where practices were left unchallenged and accepted as norms. A management system requires each business to challenge its established assumptions, knowledge and know-how in the business processes. Once all the applicable regulations, assumptions, knowledge and know-how are established and confirmed, it requires the business to operate its processes to these requirements.

The above task sounds like common sense and onerous. Many businesses are finding that regulations, standards and codes of practice may have been updated or superseded: the exact wording of the requirements is different from the norm; the product specifications were too stringent as compared to the actual client requirements, etc. Finding these issues often offers the business opportunities to reduce the energy consumption, raw materials, etc.

INTEGRATE INTO DAILY OPERATIONS

As described in Chapter 2, no processes and machines are 100 per cent efficient. Take steam from Figure PT2.1 for example, energy is lost when steam is being generated (e.g., boiler losses). Energy is also lost when steam is being distributed (distribution losses) and when it is converted by the process and machines (equipment efficiency losses). All employees are in direct control of the amount of steam used and losses.

A management system requires companies to put in place energy efficient practices in the daily operation of the business and to involve all levels of employees making up the whole company. This could be in selecting raw materials, design or modification of plant and machinery, operating procedures, training, production planning, maintenance execution and purchasing.

There is also a need to carefully craft a message to make employees understand the effect of energy reduction in relation to their work and then modify the job description of the employees. Simply telling employees to save energy does little to help employees know how their actions save energy.

Frequently, the motives of employees to reduce energy consumption are different from those of managers. As can be seen from Case Study 16.1, although the restaurant was successful in reducing energy consumption, the motivator for the senior manager is different from that of the head chef. The triggers to save energy by different employees, hence the approach to energy efficient behaviours, needs to be tailored to specific employees.

CASE STUDY 16.1   PURPOSE OF ENERGY REDUCTION IN A RESTAURANT

In a highly rated restaurant, an energy efficiency behaviour campaign was implemented throughout the kitchen and restaurant area. During the campaign, an employee behaviour survey was carried out by consultants.

Survey of the senior managers indicates that the driver for energy reduction is to reduce energy expenditure, increase working capital to ride through the recession and compliance with regulations.

When the head chef was interviewed, his team engaged with the energy reduction programme because it makes the kitchen cooler and allows the team to work closely. Communication within the team became better, resulting in more efficient work routines, better food quality, less returned food and less waste.

UTILISE APPROPRIATE PERFORMANCE MEASUREMENT

According to Andy Neely[2] 60–80 per cent of performance measurement items is useless or drives the wrong behaviour. People tend to measure too much, building very complex models to quantify the unquantifiable, or use too many non-complementary measurement models simultaneously.

---

2   This is a verbal quotation from Dr Andy Neely.

An appropriate energy performance indicator needs to be determined. This involves understanding how different levels of the workforce use energy information and what variables change the quantum of energy consumed. Care should be taken to distinguish between the absolute minimum information required and installing a lot of energy meters; between information that is continuously monitored and spot measurements.

For many managers and engineers, there is a general need to provide senior management with 'detailed' and 'unchanging' information. Using the appropriate energy performance indicators in line with a management system should allow the business to learn about their process and continually improve on the measurement when the previously measured information is no longer valid and/or when significant changes have occurred.

The means to continuously 'correct' energy performance indicators is even more important, and critical in companies embarking on energy reduction programmes where energy data and information may be lacking.

INTEGRATE INTO WHOLE LIFE CYCLE

Chapter 3 and Case Study 3.1 introduced the benefits of whole life cycle analysis. One of the key features of a management system is consider the life cycle of all investments. This could be from purchasing new, replacement and/ or modifications to existing processes and machines. It also requires businesses to inform all equipment suppliers and service providers that their quotation is assessed partly on the basis of energy efficiency.

A life cycle analysis, also known as a cradle-to-grave analysis, analyses the project through its useful life – from the initial business concept and project feasibility, operation and maintenance to its final decommissioning and disposal. Energy consumption and any non-energy related synergies such as quality improvements, waste reduction and raw material reduction are captured in this assessment. It is a useful tool for the business to appraise projects based on the overall business benefit rather than purely on the basis of capital cost.

Another trend that is developing in business is the use of cradle-to-cradle analysis. This assessment is similar to cradle-to-grave analysis with the exception that at the end of the life cycle all components are dismantled, recycled or reused in the production of new products. Some businesses are using this new tool for strategic differentiation and competitive advantage (Lee and Bony, 2009). This idea is also being extended to the use of metals, cement etc. (Dobbs et al., 2011; Allwood and Cullen, 2011).

CONTINUAL IMPROVEMENT

Continuous operation of a closed-loop management system should result in a continual rejuvenation of the planned energy reduction programme. Opportunities that were assessed and found not feasible in the past could become feasible in the future. Newer ways of working or new customer specifications could render the processes inefficient.

Joint annual surveys carried out by MIT Sloan and Boston Consulting[3] have continuously demonstrated that companies with a heavy emphasis on sustainability discover more opportunities to improve and generate additional competitive advantage than they originally expected. This could arise from:

- Aging business processes and manufacturing facilities.
- Changing energy cost.
- New (and may be more stringent) customer specification.
- New and revised regulations.
- New and revised economic incentives.
- Newer process, tools, controls and other technologies.
- Newer raw materials.
- Using less material for construction.[4]

Employees are most engaged and motivated by working on small but visible incremental progress toward a visible goal. These small wins are frequently accompanied by a sense of pride and ownership to continue working on the same goal (Amabile and Kramer, 2011).

Although not strictly elements within a management system, setting 'stretched but achievable' objectives and targets and generating opportunities for quick wins are important in helping employees assimilate energy efficient behaviours.

Collectively, a well implemented management system breaks down the people and cultural barriers. Companies that implement a good management system consistently outperform 'business as usual' scenarios (Matteini, 2011. Toffel, 2006. and Levine and Toffel, 2010).

---

3   MIT Sloan and Boston Consulting Group have carried out and published a series of reports spanning several years. These can be found on both MIT Sloan Management Review and Boston Consulting Group's websites.

4   For an introduction to this subject, see Allwood and Cullen, 2011.

17

Sustaining Energy Reduction

For sustainable energy reduction to take place, managers and change teams are required to continuously identify and monitor energy reduction efforts; link and align senior management with the workforce; and build the technical and interpersonal skills to achieve lasting energy reduction.

As mentioned in the Introduction, up to 25 per cent annual energy reduction could be achieved from more efficient behaviour and work methods without implementing new technology. Conversely, companies that ignore employee behaviours or spend little time and resources focusing on investing in technologies achieve smaller energy reduction.

A study by the Carbon Trust (2005) found that approximately £2.4 billion has been spent in the UK on energy reduction projects without realising the benefit of lower energy consumption. This roughly equates to 21 per cent of the total expenditure on energy reduction projects.

Making the results of energy reduction programmes last requires a management system that changes the way a company operates: a change in the ways of working and the introduction of a culture where energy inefficiency is not tolerated. The important differentiators between the successful organisations in managing change are:

- *Setting clear and high aspirations for change* – poor definition and 'grey' areas allow misinterpretation by employees and drift away from the original intent.
- *Engaging the whole organisation through a variety of means* – developing a positive environment for employees to succeed encourages further success.
- *Highly motivated and visible participation of senior management* – leading by 'visible and audible' example sends a powerful message to all employees.
- *A barrage of communication, encouragement, coaching and accountability.*
- *Continuity of management communication and management focus* – implementing many and disparate management change programme

slows down the success of change efforts. Consistency and continuity in management focus and communication is key.

Companies that are successful in implementing and maintaining change employ a minimum of three times more tactics and resources to drive the change (Meaney and Pung, 2008). Senior management of these companies would also recommend defining 'clearer' objectives and targets if they were to repeat the exercise again in the future.

Figure 17.1 shows the range of tactics that can be used to drive change in ways of working. They range from management tools to control mechanisms and behavioural improvements.

Figure 17.1   Range of techniques used to manage change

The Vicious Cycle of Self-Fulfilling Prophecies

Since the beginning of civilisation, humans have been treated like machines. Egyptian, Chinese, Indian, Roman and Mayan civilisations have treated their employees as 'slaves'. The lords supplied their 'employees' with food and lodging in return for high-quality, high-volume work.

This practice has carried on into the modern workplace. Employers provide adequate lighting, shelter, fresh air and comfortable work environments in exchange for the same high-quality, high-volume work output from each employee.

> *'It is not my job !!!'*
> *'I haven't got time ...'*
> *'If it's such a good idea, why it wasn't done it in the first place?'*
> *'I haven't heard of it !!!'*
> *'We'll just do what the consultant says. When he leaves, the practices will eventually return to normality anyway ...'*

These phrases have been quoted routinely since Frederick Taylor did his scientific management experiments on production efficiency between 1874 and 1893 in Philadelphia. His ideas on efficiency centred on a clear division of task, using scientific data to find the optimum way of performing a task and selecting suitable people to do it, providing method training and surveillance to conform to prescribed methods. These formed the basis of modern day management science and have led to the concept of 'lean manufacturing' (Buchanan and Huczynski, 2010). However, there is another and unreported side to his study – the human aspects. In his later days, he wrote about his own experience during his work. In his own words:

> *I was a young man in years but I give you my word I was a great deal older than I am now, what with the worry, meanness, and contemptibleness of the whole damn thing. It is a horrid life for any man to live not being able to look any workman in the face without seeing hostility there, and a feeling that every man around you is your virtual enemy. (Brown, 1963: 14)*

Similar findings were reported in many psychology, management science, social science and organisational behavioural studies.

A business is made up of people working together as a group, each with its own roles and responsibilities. All employees within an organisation influence the behaviours of the other employees. In turn, all of the employees shape the way the organisation interacts internally and externally.

Similar to the animal kingdom, employees with a lot of influence and power organise the others into a social network. These people become the alpha males and alpha females within the company, where followers begin to group together for support and to mimic their leaders in order to gain social acceptance. Some of these alphas are more competent to carry out their job and become key managerial players in the business. Other forms of alpha influences are in information hubs and social hubs.

Rationality in an Irrational Human Mindset

The barriers to energy efficiency described in Chapter 5 are resistance exhibited by the people within the business to change – the effect, not the cause of the barrier. When businesses reveal the causes of barriers, it is common to uncover the immediate causes arising from lack of visible management commitment: employees are unable to relate to the concepts described by the senior management in the workplace, blaming others for not taking action and equating means to reduce energy as applying new technology.

Contrary to popular belief, the root cause of all of the barriers is not fear of the unknown. Digging deeper, the root cause is actually fear of 'losing control' and its implications: the future job security of each employee when energy consumption has been reduced and fear of how they will be accepted in their established social standing.

A survey by Lane4 (2010) found that many employees do not trust their managers or managers their colleagues, viewing them as deceitful, foreign to the day-to-day work and not practising what they preach. This fear, a very real phenomenon, is heightened during economic hardship.

When people are under stress to deliver their work, a surge in adrenaline and cortisol in the body halts the mind's ability to perform normal functions such as reasoning and cognition (Goleman and Boyatzis, 2008). When this happens, all employee attention is fixed and directed to the new stimulus, i.e., the threat of energy reduction. The employee, therefore, falls back on old and familiar habits, no matter how unreasonable and unsuitable those traits are for addressing new challenges.

The fear is compounded by the fact that energy consumption in the workplace does not directly affect the salaries for a significant majority of employees. Apart from a number of energy use that is visible (steam leak), audible (air leak) and metered energy, a significant amount of energy consumption is hidden from view. Very frequently, employees also do not see their employers' energy bills. This invincibility hampers employees' ability to relate to energy.

Therefore, when a call for energy reduction is initiated by management, depending on who initiates the change, it causes a dynamic change through the organisation via the alphas to everyone in the business. Each change has a social, political and perceived 'psychological' safety implication between each alpha in the business. Some alphas and employees will agree wholeheartedly and follow the new direction without question. Some will not. How each alpha and their 'team' feel about each other and other teams determines how they behave and perform in relation to the new challenge.

This is very prevalent in companies that undertake multiple business initiatives simultaneously, relying on broadly themed, multiple-subject, company-wide training. Usually, these programmes are put together by consultants and contractors implementing a bunch of best practices using a cocktail of different tools within a short time frame and with little funding.

For example, a business could be implementing 5S, lean manufacturing, 6 sigma, ISO9001, ISO14001, total quality management, predictive maintenance, kaizen, gemba and energy reduction all at the same time. The simultaneous implementation of 'guru soup' programmes seldom works. This is because employees need time to assimilate the new tools, the old ways of working have to be challenged and unlearned, and new ways of working have to be established, tried, tested, improved and integrated into daily routines. This learning and implementation process takes time. It also requires senior management to provide a constant stream of the same messages and encouragement and to be seen driving the same objectives.

The constant and visible communication provides a driver for employees to accelerate the learning and implementation process. At the same time, each alpha is 'testing the waters' – finding which new tool they can excel with, which tool they can use to attract the praise from senior management. Each success and acknowledgement builds personal 'psychological' safety for the alpha. Each success also builds team admiration, further enhancing personal 'psychological' safety.

A constant shift in communication and focus on different tools provided in a 'guru soup' change programme confuses employees. Employees trying to assimilate and implement multiple tools and techniques will slow the change process. Very frequently, managers and engineers in a company using 'guru soup' programmes are also unable to assess the merits and success of individual components of these programmes, leading to an inability to account for actions and a sense of being 'out of control'.

The fear of losing control takes precedence the in minds of alpha males and alpha females in the company. This fear is less about each alpha's own capability but about fear that the 'others' are losing control and therefore impacting them.

Patrick Lencioni (2002: 188–9) puts it succinctly:

> *An absence of trust among team members stems from their unwillingness to be vulnerable within the group. Team members who are not genuinely open with one another about mistakes and weakness make it impossible to build a foundation of trust. This failure is damaging because it sets the tone for fear of conflict. Teams that lack trust are incapable of engaging unfiltered and passionate debate of ideas. Instead, they resort to veiled*

discussions and guarded comments. A lack of healthy conflict ensures a lack of commitment. Without having aired their opinions in the course of passionate and open debate, team members rarely, if ever, buy in and commit to decisions, though they may feign agreement during meetings. Because of this lack of real commitment and buy in, team members develop an avoidance of accountability. Without committing to a clear plan of action, even the most focused and driven people often hesitate to call their peers on actions and behaviors that seem counterproductive to the good of the team. Failure to hold one another accountable creates an environment where inattention to results can thrive.

In the early 1970s, Albert Hirschman, a German economist, hypothesised that when a company embarks on a change programme, employees who disagree with the new direction have three predictable courses of action.[1] The three choices are:

- Exit – resign from the requirements and carry out tasks only when instructed.
- Voice – voice their concern, seek clarification and reassurance or look to change the change itself.[2]
- Loyalty – remain loyal to the company personnel and carry out the task as a 'friendship' gesture.

Figure 17.2 shows a possible cycle where fear of losing control leads to resistance to change and eventually breaking down the company initiative. The cycle starts from a poorly communicated change, causing an individual employee to be concerned. This locks the employee into thinking about the value they add to the company and focuses their efforts on doing their originally prescribed job function. No time is spent reflecting on their own actions, planning and reviewing the intended change and its benefits to the company.

Some managers ignore their colleagues and/or subordinates, work longer hours, and become exhausted and stressed. While working extra hours could have very short-term gains, studies in the 1940s, 50s and 60s showed that the

---

1   Albert Hirschman's theory has been debated over the decades and has been generally accepted as the norm. Some scholars argue that there is a fourth predictable course of action: sabotage – carrying out actions in direct opposition to the task, to sabotage the efforts of other employees and management. For more information, see Hirschman, 1970.

2   Sometimes, people would remain silent. Many people assume that silence means agreement. There may be groups of people who would remain silent but disagree. When left alone and unchecked, there would be no action in line with the change required. Management science calls this the Abilene Paradox. For more information, see Harvey, 1988.

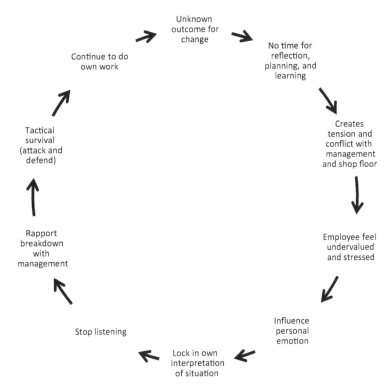

Figure 17.2   Cycle of employee resistance to change

increase in productivity decreases with the extra working time (Stillman, 2012). In the long run, such short-term results undermine creativity, efficiency, commitment and team work. Any energy efficient behaviours would be short-lived and not sustainable.

Groups of similar thinking employees come together and create tension and conflicts with management plans. Left uncontrolled, more employees will feel undervalued and stressed, leading to workplace anxiety. This amplifies and reaffirms the employees' own interpretation of the required change. Some senior managers try to resolve all tension and conflicts, while others try to silence and isolate the 'culprits'. As suggested by Hirschman, this merely moves the disagreement away from day-to-day conversations – it does not disappear or become a non-issue.

Over time, employees withdraw into familiar actions, stop listening and learn to be 'inauthentic' – they create distance between each other and disengage with the management. The work environment becomes highly political and a place of tactical survival: defending actions of 'friends' and shifting the 'blame' to others.

Generating Energy Efficiency Conversation for Initial Change

Engaging colleagues and employees to embrace energy efficient behaviours has to minimise emotional resistance. It needs to be done by building rapport with people and recognising emotional cues. Energy efficient behaviours are directly linked to each employee and are the result of interaction and rapport between the 'communicator' and each 'individual'. The interaction engages and enrols the 'individual' to make changes in thinking and in action with respect to energy consumption. Some managers and engineers are naturally better at emotional and social intelligence. This skill can be learned through conscious awareness and conscious practice.

Between 1924 and 1932, George Elton Mayo – an Australian psychologist, sociologist and organisational theorist – carried out a series of social experiments at the Hawthorne Works (part of Western Electric) in Illinois. His experiments are known loosely as the 'Hawthorne Experiments'. He studied many social and psychological aspects of the work environment in relation to work output and discovered that managers who excel at driving and maintaining high-quality production were those who:

- Were under less supervision from their own managers;
- Placed less direct emphasis on production as the goal;
- Encouraged employee participation in the making of decisions;
- Were more employee-centred;
- Spent more of their time in supervision and less in straight production work;
- Had a greater feeling of confidence in their supervisory roles;
- Felt that they knew where they stood in relation to the company.

When his findings and recommendations were analysed, the theories were well grounded and entirely rational.[3] Since that time, theories and research on change management have not changed from those found by Elton Mayo. The following are five no-nonsense simple steps to engage employees in adopting energy efficient behaviours:

- Form an energy change team.
- Build an awareness campaign that connects with each employee.

---

3   The theories of Frederick Taylor and Elton Mayo form the opposite ends of management styles and work output. As with the Jevons paradox (see Introduction, note 2) and the Abilene paradox, the balance for real business organisations lies somewhere in between and is specific for each company.

- Create a platform where employees can contribute towards energy reduction.
- Reinforce the energy efficient behaviours by integrating it into normal practices.
- Have senior management be seen reducing energy consumption.

Rob Goffee and Gareth Jones (2000) proposed a key characteristic that change teams should have: authenticity. In the context of an energy change team, this means team members with high personal integrity whose values for energy reduction are aligned with the business goals and who are perceived by employees to have high consistency between their words and their actions.

Trust is also an important factor in the workplace for job satisfaction, team work and team performance. Figure 17.3 shows what employees deemed important to built trust and what employees perceived their leaders were not doing. It is surprising to find that the action to build trust and team effort comes from simple actions that involve many aspects of human interaction.

Effecting a change by creating and utilising a team is not a new concept. Embedding a change in the normal ways of working in a business to instil energy efficient behaviours is not a simple matter of releasing employees for one-time training. It requires a range of techniques.

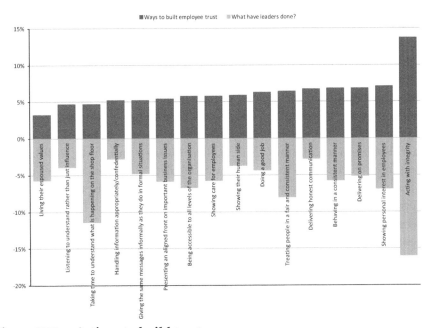

Figure 17.3   Actions to build trust
Source: Data for the figure drawn from Lane4, 2010.

In order for the change team to succeed, business managers must choose a good and reliable energy change team. John Kotter (1995), a professor of organisational change and transformation, recommends that in a small to medium sized companies, a change team should consist of between three and five people. In large businesses, 20 to 50 people is a good starting point, with the number rising to at least 2–5 per cent of employees to achieve a critical and self-sustaining participation. These change team members should:

- Exhibit enthusiasm for the role and willingness to learn.
- Have credibility at all levels of the company and 'followship'.
- Have or be given authority to organise resources, meetings and appropriate training.
- Build rapport and motivate colleagues, resolve problems and continue with progress.
- Communicate with staff and senior management and provide feedback.

Ideally, an energy change team, made up of front-line supervisors and managers, cuts across the business organisation. They typically spend more than 50 per cent of their time in the work area to coordinate and facilitate energy efficient behaviour, auditing progress and advising colleagues on ways to improve.

Selecting employees that are well respected within the company as team members sends a clear signal to all employees that the management takes the change seriously. If this team is started as a pilot project, the business has a safe environment in which to rapidly learn and improve before rolling the programme out to the whole business (Pascale and Sternin, 2005).

Many organisations put in a lot of time and attention to form the concept of change. Among the companies surveyed, only 16 per cent have successfully implemented the change as designed, on time and in full (Ghislanzoni, Heidari-Robinson and Jermin, 2010; Keller, Meaney and Pung, 2010). These organisations focused their attention on detailed plans, micro-level day-to-day issues that drive energy efficient behaviours, and were therefore better equipped to dismantle organisational barriers.

The first task of the team should be to fully understand the key drivers, key success factors, key barriers and the criteria used by the top management when allocating capital and human resources. Simple open-ended questions such as: 'How is consuming less energy important to you?' can often uncover the values and motivators of employees. There will also be times when members of the change team and other employees disagree with each other. Conflicting views and disagreements are also important. Furthermore, they reveal what each individual cares about and what motivates them.

Fundamental understanding of these issues is important to sculpt a targeted energy behaviour programme, values and vision that all employees buy into (more than their personal disagreements) and select the right energy projects for consideration. It also helps to soothe the egos of alphas within the company and make alphas feel 'psychologically' safe (Hilaire, 2011). John Kotter (2007) suggests that more than 50 per cent of businesses fail to carry out this step. If these questions are not clear and understood, the change team should speak up, challenge and seek clear and concise answers to these important questions.

Just like any clients of a business, employees need to be persuaded to buy into energy reduction. They need to be convinced that their efforts are of value to them (primarily) and to the company. Employees are very likely to be motivated by four key issues (Zohar, 1997):

1. The employee themselves (development plans, pay package and bonus, benefits, recognition etc.);
2. Working relationship with others;
3. Societal concerns;
4. Work output (good-quality production, waste, working conditions etc.

An energy reduction programme which does not meet one or more of the above 'motivators' is unlikely not to generate buy-in and the effort is wasted.

Different employees (or different function or groups of employees) are also likely to be motivated by differing combination of the four issues identified by Danah. Jargons, scare mongering and character assassinations does not work.

Naturally, the second task for the team is to set up a campaign to raise awareness of energy efficiency that meets everyone's needs. The word 'awareness' used in this context is not about employees' basic understanding of what energy is. Awareness in this context is about the activities of each employee in relation to energy consumption. Awareness begins when the employee realises that poor use of energy is within their control.

A good energy awareness campaign equips all employees with the knowledge and understanding for reducing energy consumption: they are aware of personal needs and business needs for reducing energy consumption, and understand their role and actions in the unfolding energy reduction programme. It has to convey a message that connects with everybody's needs, is worthwhile for employees to play a significant part, and has the simple tools and techniques that employees can use to participate in reducing energy consumption. The tools should be appropriate to the job functions of each employee in the company, e.g., production, maintenance, management, office etc.

Attaching a catchy name to the energy reduction programme, although trivial, can help integrate it into normal organisational routine. Film titles and historical events are good sources of inspiration.

A very good, but frequently ignored, tool is the use of an energy charter as shown in Case Study 17.1. An energy charter is a workplace 'social contract' in which the management agrees to uphold or deliver certain working conditions. Employees, in return, commit to carry out defined energy efficient 'favours' or agree to adjustments to certain defined changes to the working environment for the purpose of reducing energy consumption.

Lasting employee engagement requires a thought-out series of simple messages relevant to the business. As mentioned earlier, it also needs to identify with, anticipate and break down any defensive reasoning and routines put up by the employees (Argyris, 2994). Some of the barriers towards energy efficiency and energy reduction are described in Chapter 5, this chapter and in Chapter 18.

CASE STUDY 17.1   ENERGY CHARTER

This is our workplace energy charter – the promotion of the right of all employees* to universal access to an efficient and sustainable building service. The company is committed to:

- Reduce wasteful energy consumption patterns.
- Promote the supply of sustainable energy services.
- Service availability without arbitrary disconnection or interruption.
- Clear notification will precede any scheduled interruptions.
- Energy information and education is readily available.

Following a three week employee consultation, and as part of this commitment, the company will be replacing all windows from a single glazing to triple glazing and introducing a new air conditioning regime:

- Heating will be controlled to 19°C.
- Cooling will be controlled to 24°C.
- Humidity controls will be disabled.

As discussed and agreed during the consultation process, all employee will cooperate with the company's energy reduction programme. In particular:

- Will not use portable heaters in the workplace.
- Ensure that all doors and windows are closed at all times.
- Reporting any maintenance issues observed.
- Reducing wasteful energy consumption.

---

*   Some companies prefer to use the term 'residents' for employees within a building.

As suggested by Amabile and Kramer (2011), employees like to feel good accomplishing tasks. Focusing on small tasks over a long time allows everyone to feel good accomplishing many tasks. It also allows employees to constantly practise the new ways of working and integrate them into daily routines. Repeated success, especially successes that can be seen, touched, heard and felt builds trust, slows down organisational cultural barriers. In some organisations, employees could also begin peer policing, take an initiative to be energy efficient or request for additional accountability for more energy efficient behaviours or be involved in energy reduction projects.

Therefore, energy efficient behaviours need to be drip fed over a long period using multiple means of communication. The purpose of this step is to continue the energy efficient programme with reminders for action and to target employee efforts in looking for energy reduction opportunities, e.g., compressed air leaks, etc.

Companies that use 'positive' and 'in action' framed messages together with many good and successful examples tend to generate positive employee behaviours. Many methods are available, ranging from short refresher training sessions to suggestion boxes, free light bulbs, posters, stickers, newsletters, competition, booklets etc. The selected media should be appropriate to the business culture, appropriate to the task of the employee, and a means to allow the employee to practise and implement the new energy efficient behaviours at work. When this is used in concert with quick wins, it creates longer lasting behaviours.

Campaigns based on face-to-face authentic human contact – when the presenter is physically and emotionally present when delivering the message, able to build rapport and intellectually attentive – generate longer lasting results. These should be supplemented and/or expanded by other modes of communication (Hallowell, 1999).

The way the messages are phrased is important. Social studies on encouraging hotel guests to reuse towels showed that 26 per cent more guests reuse their towels when told that 'the majority of guests reuse their towels' compared to ' reuse the towels to save the environment' messages. The number of guests who reuse their towels jumps to 33 per cent and 45 per cent when told 'guests who stayed in this room reused their towels at least once' and 'the hotel has donated [a specified sum of money] to [a specified charity] on behalf of its guests for reusing their towel once' (Goldstein, Martin and Cialdini, 2007). Similar studies were carried out for energy efficiency and energy behaviours with similar success (Laskey and Kavazovic, 2010; Allcott, 2011).

A less used storyline for engaging employees at work is to provide information on energy reduction in a house. Some 89 per cent of UK households surveyed by EPRG in 2010 (Platchkov, L. et.al. 2011) showed that people deliberately implement energy reduction opportunities at home providing it is within their means and capabilities. A follow-on from this would be to relate energy reduction at home to energy reduction at work.

Using excessive negative messages invokes blame and creates fatigue and resistance. It does little to engage employees' passion and experience. Story lines using excessive visionary or blue sky approach can water down aspiration and impact. This is due to employees deeming the blue sky as 'unachievable' or 'non-practicable', leading to unwillingness to participate in what is perceived to be an unattainable goal. Words like 'strategy', 'efficiency', 'reliability' and 'capital plan' bear little relation to many employees and the message will be lost or ignored.

Different people analyse and interpret the same information slightly differently and at different pace. After the communication, do allow some time and space for everyone to assimilate the information. Allowing too little or too much time for employees to take action can also be a source of conflict and needs to be carefully balanced.

Finally, many companies allocate a very small sum of money (to the tune of a few thousand pounds) for promoting energy efficient behaviours and to engage employees to save energy. A sustainable and long-term employee engagement programme described above needs larger sums of money. A good starting budget figure is 1–2 per cent of the annual energy expenditure.[4] Business managers need facts and tangible benefits before sanctioning such capital. Managers and engineers at large are generally uncomfortable about proposing these studies – preferring technological improvements where facts can be obtained and verified.

The best approach to seeking funding to implement energy efficient behaviours is to use a three-pronged approach:

1.   Collect and provide many case studies available on the web.
2.   If possible, organise several site visits to successful businesses.
3.   Conduct a small-scale (pilot) energy efficient behaviour programme.

Sustaining Energy Efficient Behaviours

When employees are receptive, engaged and focused on the energy efficient messages, they are ready to receive 'advice' on the means to reduce energy consumption (Boardman and Darby, 2000). This 'advice' is described in Part 2 and Part 3.

---

4   This is a verbal quotation from John Mulholland.

Communication plays an even more important role in sustaining energy efficient behaviours and energy reduction. John Kotter (1995) recommends at least ten times more communication than during the initial stage. If the new behaviour is not reinforced and integrated into everyday work, employees are less likely to practise it continuously and consistently. Furthermore, if the behaviour is not part of the performance appraisal and reward of each employee, employees will soon lose their motivation and ignore the energy reduction programme. It is important to incorporate the behaviour into everyday tasks such as:

- Frequent performance monitoring of energy consuming equipment;
- Thinking about energy efficiency when replacing or buying new equipment;
- Ensuring energy reduction projects are understood and widely used;
- Induction training and refresher courses;
- Visibility of senior management engagement and participation in energy efficiency;
- Compliance with operating procedures;
- Incorporating energy efficiency into job descriptions and performance appraisals.

Other motivators to encourage and sustain energy efficient behaviours are:

- Publish energy performance to track the progress of energy reduction;
- Continued encouragement, commendations and recognition of employees efforts;
- Complement good efforts with non-financial rewards;
- Provide simple opportunities for employees to practice energy efficient behaviours;
- Provide means for employees to access resources (time, money, skills/ training/guidance, tools, information, space and authority) to raise and/or implement opportunities.

If the business uses contractors, it is very common for them to be left out of energy reduction programmes. Contractors should be included in the drive to reduce energy consumption. Case Studies 17.2–17.4 highlight the importance of including contractors in energy reduction programmes.

CASE STUDY 17.2   ENERGY LOSS OCCURRENCE IN KITCHEN

In a petrochemical company, the site generates 10 tonnes/hour of steam. During an energy audit, the auditors and the site personnel could only account for 7 tonnes/hour of steam being used by the business. After several months of investigation, it was found that the kitchen, operated by a contractor, consumed 3 tonnes/hour of steam.

CASE STUDY 17.3   UNAUTHORISED ENERGY USE BY CONTRACTORS

In a chemical plant, a capacity expansion project was approved by the executive team. During the 17-month construction phase, the energy consumption was consistently 10 per cent more than the budgeted energy consumption. When investigated, many of the contractors used energy inefficiently.

CASE STUDY 17.4   LIGHTING LEFT ON BY CONTRACTORS

During a night-time survey of an office block, it was observed that the majority of office employees turned off the lighting at the end of day. When the survey teams walked around the offices at night, the lights were left on throughout the night. Follow-up investigation found that the lights were left on by the night-time cleaning contractors.

18

Using Data to Manage Energy

Since the dawn of civilisation, people have used maps as a feedback of where they are in relation to where they want to go. Feedback is one of the most important building blocks of behavioural change programmes. In an energy reduction programme the feedback is information on energy consumption. Energy feedback allows management, change teams and employees to:

- Identify and understand its processes;
- Ensure decisions are made based on facts and figures rather than emotions and feelings;
- Show whether or not planned actions and improvements were actually realised, and take any necessary corrective and preventive actions;
- Use it for historical reporting and forward planning.

However, communication and feedback are among the most poorly executed phases of energy management and energy reduction programmes: 56 per cent of employees thought their managers (1) did not communicate clearly with them; (2) often used incomprehensible language that confuse the message; and (3) got feedback from colleagues not directly connected to the employees receiving the message (Goodman, 2010).

Many managers and engineers fail to communicate effectively information relating to energy consumption and progress of energy reduction projects. This could arise from not having energy information; fear that the energy information returns an 'unfavourable' result; presenting too much information; or presenting information that is technically too complex for the target audience.

In a manufacturing business, production personnel readily relate to feedback such as flows, temperatures, pressures etc. However, a manager in the same business relates to other parameters depending on their function within the business. For example:

- A maintenance manager relates to availability of the plant – a means to reduce idle time, which in turn is related to energy consumption.

- A production manager relates to the raw materials, throughputs, quality and waste.
- The energy manager, on the other hand, readily relates to the business's total energy consumption.

Different employees need different information to play their part in minimising the energy consumed within the business. It is important to tailor the construct of the feedback in such a way that it is easily understood by each employee. Figure 18.1 shows a visual example of the different functions and job requirements of a typical manufacturing business.

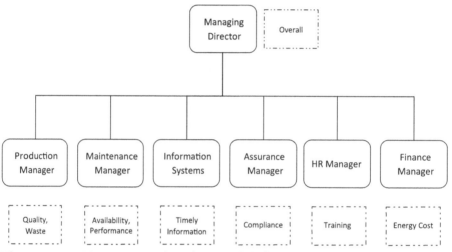

Figure 18.1   Management functions and their links with energy consumption

Generating the same set of energy data as feedback means that many employees within the business will not be able to relate the information to their work. That piece of energy data is, therefore, a waste of time and effort, and the energy reduction programme is heading for failure. Some managers and engineers install a lot of energy meters. Very frequently, most employees would still be none the wiser about the use of the energy readings.

More than 56 per cent of employees surveyed do not know where to find the information they need to use every day. Of those that do, 62 per cent do not know how to use the information correctly (Shah, Horne and Capella, 2012).

One tool to identify the information needs of each employee is the use of success maps developed by Robert Kaplan. Figure 18.2 shows an example from a fictitious manufacturing company. For ease of explanation, let us assume that the air dryer is one of the processes in the plant and the main energy use is steam. In order to develop a success map for this air drying process, ask:

Q) What causes the steam consumption in the air dryer to change?
A) Four parameters: feed throughput into the air dryer, product specification, solvent concentration and ambient air temperature.

Let us assume that the feed throughput and product specification are controlled by processes before the air dryers and are not controllable variables in the drying process. Another variable which is not controllable is the ambient air temperature. The hotter the ambient air, the less steam will be used to heat the air to the operating temperature. The reverse logic applies to cooler ambient

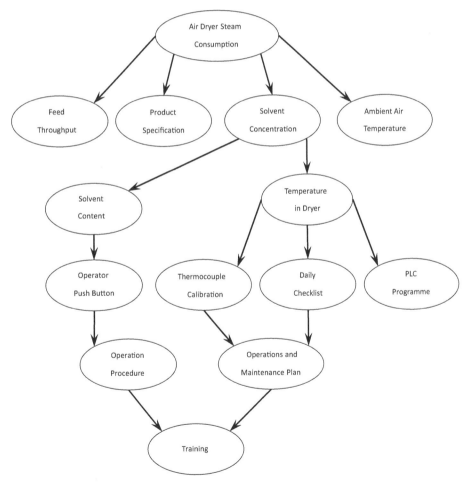

Figure 18.2   Success map of a drying operation

air temperatures. Although the ambient air temperature is measurable, it is not practical to control the ambient air temperature.

Some of the variables that can cause the energy consumption of a plant to vary are:

- Legal requirements.
- Code of conduct and guidelines.
- Product standards.
- Product formulation.
- Production rate.
- Key plant operating conditions.
- Weather (heating, cooling, humidity).
- Occupancy rates.
- Public commitments.
- Voluntary agreements, etc.

Continuing from the example above, a similar question is used again:

- Q) What causes the solvent concentration to change?
- A) Two factors affect the solvent concentration in the dryer: solvent content on product from the previous process and the temperature in the dryer.

A similar question and answer method is used to whittle down the reasons why energy use varies in the air dryer until it reaches human intervention. This success map now serves as a guide showing how each employee uses the information to operate the process. It also serves as an aid to communicate each action that can have an impact on energy consumption.

In the example above it is important that all personnel operating the air dryer follow the operating procedure to accurately push the solvent button. This in turn minimises the solvent content and steam required to operate the air dryer. Similar lines of communication can be used for the processes upstream of the air dryer to minimise solvent use due to feed throughput and product specification.

This map also serves as a tool to identify areas where energy efficient behaviours can be added to operating procedures and as a prompt when reviewing operational checklists and when locating any additional meters and measurement instruments. This success map can be expanded to include the full process plant in order to show all the interrelated linkages to minimise energy consumption.

When energy information is provided this way – a form that can be readily related to everyone within the business – the information becomes useful and employees can respond to the energy feedback. For example, if a production worker is told that they are using too much steam pressure or processing the product for too long, it is information the said employee can respond to and take corrective action on immediately. If a maintenance manager is told that using poor-quality parts is causing unreliability in the process, leading to long idle time and associated cost (including energy), it is a piece of information that they could use and take action on.

Businesses that are office based or service based have similar measurable energy-related parameters and can derive similar energy success maps using the same method.

Relating Operational Data to Minimise Energy

Day-to-day management of energy requires a thorough understanding of how the business consumes energy. Some of the available energy data would have been identified when preparing a success map. Similar to accounting practices, many managers and engineers rely on month-end, quarterly or year-end energy data to review energy consumption. This means that the equivalent amount of time would have lapsed before any corrective action could be identified and applied.

When managers and engineers think about managing energy on a daily basis, many would immediately think about installing energy meters. Energy metering should not be used to mean buying and installing energy meters and automated data logging systems in every location within the business. As demonstrated by the use of success maps, there are many other parameters that are almost always available to the business: flows, weight or volume, temperature, time 'ON' or 'OFF' status, conductivity, power factor etc. Many of these measurements are already available from gauges installed locally to the equipment. Others could be located in control panels, control rooms, building management systems (BMS), energy management systems (EMS) and distributed control systems (DCS).

These parameters can be used to calculate energy consumption and energy efficiency. Very frequently, energy consumption can also be measured or inferred by other means. For example, the amount of steam used in a heat exchanger can be quantified by measuring:

- Steam flow into the heat exchanger (direct method).
- Condensate flow out of the heat exchanger (indirect method).
- The flow liquid to be heated and its inlet and outlet temperature (inferred).

BMS, EMS or DCS use the measurements to automatically adjust the process or building controls. This is essentially taking the inputs from the measurements, running through a series of predefined programmes (also called programmable logic controllers, or PLCs) and sending a pre-programmed action sequence to other devices – e.g., to open or close a valve.

If no metering is available, additional meters can be installed. When used correctly, metered information helps an organisation create a set of energy performance indicators. Figure 18.3 shows a range of metering options, users of the metered information and frequency of use.

Figure 18.3   Various forms of energy feedback

When installing new meters, it is important to understand and remember the following:

1.   Energy meters (natural gas meters, thermal energy meters and electricity meters) form only a small part of energy consumption information.

2. Energy meters do not think or take action – people do. Energy metering does its job best when it support employees to analyse data and take the appropriate action.

3. Installing energy meters does not save energy. Employees analysing the energy data, recognising an energy reduction opportunity and implementing the opportunity leads to energy reduction.

Any additional meters should be assessed based on the risk of undetected deviation leading to unnecessary energy consumption.

1. Estimate the annual cost of the energy consumption.
2. Decide on the level of risk factor:
   – 20 per cent – highly intermittent or very variable loads, or allowed to operate 'flat out' when its output ought to modulate in response to changes in demand;
   – 5 per cent – failure of controls would become apparent quickly;
   – 1 per cent – any failure would be immediately detected and rectified.

3. Multiply the annual cost and risk factor to get an estimate of the likely energy cost due to undetected deviation. This figure can be used by the business to budget for metering needs.

Using a cooling system as an example, the energy cost could be £50,000 per annum. The cooling system is used only for comfort cooling and is therefore highly seasonal. The risk of undetected deviation is £50,000 × 20 per cent = £10,000 per annum. The cost to install a flow meter and the supply and return temperature probe costs £1,500. At a cost of £1,500, the metering system – when installed and used appropriately – can prevent a potential deviation worth £10,000.

Other factors that may need to be considered are:

• Most direct metering devices will cause a drop in pressure inside the pipe. Choose the metering device that gives the lowest pressure drop.
• All metering devices have an intended operating condition. Check that the minimum, normal and maximum values of the proposed metering device meet the requirement of the utility to be metered. If necessary, use a portable meter to determine the minimum, normal and maximum values before specifying the correct measuring device.
• With the exception of electrical measuring devices, all other devices have an optimum installation location. For flow metering, this could

be the straight distance from (and to) a bend, valve, fittings etc. in relation to the proposed metering device location.

For a significant majority of metering needs, there is a suitable metering device for all foreseeable installation challenges and requirements.

Purchasing an unsuitable metering device may lead to poor energy information and could cost the business to make the meter information right. When a meter is installed, it needs to be installed in the correct location and maintained to a standard as specified in the operation and maintenance manual (Case Study 18.1).

CASE STUDY 18.1   INSTALLING NEW METERS IN THE WRONG LOCATION

A pharmaceutical manufacturing site with four steam boilers replaced all steam meters, natural gas meters and water meters. The old meters, installed 30 years ago, were replaced because the internal parts of the meters are corroded and there are no spare parts available. Following the replacement, it was found that these meters are consistently reading 12 per cent higher than the previous readings.

The new meters were purchased based on cost and installed in the same location as the old meters. Following a protracted discussion with the manufacturer, it was agreed that the meters were not installed in a location as specified by the manufacturer's installation guide. As a result, the readings were not accurate. In order to obtain accurate and repeatable information, two options were available:

- Replace all the new meters with meters made by a different manufacturer. This would cost 50 per cent more than the ones purchased.
- Rework the pipe work to fit the conditions required by the manufacturer of these new meters. This would cost the site four times more to make the meters work.

Option 1 was chosen by the site and the installed meters were disposed of as meters could not be restocked or resold.

Ensure that all energy feedback provides useful information to somebody within the business. It is also very common to find top-of-the-range, state-of-the-art metering solutions installed within a business where there are no users using that information or the information is presented in a form that is not usable by anyone within the business.

For all additional measurements the business chooses to install, they need to be implemented in line with the following guidelines:

1.   There is a valid user for the measured data.
2.   It is installed in the correct location.
3.   It is displayed in an accessible location.
4.   There is a means to ensure continuous accuracy and repeatability.
5.   It visually presents relevant, clear and useful information.
6.   It highlights areas that need corrective action.
7.   It is appropriate to the business.

A simple guide for designing the energy metering and for monitoring and targeting can be found in Figure 18.4.

While the capital cost of these metering devices are a one-off cost, the cost to operate, maintain and ensure accuracy and repeatability of these measuring devices is a recurring cost to the business. In general, when more and more direct metering devices are chosen correctly, installed in the right location and routinely maintained, data accuracy and data reliability is improved.

If there is a need to store this data – e.g., it needs to be kept in a secure environment for later analysis, reporting etc. – an automatic meter reading (AMR) system is required. Create a list of metering devices and discuss them with the IT department to decide which devices and systems can be supported from the existing infrastructure. An AMR involves five components:

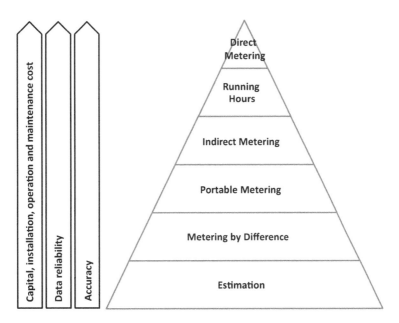

Figure 18.4   Accuracy, data reliability and cost of measurement methods

CASE STUDY 18.2   USERS NOT TRAINED TO OBSERVE AND REPORT ON ENERGY DEVIATION

An industrial site has multiple boilers of similar make and capacity. As part of a metering, monitoring and targeting programme, many parameters from each boiler are monitored, and composite boiler efficiency is displayed and trended.

At the end of the year all boiler efficiency trends were reviewed. Figure 18.5 shows the efficiency trend over a full year for one of the boilers. There is an apparent drop in boiler efficiency sometime in August. The trend on all other boilers did not show this drop in efficiency.

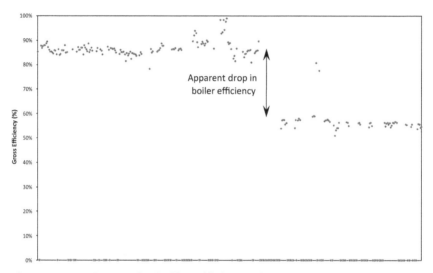

Figure 18.5   Composite boiler efficiency data

Even though the boiler efficiency was trended, a total of five months lapsed before the deviation was detected. It was lucky that the cause of the apparent drop in efficiency was traced to poor calibration of the meters. This was confirmed by the amount of natural gas purchased and the amount of water consumed by the said boiler.

If it had been a real drop in efficiency, the company would have incurred a significant amount of energy use for a full five months before the deviation was detected. This case study shows the importance of ensuring that the energy data is understood by the people within the organisation, and the need for ongoing and continual monitoring of the recorded data.

1.   The measuring device;
2.   A transmitting device (typically pulse output, 0–10 V output, or 4–20 mA output);
3.   A communications device (typically, RS323/RS485/RS422, Ethernet, wireless or any other communication protocol);
4.   A data logging device;
5.   A database for energy data storage.

If records for the energy data are business critical or important for business continuity, uninterruptable power supply (UPS) and data backup facilities will also need to be included in the automatic meter reading system.

Energy data can also be analysed by computers and generate reports. Such systems are called automatic monitoring and targeting systems (aM&T). An aM&T system requires all of the items described above and software to analyse the energy data.

Designing Dashboards to Monitor Energy Consumption

As mentioned in Chapter 16, 60–80 per cent of performance measurement items are useless or drive the wrong behaviour and outputs from a business. In a separate study, Ron Howard found that many companies trying to measure detailed information unknowingly spend more than 10 times the economic value of the information being measured. In fact these extra costs did not cause any change in the output of the measurement or the decisions that would have been made by the management in light of the new information (Savage, 2009).

In general, companies monitor:

* Nothing.
* Everything.
* The right energy performance indicator wrongly.
* The wrong energy performance indicator rightly.
* In very limited cases, the right energy performance indicator rightly.

There are more than 30 reputable commercial and industrial energy aM&T systems on the market. This list is constantly growing. Many of these packages provide flashy and complicated displays similar to those shown in Figure 6.5. However, if these displays do not provide clear, accurate, concise and easy to understand energy management information or information that highlights problem areas at a glance, employees within the business will soon stop using the aM&T system. Furthermore, many aM&T systems are only used by the energy manager as a corporate energy measurement and reporting tool. As other employees do not use them, many aM&T systems become expensive white elephants.

This is not a failure in the aM&T technology. This is a failure of:

1. energy managers not designing the management systems with insight, thus being unable to decipher the measurements that give meaningful information;
2. managers, engineers and scientists not writing up detailed requirements of an aM&T system to support people within the business to use the energy information;
3. software designers to understand data visualisation techniques for business operations.

CASE STUDY 18.3   AN AM&T SYSTEM WITH ONLY ONE USER

In an industrial plant, steam is monitored and trended on the SCADA screen. The SCADA is routinely monitored by maintenance technicians. As part of a steam demand reduction campaign, all maintenance technicians are required to investigate and record reasons for peak steam demand. The technicians use this record to (1) investigate planned and unplanned steam use according to production schedule and (2) identify opportunities to reduce steam consumption.

After the study was completed, the technicians continued to use this method to drive energy efficient behaviours. When there is a change in steam demand but there is no change in planned activities, the technicians investigate the plant to identify the cause of an increase in steam consumption. Prolonged and routine visits by the technicians to the production operators have resulted in changes to several operating procedures and production planning.

George Miller (1956), a Harvard University psychologist, found that human beings have a short-term memory and proposed that on average a human being could remember 7±2 pieces of information at a time. Effective energy information needs to:

1. match the way the business uses and analyses data;
2. provide high-level data, ideally within 7±2 pieces of energy information that can be scanned quickly by the relevant user;
3. highlight any areas that require attention or intervention in a short period of time;
4. if appropriate, provide a means to allow further analysis of the data.

The previous section provided a framework to design energy performance measurement that is relevant to the business operation. The remaining section provides a framework for developing good visual techniques to analyse energy data and for monitoring energy consumption. When there is a visible deviation, troubleshoot the cause of the deviation and rectify the root cause of the issue. The development of this tool also builds insight into how the business can use energy information and allows the managers and engineers to specify a good aM&T system.

Energy data analysis can be done for any time interval. Common time intervals for energy analysis are:

1.   Seconds.
2.   Minutes.
3.   Half-hourly (natural gas and electricity supply are frequently measured in this time interval).
4.   Hourly.
5.   Daily.
6.   Weekly.
7.   Monthly.
8.   Yearly.

The simplest form of energy data visualisation technique that can be used to monitor energy consumption is tabular information or pie charts. Tabular information and pie charts are good for providing snapshot information. They can provide information about the energy mix, i.e., where energy is consumed in one time period. They do not give information about the energy mix compared to other time periods. Several pie charts are required to provide a picture on the trend. A better representation of energy trends is to use a bar or line chart, as shown in Figure 18.6.

Another alternative, shown in Figure 18.7, shows the spread of energy data depicted as the minimum, 25-percentile, mean, 75-percentile and maximum energy consumption within the sample period.

This is an ideal starting point to plan for energy sub-metering throughout the business. The data representation above can be recomputed to provide information on the consumption of different utilities by the respective area. This representation also allows comparison of energy use in different business areas across multiple time intervals.

At this stage there is insufficient information to analyse and confirm whether or not the proportion of utility consumption is representative of the demands for energy. In order to understand the variation of energy consumption in day-to-day operation, the variables that would cause energy consumption to vary

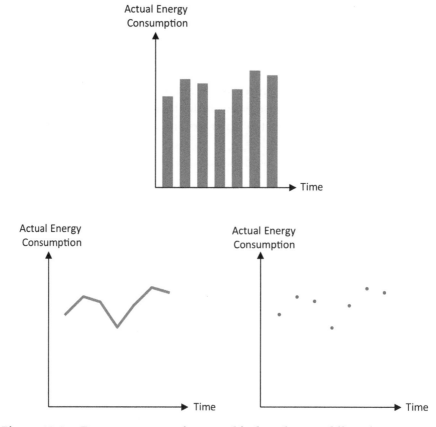

Figure 18.6   Energy consumption trend in bar chart and line chart

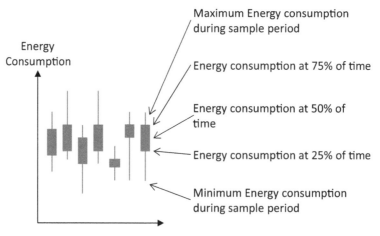

Figure 18.7   Energy consumption trend in box-and-whisker/candlestick chart

need to be identified, measured and verified. The success map described earlier has identified these variables.

Understanding the implications of these energy variables brings forth the concept of expected energy consumption and forms the basis of an aM&T system and an energy baseline where the energy reduction programme and projects can be measured.

The process of developing this model is an iterative process and is summarised in Figure 18.8. There are many ways to develop a model to predict the energy consumption for the business. They are:

- *Theoretically*: by carrying out a full material and energy balance, summing up all of the variables from the operation of individual equipment.
- *Statistically*: analysis of plant data and fit the data into a suitably identified curve.
- *Hybrid method*: a judicious mix of theoretical and empirical formulation.

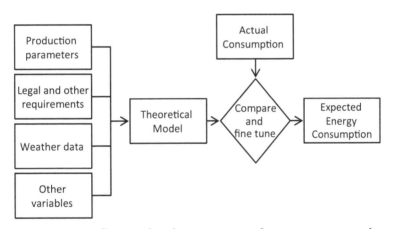

Figure 18.8   Process flow to develop an expected energy consumption formula

Consider a plot of actual energy consumption vs. production throughput as shown in Figure 18.9. This is a linear relationship where the energy consumed is directly proportional to the production throughput.

Energy profiles of this type can be described by a straight line equation taking the form:

$Y = mX + C$

Energy consumption = Slope × Production Throughput + Constant

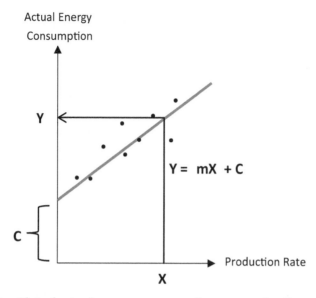

Figure 18.9   Plot of actual energy consumption vs. production rate

There are four types of information that can be extracted from this relationship. The first is that a business that follows this linear relation can use it to predict, and therefore budget for, the energy to be consumed by the production facility. With a known production volume (X), the equation would estimate the expected energy consumption (Y).

The second piece of information obtained is the quantity of energy consumption not related to production, i.e., the fixed load. This is depicted by the value C. A large C value in proportion to the total energy consumed indicates that a large quantity of energy is not used to manufacture products and that the marginal energy used per unit of product output is small and vice versa.

Figure 18.10 shows the expected energy consumption from a manufacturing plant. The fixed load for Utility 1 and Utility 2 is 1,924,890 and 64,147 units of measurement respectively. It is important to identify and quantify the makeup of these energy base loads.

In some businesses the fixed load energy consumption cannot be minimised. Fixed loads could also be business critical and therefore could not be turned down or turned off. Examples of business critical operations are data centres or server rooms and large UPS rooms.

In other areas, they are good quick win opportunities and should be a target area for energy reduction. Typically, they can be found in machines that are standing idle for significant periods of time, ventilation systems, laboratories, lighting, staff facilities, kitchens and offices.

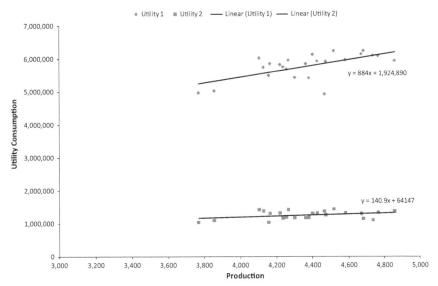

Figure 18.10   Expected energy consumption from a plant

In real-world businesses not many businesses conform to a straight line relationship. Figure 18.11 shows the different types of curve that can be expected and their meaning.

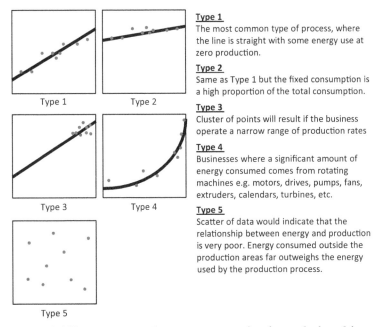

Type 1
The most common type of process, where the line is straight with some energy use at zero production.

Type 2
Same as Type 1 but the fixed consumption is a high proportion of the total consumption.

Type 3
Cluster of points will result if the business operate a narrow range of production rates

Type 4
Businesses where a significant amount of energy consumed comes from rotating machines e.g. motors, drives, pumps, fans, extruders, calendars, turbines, etc.

Type 5
Scatter of data would indicate that the relationship between energy and production is very poor. Energy consumed outside the production areas far outweighs the energy used by the production process.

Figure 18.11   Different types of energy vs. production relationships

Some businesses have several multiple business streams operating on the same site or use the same machines to manufacture different products. These relationships should be established independent of each other and then brought together into a multivariable (sometimes known as multivariate) regression analysis. Many statistical packages are available on the market. The key is to apply common sense in these analyses.

The third type of information that can be obtained is the slope of this relationship. It is the variable load energy consumption, also known as marginal energy consumption or specific energy consumption (SEC). SEC is used in benchmarking exercises and frequently quoted by licensed processes. Many factors can change the SEC value within a business. Typical examples are:

- Change in production levels.
- Change in quality of input materials, production formulation and specification.
- Producing components of higher or lower energy intensity.
- Changing plant running efficiency.
- Change in ways of operation to meet health, safety and environmental regulations etc.
- Poor-quality (graded) production or loss of skilled employees
- Extremes of weather.

A significant majority of managers, engineers and even energy specialists and management consultants make two common mistakes when computing SEC:

1. By computing it as the ratio of total energy consumption and good production output. This has led to a lot of confusion, misleading plant performance and energy consumption. A better way to calculate SEC is as the ratio of total energy consumption and total production output.
2. Forgets that SEC is marginal or variable energy consumption and that there is fixed energy consumption. Any resultant analysis means that at zero production, there is no energy consumption. As seen from the examples shown above, this is clearly not the case! SEC figures are only valid when the production output or range is also specified.[1]

Therefore, the use and publication of SEC information needs to be done cautiously. The following are some of the common issues when using SEC.

---

1   For licensed processes, the plant or machinery is designed for a fixed range of applicability. Therefore, the SEC quoted is bound by this design range only. On many instances, the machines or equipment is not capable of operating outside the design range.

1.   Reduction in SEC could arise from an increase in good production,
      reduction in waste or reduction in energy consumption. Using SEC to
      indicate energy reduction is not strictly true as a reduction in SEC can
      also be achieved via several means.

2.   Scaling of energy consumption based on SEC assumes energy
      consumption varies in proportion to production. When there is no
      production, there is no energy consumption. This does not happen in
      real manufacturing plants as there is always base load consumption.

3.   Using SECs in benchmarking prejudices the quality of energy produced
      and used on site: i.e., 1 kg of steam at a pressure of 10 barg consumes
      more energy to produce (hence has higher SEC) when compared with
      1 kg of steam at a pressure of 2 barg. As another example, pumping
      water at 5 barg will consume more electricity than pumping the same
      amount of water at 2 barg.

The fourth kind of information that can be extracted from the energy
consumption vs. production relationship is by plotting the SEC vs. production
(sometimes known as the differential SEC relationship). This gives an indication
of the optimal production level that yields the lowest energy consumption.
Operating a manufacturing plant at or near this optimal point would consume
the least amount of energy. Figure 18.12 shows the different types of differential
SEC relationships that can be encountered. Ultimately, the choice of production
rate is a management decision.

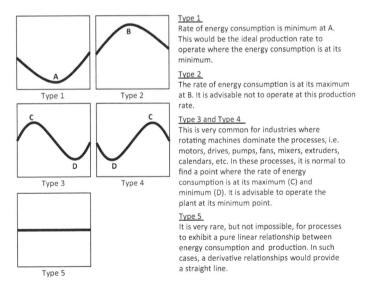

Type 1
Rate of energy consumption is minimum at A.
This would be the ideal production rate to
operate where the energy consumption is at its
minimum.

Type 2
The rate of energy consumption is at its maximum
at B. It is advisable not to operate at this production
rate.

Type 3 and Type 4
This is very common for industries where
rotating machines dominate the processes, i.e.
motors, drives, pumps, fans, mixers, extruders,
calendars, etc. In these processes, it is normal to
find a point where the rate of energy
consumption is at its maximum (C) and
minimum (D). It is advisable to operate the
plant at its minimum point.

Type 5
It is very rare, but not impossible, for processes
to exhibit a pure linear relationship between
energy consumption and production. In such
cases, a derivative relationships would provide
a straight line.

Figure 18.12   Different types of differential SEC relationships

Another common variable that changes energy consumption is the weather. Let us consider the energy input into a building. To simplify the description, we assume that this building is a cube shown in Figure 18.13.

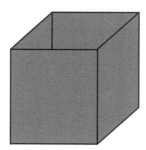

Figure 18.13   Simplified building model

The heat gained or lost by this building is determined by natural laws of conservation. Recalling Chapter 2, the law is summarised below and shown graphically in Figure 18.14:

Energy Input + Energy Generated = Useful Energy + Waste Energy

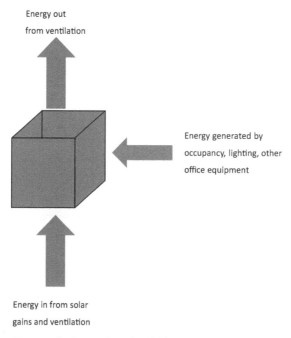

Figure 18.14   Energy balance in a building

Energy input to the building is from the solar gains, air used to ventilate the building and either heating or cooling the incoming air. The energy generated from the building is the heat generated by each occupant, heat from lighting and all other office equipment. Some of the energy input and energy generated is termed useful energy: it is necessary to create a comfortable working environment. For example, heating the incoming air during winter is considered useful when it maintains a comfortable office environment and meets health and safety requirements. Other forms of energy are classified as wasteful when not used efficiently. Using the same air heating example, excessive heating of air above the temperature set point is deemed energy waste.

For a known occupancy and IT equipment, the amount of energy input to a building changes according to ambient conditions, e.g., amount of sunlight, time of day, season of the year and the temperature (or other) set points inside the building.

Consultants and contractors would be able to calculate the energy requirements either with historical temperature data or degree-day data. The use of daily or hourly historical data would be most accurate but involves a very large sample of data points for analysis. Degree-day data is a simplified form of historical weather data available on a weekly and monthly basis for heating and cooling at several base temperatures – i.e., the temperature set point inside the building. The commonly found base temperatures available from the internet are:

- Heating: 10°C, 15.5°C, 18°C.
- Cooling: -20°C, -5°C, 0°C, 5°C.

A lot of degree-day data at other base temperatures can also be found. Figure 18.15 shows the different types of energy consumption vs. degree day relationships that can be encountered.

In limited cases, e.g., a carbon adsorption process, the slope will be negative. This is because, during warmer months, carbon molecules will preferentially adsorb water, giving less capacity for its normal production and necessitating additional regeneration.

The computation of degree-day is formulated based on several assumptions. The two key assumptions are:

- Continuous 24 hours per day/7 days per week operation.
- The building or process is temperature controlled.

Therefore, the application of degree-day must be done with caution. Some of the common mistakes when using degree-day data are:

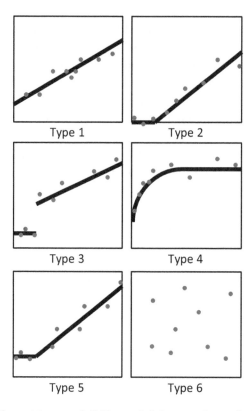

Figure 18.15   Different types of differential degree day relationships

1.   In some buildings and processes, it does not operate continuously. These businesses may have utilities turned off at night and at weekends. For these businesses, direct application of degree-day will yield the wrong results.

2.   Some businesses use publicly available degree day data which is not representative of the business. Businesses operating to different work environments have different heat gains – e.g., occupancy, building materials and orientation may have different base temperatures from those available in the public domain. Different countries also have different base temperatures. The key is to match base temperatures to the building and/or manufacturing process.

3.   Some businesses may not be controlled solely by temperature. Some examples are data centres and some labs where relative humidity is the main parameter of control. In these buildings, degree-day will have a poor correlation with the energy consumption.

4.   As seen in Figure 18.15, there are many forms of degree-day relationships. The majority of spreadsheet software is not capable of

identifying the patterns. Human interpretation of the trend may be required to decipher the degree-day analysis.

5.   For energy data collected manually or via invoices, the timing of any energy data will be important for accurate allocation of energy consumption.

Analysis of energy consumed vs. production levels and vs. weather are only two of the available measures to assess the relationship between energy and an external variable. Many other measurement indicators and variables are available and should be considered if applicable for the business. With the advent of computer technologies and advanced software, degree-days are slowly being replaced by actual records of temperature.

The dots shown in Figures 18.9, 18.11, 18.12 and 18.15 are purposely drawn such that there is no perfect correlation. In real businesses there are very few processes that exhibit perfect correlations. Many managers and engineers are familiar with using spreadsheets to generate the 'best fit' lines, displaying equation of best fit and the correlation of determination (also known as the r-square value).

A best fit line is drawn by finding a 'line' where the sum of the difference of all data points to the best fit line equals zero. An r-square value is a theoretical statistical tool that describes the correlation of two things being compared. Many managers and engineers look for a 'magic' r-square value of 0.75, or 75 per cent, as the cut-off point – any correlation less than 75 per cent is deemed to be non-existent and any correlation more than 75 per cent is deemed to be good.

In a large sample of data, a low r-square value may still be practically significant. A simple test would be to determine the probability of a chance result or an erroneous result. This has been studied and computed by Rummel (1976). The relationship between r-square and probability of error is dependent on the number of data points used in the analysis and is shown in Figure 18.16. Based on Figure 18.16, for an r-square value of 0.8:

- If there are five data points, the probability of error is 1 in 20 (5 per cent).
- If there is 12 data points, the probability of error is between 1 in 200 (0.5 per cent) and 1 in 2,000 (0.05 per cent).

As a rule of thumb, for energy data to be practically significant, an error probability of 1 in 40 (2.5 per cent) is a suitable starting point.

Monitoring, comparing and setting budgets based on expected energy consumption or energy baseline is known as energy monitoring and targeting. Examples of these are deviation from expected chart (Figure 18.17), control

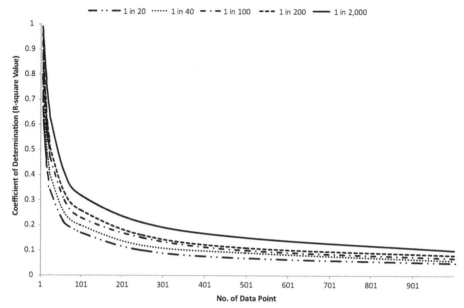

Figure 18.16   Odds against an erroneous result
Source: Data for the figure drawn from Rummel, 1976.

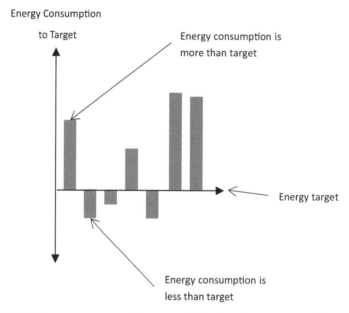

Figure 18.17   Energy consumption as a deviation from expected consumption chart

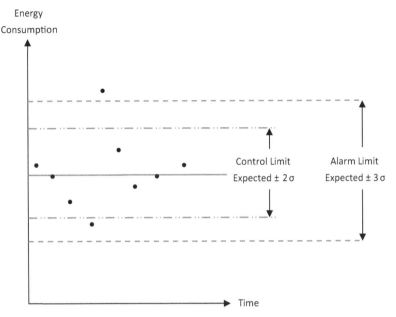

Figure 18.18   Energy consumption as control chart

chart (Figure 18.18) and CUmulative SUM of deviations/differences (CuSUM) chart.

CuSUM is a simple statistical technique used in Total Quality Management (TQM). It involves plotting the difference between actual consumption and expected energy consumption. This technique allows small changes in energy consumption to be easily seen. A CuSUM chart looks for the changes in slope as indicators of change:

- Horizontal slope means that the energy consumed is as expected.
- Slope upwards means that the energy consumed is more than expected.
- Slope downwards means that the energy consumed is less than expected.

A change of direction in a CuSUM indicates an 'event' has occurred with relevance to energy consumption. A change in slope could mean a planned energy reduction project is on target, some equipment is showing signs of deterioration or the effect of energy awareness campaign are starting to wear off etc.

If a change in slope is unplanned, it indicates that the cause of changes in energy consumption needs to be identified, investigated and eliminated. If the cause is for a valid purpose, the cause needs to be recorded and the CuSUM

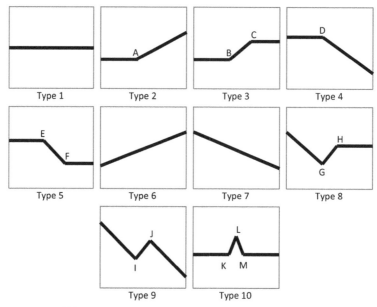

Figure 18.19   Different types of CuSUM relationships

re-plotted from that point onwards. Figure 18.19 shows the range of CuSUM relationships that is available.

Very frequently, a CuSUM needs to be read in conjunction with a trend chart. Trend charts pick up short-term isolated results better than CuSUM. However, CuSUM is more sensitive to smaller changes over a long period.

Some consultants and contractors take the concept of CuSUM a step further by identifying 'aggressive yet achievable' energy targets. This aggressive yet achievable target is usually based on 8–12 sustained downward data points from the original CuSUM chart plotted above. Care should be taken when using aggressive yet achievable targets. The reason for the sustained reduction in energy has to be identified, otherwise, the new target would not be achievable.

19

Policy, Objectives and Targets for Energy Management

When it comes to setting good policy, objectives and targets, many managers and engineers are familiar with the SMART framework. SMART is an acronym that describes the key characteristics of good objectives, namely: Specific, Measurable, Achievable, Realistic and Time-bound.

SMART Framework

The reality is that managers, engineers, consultants and contractors can use the SMART framework and still set bad objectives and targets. In fact, there are more badly set objectives and targets than good ones. The two primary reasons for setting bad objectives and targets arise from (1) confusion about what is defined as objectives, targets etc. and (2) misinterpretation of the requirements of SMART.

A policy is an over-arching goal to be achieved. It is to be used as a decision road map for managers within the organisation in terms of energy reduction. This is not to be confused with the term 'strategy' or 'procedure'. Under the policy, there could be several objectives designed or planned to achieve the results specified by the goal. The relationship between policy, objective, target, plan and tasks is best described pictorially. Figure 19.1 is another adaptation of Robert Kaplan's success map shown in Chapter 18.

Some experienced managers and engineers will be familiar with different the ways of specifying a goal: 'towards' goals and 'away from' goals and the relative benefits of using the former over the later. The use of 'towards' goal and 'away from' goals is a subject of word play and the psychological attitude attached to such goals. It is normally used in Neuro-Linguistic Programming (NLP) and is beyond the scope of this book.

Recapping the ideas in this book, we have looked at strategies for energy reduction, developed a simple framework for implementation, and identified the barriers, merits and demerits of various tools and techniques for identifying

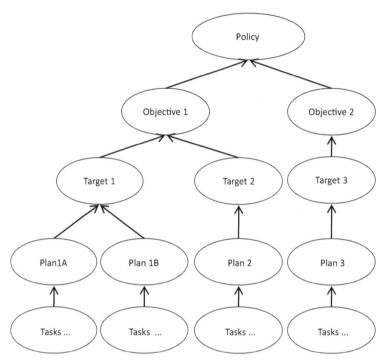

Figure 19.1   Relationship between policy, objective and target

energy reduction, quick wins and the various managerial aspects of an energy reduction programme.

Once all of the information gathered from Parts 1, 2, 3 and 4 of this book has been analysed, the task for developing an energy policy, objectives and targets for energy reduction is to bring all of the information together. The most important point is to select a goal without neglecting the purpose of the business – to provide quality product and/or services to its customer. Focusing on energy reduction to the extent of neglecting the business purpose will lead to business issues. The second important point is, if the chosen goals are the right goals for the company, focus on its implementation to achieve the goals.

Communication approaches similar to those described in Chapter 18 can be used such that all managers and employees are clear about how their roles and responsibilities fit together in the big picture. When supported by visible and audible examples from senior management, this creates organisational alignment, commitment to implement and sustains long-term results.

The SMART framework is still a good tool and can be used to set good policies, objectives and targets.

- *Specific* (well-defined, focused, detailed, concrete) – Who is going to do what? When do we need it done? How are we going to do it? How much time and money is required? Do we need external support?
- *Measurable* (kWh, time, money, percentage etc.) – How will we know when this goal has been achieved? How can we make the relevant measurements?
- *Achievable* (feasible, actionable) – Is there a plan of works? Can it be done within the timeframe? Do we understand the constraints and risk factors? Has this been done (successfully) before? What resources (human, time, monetary, educational and other external resources) are required?
- *Realistic* (in the context of the resources that can be made available) – Do we currently have the resources required to achieve this objective? If not, can we secure extra resources? Do we need to reprioritise the allocation of time, budget and human resources to make this happen?
- *Time-bound* (defined deadline or schedule) – When will this objective be accomplished? Is the deadline unambiguous? Is the deadline achievable and realistic? Try to set deadlines that create just the right amount of urgency to get the work done.

Continual Improvement

In line with any good management system, the effectiveness of the policy, objectives and targets should be routinely examined. They are measured in terms of:

1. The quantum of energy reduction or progress achieved vs. the expected energy consumption and target for the project.
2. The promotion and continuous adoption of energy efficient behaviours.

Such routine assessments form a good basis to review progress and identify any corrective and preventive actions needed to steer the energy reduction programme on target to meet its goals.

Part 4 has explored the human aspects of energy efficiency and options to sustain energy reductions. Human factors related topics were written here as the last but the *most important* topic. It is hoped that reading this part last will help managers and engineers remember the importance of employee engagement in the context of energy reduction.

Epilogue: Managing Energy in Real Companies

Throughout this book, we have developed many aspects to achieve and sustain maximum energy reduction. These concepts are grouped into four themes:

1. In Part 1, we explored the need for energy reduction, a framework for achieving sustainable energy reduction and barriers to increasing energy efficiency.
2. The various tools and techniques used by consultants and contractors for assessing and recommending energy reduction were explored in Part 2.
3. Part 3 focused on the maintenance and ideas for generating quick results. These opportunities are typified by large quantities of small energy reduction opportunities requiring no or low capital costs. These opportunities should be implemented as soon as possible. Aspects for selecting a good consultant and contractor to meet business needs have been highlighted.
4. Finally, in Part 4 we explored the management aspects of gaining senior management commitment and a management system to ensure long-term energy reduction. We continued to examine the employee–manager characteristics necessary to design an energy reduction programme meeting the needs of both the management and the workforce. The part concluded by demonstrating a simple energy monitoring system that is informative and relevant to the business.

When described in isolation, the above concepts are easy. In practice, managers and engineers have their daily roles, responsibilities and accountabilities within the business. Energy reduction may only form part of their routine function.

The Prologue pulled together all of the concepts covered in this book using a fictitious case study in order to mimic a real-life manufacturing environment.

The following is a commentary giving an example of how the concepts covered in this book can be applied.

Wesh Pharmaceutical – Case Commentary

Wesh Pharmaceutical is a 50-year old operation. Based on a typical pharmaceutical site, the energy cost is typically 5 per cent of the site's total operations cost. From the information provided, the total energy cost would equate to £2.8 million and an estimated total operational cost of £56 million per annum. Assuming that when the energy cost rises and no other costs change, the cost of operations will increase by 2.5 per cent.

Wesh have been implementing energy reduction projects on an adhoc basis. There have been no efforts to improve the plant. All maintenance was carried out reactively and to maintain, as the case study puts it, the 'status quo'. There have been several projects implemented but there is no structure or systems in place to monitor and provide any substantiated evidence that the various projects have worked.

ENERGY PERFORMANCE INDICATOR

Jimbo's worries of a 4 per cent year-on-year energy increase have been unfounded. Analysis of the energy and production data shows that Jimbo has been using specific energy consumption (SEC) as the energy performance indicator. Detailed investigation shows that there is no change in availability, machine performance and good production output. The source of the increase in specific energy consumption seems to be coming from 4 per cent additional total production throughput, which is translating directly into a 4 per cent increase in poor-quality production by the site.

1. Jimbo has used a wrong energy performance indicator:
    - He has been focusing only on the availability and machine performance parameters within the OEE calculation at the expense of quality parameters.
    - SEC is also very susceptible to computational errors. It may be better to identify an alternative performance indicator. If none is available, the use of total energy consumption per total production is a better option.
2. The causes of increasing poor production have to be investigated. If there have been no other changes apart from higher production

volume, a reduction in throughput will save the company energy, raw materials and waste disposal.

JIMBO, THE ALPHA MALE

Wesh also rely heavily on Jimbo's skills and historical experience with the plant. He knows he needs to improve and is internalising his frustration. It is not clear if he has verbalised his thoughts to his management team. He has a concept of how to improve the business and energy performance, but there is much evidence in the case study that he could not or does not know how to translate his concepts into reality.

Wesh's management team's reliance on him has also led to Jimbo becoming one of the 'alpha males' in the company:

- Despite having management team meetings, all decisions are channelled through Jimbo. He effectively becomes the bottleneck for all decisions required in the business. This is typified by the 'ever expanding pile of papers'.
- Furthermore, when challenged by two other 'alphas', Cameron and John, Jimbo very quickly dismisses their ideas and concerns.

LACK OF ACCOUNTABILITY

Looking at the management team structure, everyone is measured on plant OEE and energy reduction. However, no one has absolute accountability and responsibility for OEE and the overall site energy reduction.

- Al, Jodie and Peach have no influence over OEE or site energy consumption.
- John provides energy information – although he has not done much at Wesh.
- Cameron can improve energy consumption via new or modification projects, but he himself does not affect OEE and energy consumption.
- Ben's role could affect two components of OEE (time available for production and production that is right first time) and energy consumption.
- Sam manages the facilities and could affect one component of OEE (time available for production) and energy consumption.
- It is unclear what Derek does. It is also not clear who is responsible for human resources and for production and scheduling – this person

is the user of all raw materials, energy and maintenance. He has the largest contribution to OEE and energy consumption.

As a result, many people become uninterested in, unaware of or unable to relate to energy reduction. This arises from a combination of low awareness level, poor employee engagement and 'not my responsibility' attitudes.

There is much evidence of Wesh employees lacking awareness of where energy is not used efficiently. There is also a general lack of engineering understanding of energy consuming machines. Many of the routine failures such as the chilled water pumps and bearings failure could have been avoided by engineering the problem away, e.g., removing the heat source from the motors etc.

LACK OF CAPABILITY

The lack of capability to identify and resolve the root cause of failures, neglect of plant asset and a high level of inefficiency could have contributed to Wesh being an easy target for sales personnel selling products and services. For example:

1. Replacing the entire population of 'holed' steam traps with a steam trap variant with an orifice (a hole) does not reduce energy consumption.
2. Inability to set and use the correct performance indicators for production and energy consumption.
3. Purchase of a state-of-the-art monitoring and charting system that no one knows how to use.

Furthermore, evidence put forward by Cameron suggests that the frequency of steam trap blockages has increased. This highlights that there could be an inherent problem prohibiting the condensate draining away at sufficient speed, the orifice could be too small (compared to the hole drilled by Wesh employees) or something is blocking the pipe work. Based on the age of the plant (~50 years), it is highly likely that the blockage is loose rust from the pipe. Regardless, the root cause needs to be found and resolved to the correct problem. If the pipe work is corroded it could potentially imply the limited remnant life of the asset and a need for asset replacement planning.

UNCONTROLLED MODIFICATIONS

Several employees, including Jimbo, change the settings and set points of machines, heating and cooling system and, without understanding the cause, resolve the cause of the problem. These changes are implemented without the appropriate change controls, in accordance with operating procedures. They were also not recorded. This is in violation of pharmaceutical Good Manufacturing Practice (GMP) protocol.

SHORT-TERM RETURN ON INVESTMENT

Wesh uses a two-year simple payback as a measure for returns on investment. This short-term requirement limits the opportunities for long-term energy reduction. It is prudent for Jimbo to explore and seek clarification from the Wesh family or obtain permission to extend the need for short-term payback. If the plant is near the end of its planned life and the Wesh family do not intend to keep the plant, it could explain the need for short-term payback.

In the case of funding for the new boiler, the company also considers the benefits of reliability. In order to boost the economic benefits of a new boiler, the cost of down time should also be included in the analysis. However, in order to do this, the root cause of unreliability must be determined and designed out.

MISSED OPPORTUNITIES

Besides John's obsession with deciphering the performance of each line, there are many energy reduction opportunities within the case study that, collectively, will exceed the 2 per cent year-on-year reduction required in the short to medium term. These opportunities can be progressed without the need for machine performance data. They are grouped into the following.

1.   Based on the data presented, as there is no change in availability and performance of the machines; reducing the production throughput by 4 per cent reduces raw material and energy consumption and avoids waste.

2.   One of the largest energy reduction opportunities may have already been identified by Cameron. This, if successful, could result in a 33 per cent reduction in natural gas use and could result in a smaller replacement boiler – a capital saving.

3.   The site utilises 73 million kWh of natural gas and 17 million kWh of electricity. Assuming the site operates 24 hours a day seven days a week, this gives a good opportunity to use a combined heat and power (CHP) system. CHP generates electricity and heat simultaneously. Although the site will consume more natural gas to operate the machine, it is offset by a reduction in electricity purchased. On a

continuous plant, CHP typically has a return on investment of four to five years.

4.   As the site has not applied any new technologies during the 50 years of operation, variable speed drives (VSDs) have become a proven technology. There are bound to be applications where VSDs will be beneficial. In addition, the site has had many motor failures. They would have been, over the years, rewound many times. It may be more economical to replace the failed motors with high efficiency variants.

5.   Switch off lights in the car park during the day or use lighting level sensors.

6.   Switch off lights or use occupancy detectors in the office.

7.   Turn off heating, ventilation systems, printers and photocopiers in the office overnight and at weekends, or use a timer control.

8.   Use management team energy awareness to stop behaviours such as (1) turning on lighting and closing blinds; (2) turning heating and cooling on simultaneously; and (3) excessive ventilation. Alternatively, an interlock could be used to inhibit the start of air conditioning if the heating is on or the window is open.

9.   When comparing the two proposals for boiler improvement, both have similar return on investment. Continued delay in making a decision will lead to a loss of energy savings.

10.   Find the root cause and fix the problem to stop the need to drill a hole through a steam trap or use orifice steam traps. It could also lead to larger asset longevity issues.

11.   Move the compressed air exhaust away from the chilled water pump. Pumps and motors need cooling and ventilation to operate efficiently and reliably. Removing the heat source from the chilled water pump saves the cost of maintenance. If chilled water is a critical manufacturing requirement, the availability of the process will also increase.

12.   Some 86 per cent of energy input into an air compressor turns into heat. The hot compressor exhaust could be used for office or factory heating. Alternatively, it can be converted and used as hot water. Using the hot exhaust for heating or hot water reduces the energy required for heating and hot water generation.

13.   Find the root cause and fix the problem leading to continued bearing failure. Bearing failures on pumps are usually caused by misalignment between the motor and pumps. The symptoms are heat and bearing failure. Using compressed air to cool the pump and replacing the motor with a bigger motor lead to two additional energy inefficiencies and increases the energy consumption. In another case, instead of

tightening the slack belt on a motor, Derek squirts XE50. Leaving it in a loose position reduced the contact between the motor and the pump or fan. In itself, it does not consume more energy. If the pump or fan is sufficient to provide the required duty even with the slack belt, it provides an opportunity to turn down after the slack belt is repaired. If the pump or fan is insufficient to provide the required duty, it could translate into poor production.

14.   Apply insulation to production machinery, steam and condensate pipes, valves, strainers and other fittings. Because of the heat lost to the cooler environment, the production equipment has insufficient heat for production.

15.   It is not clear from the case study whether the condensate is contaminated and not suitable to be reused in the boiler – or 'clean'. If the condensate is clean, it should be returned to the boiler and reused. If it is 'dirty', recovering the heat, as proposed by Sam, is the right thing to do.

16.   The awareness of many employees of machine reliability, energy efficiency and energy reduction is low. Many employees have differing ideas about energy reduction. The general awareness and energy education of employees needs to be aligned and improved.

The Needs of Wesh Pharmaceutical

Bearing in mind all of the issues described above, in order to create a platform where energy reduction can be sustained and verified over the long term and also to meet the requirements of the Environment Agency, the issues of plant failure/reliability should be addressed while implementing energy reduction. Jimbo has to instil a culture of solving problems at the source rather than treating the symptoms. Daily operational decisions should be delegated to the management team – although this might be harder to achieve because of Jimbo's skills and personal interest.

More importantly, Jimbo and his management team need a lot of guidance to identify and implement – and the means to verify – the improvements needed at Wesh. In the case study, it is not clear how Jimbo intends to achieve the energy reduction: (1) long-term consultancy; (2) the services of an energy service company; or (3) an in-house resource. An action plan for Jimbo for the next 12 months would be as follows:

1.   Reduce production throughput by 4 per cent. This has no impact on saleable production and decreases energy, raw material consumption and waste.

2. Investigate the opportunity identified by Cameron. Establish the natural gas reduction that can be achieved without compromising production quality and GMP requirements.

3. Commission an external consultant to carry out a root cause analysis on the problems associated with the boiler. It is important to identify the root cause in order to prevent similar issues from recurring. At the same time, study the feasibility of installing a CHP, replacing the site boilers or both.

4. Identify a person responsible for managing production and a person responsible for human resources.

5. Consider the use of an experienced coach in energy and engineering from whom Jimbo could get advice and to challenge the management team.

6. Commit to and chair the development and implementation of ISO50001. Specifying a dateline, e.g., one year to certification, provides an end point and urgency for change to occur.

7. Organise several 'best practice' visits where the management team can observe best practices and results from other companies. Bring those ideas back to Wesh for implementation.

8. There is a need to rethink whether each manager is the right person for the job, with the right skills, knowledge, experience and aspirations for the management roles. Cameron seems to be more suited to being an energy manager than John, the production manager. Appointment of the right person with the right skills, experience and aspirations facilitates and accelerates the improvement process.

9. Jimbo should prevent himself from stepping in and micromanaging the management team. He should delegate, coach and routinely monitor the following tasks to specific managers. All managers to receive training in equipment reliability and energy efficiency. The managers can then roll out the training to all employees and contractors.

• Production manager and facilities manager
    i. Review all operating procedures and production planning;
    ii. Return all operating parameters back to 'as specified' or 'as designed' condition;
    iii. Work with quality manager to ensure that the changes do not change the validation requirements and production quality;
    iv. Work with the maintenance manager to prioritise a list of maintenance requirements.

- Quality manager
    i. Compile and obtain the latest copy of all relevant codes of practice, product specifications, regulations and other requirements having an impact on site operations and energy consumption;
    ii. Compare these documents with current practice to prioritise urgent work to be carried out;
    iii. Review the key operating parameters that ensure continued compliance with pharmaceutical regulation and guidance such as GMP.

- Maintenance manager
    i. Provide the maintenance team with root cause analysis and preventive maintenance training;
    ii. All maintenance has to be carried out by resolving the root cause of the symptoms;
    iii. When carrying out maintenance, replace old motors with high-efficiency variants. Use appropriate alignment techniques to prevent reoccurring failures.

- Energy manager
    i. Identify the type and quantities of energy and utilities used by all energy consuming equipment at Wesh;
    ii. Identify key parameters that change the amount of energy used by each machine;
    iii. Specify energy performance indicators that allow quantitative operational and energy measurement;
    iv. With the aid of an energy map or flow chart, review the location of existing metering set-up;
    v. Carry out a gap analysis on the measurements recorded by the automatic charting system and prioritise a list for improving the automatic charting system.

- Project manager
    i. Investigate and implement the opportunities identified above.

- Human resources manager
    i. Review the roles and responsibilities of the whole management team. Ensure that the performance measurement for each manager is (1) specific to the roles and responsibilities of each manager; and (2) aligned with the overall business objectives;

     ii. Work with the energy manager to incorporate energy efficiency behaviours into the performance appraisal of each employee;

     iii. Prepare a communication plan to roll out impending changes. Constant and varied communication technique is important to the success of the change. It may be necessary to tap into the sales and marketing skills of the commercial manager;

     iv. Come up with a plan to diffuse potential complaints about the changes that are about to happen.

- Commercial manager
  - i. Have an overview and input into all plans developed by the departmental managers to ensure that any potential disruptions to production and customer satisfaction can be minimised;
  - ii. If disruption cannot be minimised, prepare a communication plan with external clients and other parties;
  - iii. Work with the human resources manager to create an internal change management communication plan.

10. Using the management team as the change team, compile all lists into a master list, prioritise a programme for implementation and launch the change programme.

11. Require all action items to be executed in a manner visible to all employees within Wesh.

12. Set up a platform where progress and action plans can be reviewed, discussed, monitored and corrective action applied.

The activities set out in this 12-point plan to achieve ISO50001 will be challenging for Wesh over the next 12 months. All activities must be focused on the end goal – achieving certification. By gaining this certification, a workable plan would have been identified and put in place. All reliability and energy reduction activities will be well underway. It may also add credibility with the Environment Agency.

In order for Wesh Pharmaceutical to achieve the programme within 12 months, it is important for Jimbo and the management team to acknowledge and discuss the possibility of increasing resources to help implement the additional work required. Ignoring and sidelining this is equivalent to not allocating the appropriate resources or setting unrealistic timeline. Alternatively, Jimbo could consider a longer time frame, e.g., 18 months.

A lot of discipline will be required from all parties to drive the change. Intolerance towards inefficiencies needs to be driven through the entire organisation before the new culture settles into the 'new' ways of working.

It is also recommended that extra communication and encouragements are provided to all of the management team and employees at regular intervals and when milestones are achieved.

References

Allcott, H. 2011. Social Norms and Energy Conservation. *Journal of Public Economics*, 95(9–10): 1082–95.

Allwood, J.M. and Cullen, J.M. 2011. *Sustainable Materials: With Both Eyes Open*. Cambridge: UIT. also available at: www.withbotheyesopen.com.

Amabile, T. and Kramer, S. 2011. *The Progress Principle: Using Small Wins to Ignite Joy, Engagement, and Creativity at Work*. Boston, MA: Harvard Business Review Press.

Argyris, C. 1994. Good Communication That Blocks Learning. *Harvard Business Review*, July–August.

Barker, R. 2010. No, Management is Not a Profession. *Harvard Business Review*, July–August.

Barker, T. and Foxon, T. 2006. *The Macro-Economic Rebound Effect and the UK Economy*. Report written by the Cambridge Centre for Climate Change Mitigation Research (4CMR) for the Department for Environment, Food and Rural Affairs.

Bell, V. 2011. *Sustainability Update*. Presentation from BSI Associate Consultants Programme: ACP Meeting. Milton Keynes, 9 December.

Boardman, B. and Darby, S. 2000. *Effective Advice: Energy Efficiency and the Disadvantaged*. Oxford: Environmental Change Institute, University of Oxford.

Bower, J. 2011.*The Most Successful CEOs Come from Within* [Online, 30 September]. Available at: blogs.hbr.org/hbsfaculty/2011/09/most-successful-ceos.html [accessed: 23 February 2012].

BRESCU [Building Research Energy Conservation Support Unit]. 1995. *Organisational Aspects of Energy Management: A Self-Assessment Manual for Managers*. Energy Efficiency Best Practice Programme Good Practice Guide 167. London: HMSO.

BRESCU. 2001. *Energy Management Priorities: A Self-Assessment Tool*. Energy Efficiency Best Practice Programme Good Practice Guide 306. London: HMSO.

Bressans, F., Farrell, D., Haas, P. et al. 2007. Curbing Global Energy Demand Growth: The Energy Productivity Opportunity. *McKinsey Global Institute*, May.

British Gas. 2012. *British Gas Warns Business Wasting 50% of Electricity* [Online]. Available at: www.britishgas.co.uk/business/what-we-do/our-business/bgb-news.html [accessed: 3 April 2012].

Buchanan, D.A. and Huczynski, A.A. 2010. *Organizational Behaviour*. 7th Edition. Harlow: Financial Times/Prentice Hall.

Brown, J. 1963. *The Social Psychology of Industry*. Harmondsworth: Penguin.

Business Line. 2011. *Carbon Credit Capital Plans $100-M Fund for Renewable Projects* [Online]. Available at: www.thehindubusinessline.com/todays-paper/tp-logistics/article1689174.ece [accessed: 18 April 2012].

Carbon Trust. 2005. *Creating an Awareness Campaign: Energy Awareness in Your Business*. London: Carbon Trust.

Carbon Trust. 2010. *The Business of Energy Efficiency: A Paper from Carbon Trust Advisory Services*. London: Carbon Trust.

Casciaro, T. and Lobo, M.S. 2005. Competent Jerks, Lovable Fools, and the Formation of Social Networks. *Harvard Business Review*, June.

Courtney, H. 2000. Games Managers Should Play. *McKinsey Quarterly*. June: 91–6.

Courtney, H., Horn, J. and Kar, J. 2009. Getting in Your Competitor's Head. *McKinsey Quarterly*, February: 129–37.

deRond, M. 2011. *Cambridge Ideas: The Perfect Crew* [Online]. Available at: www.sms.cam.ac.uk/media/537167;jsessionid=2BFB458B7CE46FBA8D6711B1D9310801 [accessed: 23 February 2012].

Dobbs, R., Oppenheim, J., Thompson, F. et al. 2011. Resource Revolution: Meeting the World's Energy, Materials, Food, and Water Needs. *McKinsey Global Institute*, November.

Economist, The. 2009. *Carbon Markets in China: Verdant?*[Online]. Available at: www.economist.com/node/14258926 [accessed: 18 April 2012].

Economist Intelligence Unit. 2011. The Complexity Challenge – How Businesses Are Bearing Up: A Survey by Economist Intelligence Unit. *The Economist*.

Enkvist, P. and Vanthournout, H. 2007. How Companies Think About Climate Change: A McKinsey Global Survey. *McKinsey Quarterly*. December.

Enkvist, P., Naucler, T. and Riese, J. 2008. What Countries Can Do About Cutting Carbon Emissions. *McKinsey Quarterly*, April.

Farrell, D. and Remes, J. 2008. How the World Should Invest in Energy Efficiency. *McKinsey Quarterly*, July.

Ghislanzoni, G., Heidari-Robinson, S. and Jermin, M. 2010. McKinsey Global Survey Results: Taking Organizational Redesign from Plan to Practice. *McKinsey Quarterly*, December.

Goffee, R. and Jones, G. 2000. Why Should Anyone Be Led by You? *Harvard Business Review*, September–October.

Goldstein, N.J., Martin, S.J. and Cialdini, R.B. 2007. *Yes! 50 Secrets from the Science of Persuasion*. London: Profile Books.

Goleman, D. and Boyatzis, R. 2008. Social Intelligence and the Biology of Leadership. *Harvard Business Review*, September.

Goodman, G. 2010. *Ways to Be Clear, Be Convincing and Be Done* [Online]. Available at: http://ezinearticles.com/?5-Ways-to-Be-Clear,-Be-Convincing,-and-Be-Done!&id=3538101 [accessed: 23 March 2012].

Hallowell, E. 1999. The Human Moment at Work. *Harvard Business Review*, January–February.

Hartmann, A., Farrell, D., Graubner, M. et al. 2008. Capturing the European Energy Productivity Opportunity. *McKinsey Global Institute*, September.

Harvey, J. 1988. The Abilene Paradox: The Management of Agreement. *Organizational Dynamics*, 17(1): 16–34.

Herring, H. 2006. Energy Efficiency: A Critical View. *Energy*, 31(1): 10–20.

Hilaire, C.S. 2011. *27 Powers of Persuasion: Simple Strategies to Seduce Audiences and Win Allies*. London: Vermilion.

Hirschman, A.O. 1970. *Exit, Voice, and Loyalty: Responses to Decline in Firms, Organizations and States*. Cambridge, MA: Harvard Business School Press.

Ipos MORI. 2006. *Energy Efficiency: What Business Really Think*. A Survey by Ipos MORI for British Gas Business, December. Ipos MORI.

Ipos MORI. 2010. *Skills for a Sustainable Economy: The Business Perspective*. A Survey by Ipos MORI for Business in the Community and EDF Energy, June. Ipos MORI.

ISO. 2011. *Energy Management System – Requirement with Guidance for Use: ISO 50001:2001(E)*. Geneva: ISO.

Janda, K.B. 2009. *Buildings Don't Use Energy: People Do*. 26th Conference on Passive and Low Energy Architecture, Quebec City, Canada, 22–24 June.

Kaplan, R.S. and Norton, D.P. 2008. Mastering the Management Systems. *Harvard Business Review*, January.

Kauffman, C. and Coutu, D. 2009. *The Realities of Executive Coaching*. Harvard Business Review Research Report (January). Boston, MA: Harvard Business Review Press.

Keay, M. 2011. Energy Efficiency: Should We Take It Seriously? *European Energy Review* (December).

Keller, S., Meaney, M. and Pung, C. 2010. McKinsey Global Survey Results: What Successful Transformations Share. *McKinsey Quarterly*, March.

Kotter, J. 2007. *Leading Change*. Boston, MA: Harvard Business School Press.

Kotter, J. 1995. Leading Change: Why Transformation Efforts Fail. *Harvard Business Review*, March–April.

Lane4, 2010. *A Question of Trust: A Current Look at Trust in Leaders*. Buckinghamshire: Lane4.

Laskey, A. and Kavazovic, O. 2010. OPower: Energy Efficiency through Behavioral Science and Technology. *XRDS Magazine*, 17(4): 47–51.

Lee, D. and Bony, L. 2009. *Cradle-to-Cradle Design at Herman Miller: Moving Toward Environmental Sustainability*. Harvard Business School Case Study 9-607-003. Rev: 16 December.

Lencioni, P. 2002. *The Five Dysfunctions of a Team: A Leadership Fable* (J-B Lencioni Series). San Francisco, CA: Jossey-Bass.

Levine, D.I. and Toffel, M.W. 2010. Quality Management and Job Quality: How the ISO 9001 Standard for Quality Management System Affects Employee and Employers. *Management Science*, 56(6): 978–96

Lockwood, C. 2006. Building the Green Way. *Harvard Business Review*. June.

Luehrman, T. 1997. What's It Worth? A General Manager's Guide to Valuation. *Harvard Business Review*. May–June 1997.

Mackay, D.J.C. 2009. *Sustainable Energy: Without Hot Air*. Cambridge: UIT. Available at: www.withouthotair.com.

Magretta, J. 2012. *Understanding Michael Porter: The Essential Guide to Competition and Strategy*. Boston, MA: Harvard Business Review Press.

Mankins, M.C. and Steele, R. 2005. Turning Great Strategy into Great Performance. *Harvard Business Review*, July–August.

Matteini, M. 2011. *Why ISO 50001 and Energy Management for Industry of Developing Countries and Emerging Economies*. United Nations Industrial Development Organization, Industrial Energy Efficiency Unit. 17 August

Meaney, M. and Pung, C. 2008. Creating Organizational Transformation: Mckinsey Global Survey Results. *McKinsey Quarterly*, July.

Miller, G. 1956. The Magical Number Seven, Plus or Minus Two: Some Limits on Our Capacity for Processing Information. *Psychological Review*, 3(2): 81–97.

Mintzberg, H. 1994. The Fall and Rise of Strategic Planning. *Harvard Business Review*, January–February.

Mintzberg, H. 2009. *Managing*. Harlow: Financial Times/Prentice Hall.

Neely, A., Yaghi, B. and Youell, N. 2008. *Enterprise Performance Management: The Global State of Art*. A Joint Survey by Cranfield University School of Management and Oracle.

NIFES Consulting Group, 2002. *Undertaking an Industrial Energy Survey: Advice for End-Users on Finding Energy Cost Savings*. Energy Efficiency Best Practice Programme Good Practice Guide 316. London: HMSO.

Neufville, R. and Scholtes, S. 2011. *Flexibility in Engineering Design*. Cambridge, MA: MIT Press.

Orsato, R. 2006. Competitive Environmental Strategies: When Does It Pay to Be Green? *California Management Review*, 48(2): 127–43.

Pascale, R.T. and Sternin, J. 2005. Your Company's Secret Change Agents. *Harvard Business Review*, May.

Pfeffer, J. and Sutton, R. 1999. The Smart-Talk Trap. *Harvard Business Review*, May–June.

Platchkov, L., Pollott, M. and Reiner, D. et.al. 2011. *2010 EPRG Public Opinion Survey: Policy Preferences and Energy Saving Measures*. Electricity Policy Research Group Working Paper. University of Cambridge

Rosenzweig, P. 2007. *The Halo Effect … and the Eight Other Business Delusions That Deceive Managers*. New York: Free Press.

Rummel, R.J. 1976. *Understanding Correlation* [Online]. Available at: http://www.hawaii.edu/powerkills/UC.HTM [accessed: 7 April 2012].

Savage, S. 2009. *The Flaw of Averages: Why We Underestimate Risk in the Face of Uncertainty*. Hoboken, NJ: Wiley.

Shah, S., Horne, A. and Capell, J. 2012. Good Data Won't Guarantee Good Decisions. *Harvard Business Review*, April.

Stillman, J. 2012. *Why Working More Than 40 Hours a Week is Useless* [Online]. Available at: www.inc.com/jessica-stillman/why-working-more-than-40-hours-a-week-is-useless.html [accessed: 22 March 2012].

Strong, D. 2009. Air Source Heat Pump. *Green Building Magazine*, 19(2).

Toffel, M.W. 2006. *Resolving Information Asymmetries in Markets: The Role of Certified Management Programs*. Harvard Business School Working Paper 07-023. Harvard Business School.

Vesma, V. 2006a. *Combustion Gadgets are Rubbish* [Online, May]. Available at: http://www.vesma.com/tutorial/fuel_gizmo.htm [accessed: 8 March 2012].

Vesma, V. 2006b. *Voltage Reduction as an Energy-Saving Measure* [Online, July]. Available at: http://vesma.com/enmanreg/voltage_reduction.htm [accessed: 8 March 2012].

Vesma, V. 2010. *The Future of Energy Management in the UK*. A Report Commissioned by Schneider Electric. Schneider Electric.

Willard, B. 2004. Teaching Sustainability in Business Schools: Why, What and How, in *Teaching Business Sustainability Volume 1: From Theory to Practice*, edited by C. Galea. Sheffield: Greenleaf Publishing, 268–81

Zohar, D. 1997. *ReWiring the Corporate Brain: Using the New Science to Rethink How We Structure and Lead Organizations*. San Francisco, CA: Berrett-Koehler.

Appendix A
Examples of Questions Asked for Energy Benchmarking

Site/Plant Manager

- What is the company philosophy and views on energy efficiency?
- To what extent do the business/site interpret the company's environmental policy relating to energy?
- Does an in-house energy management programme exist?
- Who is responsible for coordinating, implementing and monitoring the energy management aspects of corporate policy and, in particular, the business impact of energy/environmental issues?
- What are the expectations from the energy audit exercise?
- What are the site's total energy consumption and costs? What proportion of the total production costs is this?
- Based on the current business plans, what is the likely pattern over the next five years of the site in terms of:
  a) Total energy consumption?
  b) Total emissions of CO_2, SO_x, NO_x etc.?
  c) Total energy costs and their percentages of manufacturing cost and profits?
- What measures are taken to ensure that all managers understand the energy management aspects of the company's environmental policy and their individual roles in its implementation?
- How frequently are energy management issues reviewed at a business/site level?
- What lines of communication exist to bring legislative and environmental issues that affect energy management to the attention of management?

Energy Manager

- What is the structure of in-house energy management programme, chain of command and position of energy manager within the corporate organisation?
- What are the goals and the status of any energy management programme?
- Are there any works completed under the programme, including monitoring reporting systems?
- What procedures and systems are used to collect data within the plant on energy consumptions and emissions?
- Over what period of time does the plant measure energy consumption? What is the current annual rate of improvement in energy efficiency after allowing for changing product volumes and product mix?
- Has the plant conducted any energy audit previously?
- Does the plant have an energy database and/or action plans for energy conservation?
- What ongoing actions are undertaken to maintain and improve energy efficiency and to implement new opportunities?
- Have waste materials produced by the company been studied for possible use as energy source?
- What steps are taken to make line managers responsible for energy consumption in their areas? What is done to make staff at all levels aware of the importance of energy management? How does the company provide the appropriate training?
- What information, training and resources are provided to ensure that staff recognise and act on opportunities for energy saving that arise daily in routine operations?
- What incentives, if any, are provided to encourage staff to seek energy saving opportunities?
- Review and validation on:
  a) confirmation of energy and utility bills;
  b) size, age of unit/equipment, name and location of operating departments;
  c) schedule of operating hours of each department;
  d) functions and energy consumption of major energy consuming systems;
  e) how the total energy consumption, demand charges and power factor penalties are determined for the plant;
  f) original equipment ratings and any changes in them.

Maintenance Manager

- Are maintenance objectives defined? What are the KPIs and how are they monitored? What is the level of management commitment (e.g., tolerance of non-compliance)? How are maintenance and inspection budgets set?
- Are there any maintenance procedures? Complex-specific or site-wide?
- Maintenance practices and standards – how are critical activities controlled? Are engineering specifications available and used (e.g., gasket standards)?
- Inspection policy, procedures and practices – how are critical assets identified and monitored? How are plant experience and inspection findings used to review inspection and maintenance approaches?
- Turnarounds – how is the need for a turnaround determined (e.g., what determines turnaround intervals)? How are turnaround work scopes defined (e.g., to reduce turnaround duration)? How effectively are they managed (e.g., do turnarounds take longer than planned, what are the problems during recommissioning)? Is a copy of a recent turnaround work list available?
- Spares – how are critical spares identified and controlled (e.g., reorder levels, how accessible are local or central stores)?
- Documentation – design, maintenance, inspection/testing. What system is used, how accessible is it, is it used, how is it updated?

Finance Manager

- Confirmation of energy and utility consumption and cost.
- Expenditure of operation and maintenance.
- Force outage expenditure.

Operations Technology/Technical Service Manager

- How is engineering knowledge and experience maintained and updated?
- How are modifications designed and controlled?
- Learning from past events, incidents, accidents and failures – are incidents investigated?
- What procedures are used to set priorities for internal technical development work? What importance is attached to energy and environmental issues?

- What steps are taken to ensure that developments that could achieve major energy savings are applied to:
  a) existing plant?
  b) minor plant modification?
  c) retrofits and revamps?
  d) new projects?
- How familiar are managers and staff with the energy auditing and energy efficiency programmes?
- To what extent will the installation of pollution abatement equipment for combustion-related and other emissions increase the plant's energy consumption?
- What procedures are used to audit the results of implementing energy efficiency and pollution control measures?

Production Manager

- To what extent does production planning take account of energy efficiency and its environmental implications?
- To what extent are energy consumption targets set for individual elements? Do these targets include electricity as well as heat energy? How often are these targets reviewed? What action is taken when the targets are not met?
- Is the metering of energy consumption adequate for the purpose of monitoring and setting of targets?
- What is done to ensure that plant and equipment is maintained with due care and regard to energy efficiency considerations?
- To what extent are energy audits carried out? What steps are taken to follow up their results?
- Review and validation on:
  a) specifications of materials before and after the production process;
  b) actual operating rates (production rates, quality, temperature, pressure, cycle times);
  c) standard operating procedures.
- Does the production team understand the operating limits of the equipment?
- How does the production team ensure it keeps within the operating limits, and how are deviations monitored/reported and assessed?
- What is the level of team-working and communication between production and maintenance?

Appendix B
Day-to-Day Items that Inform Consultants of Plant Performance

As a guide to support building up a picture of how the plant is operated and maintained, the consultant and contractor may want to look at the following items to gather a general impression and to identify further areas for investigation.

1. Are the plant areas tidy?
2. Are there any areas of health and safety concerns?
   a) ladders without cages;
   b) locations of alarms, fire extinguishers, safety showers etc.;
   c) hoses or other obstacles in walkways;
   d) gas detectors;
   e) evacuation routes.
3. Is there any evidence of ongoing or repetitive maintenance activities?
   a) equipment laid out ready to use to clear process line against chokes or blockages;
   b) ready to use spares or special tools (gaskets, bolts etc.) held close to the equipment;
   c) permanently erected scaffolding or access platforms;
   d) flanges or holding down bolts missing (e.g., two out of four on a flanged joint).
4. Is there any evidence of steam leaks, process leaks or product on the floor?
5. Is there any evidence (e.g., injection points, clamps) of regular use of 'on-line' leak sealing techniques?
6. Are all drains clear?
7. What is the cooling tower operations and colour of cooling water?

8.   Are there any signs of overheating/overcooling, hot spots/cold spots?
9.   Is there a lubrication store?
      a) clearly labelled drums or containers;
      b) clean and tidy;
      c) dedicated equipment to top up oil levels in the field (oil cans, hand pumps etc.).
10.   Pipe work:
      a) missing insulation;
      b) leaks;
      c) missing or badly maintained supports;
      d) evidence of external corrosion;
      e) inaccessible valves;
      f) vibrating/shaking piping;
      g) steam/water hammer;
      h) evidence of stiff or sticking valves (use of extension levers such a scaffolding poles).
11.   Machinery:
      a) missing guards;
      b) leaks;
      c) new bolts (shows it has recently been maintained);
      d) steam flexes dispersing leaks or keeping mechanical seals from blocking;
      e) newly painted items (e.g., new motor on old pump).
12.   Vessels:
      a) missing insulation;
      b) leaks;
      c) missing or badly maintained supports;
      d) evidence of external corrosion;
      e) heat damaged paintwork.
13.   Workshops:
      a) Is there lots of work in progress?
      b) What equipment is being worked on in the workshops (pumps valves, instruments etc.)?
      c) Is there any evidence of technicians with nothing to do?
14.   Materials handling:
      a) product on floor;
      b) impact damage ('hammer rash') indicative of need to clear chokes or blockages;
      c) evidence that joints and connections are repeatedly made and remade (loose bolts, incomplete bolts, new bolts and 'process operable' connections);

      d) evidence of use of bypass or dump points.

15.   Control room:

      a) Does everything look under control (calm atmosphere, no constant sound of audible alarms etc.)?

      b) Is there any evidence of 'trip defeats' (keys in panels or bypass alarms on a distributed control system (DCS))?

      c) Are the 'outside operators' constantly dashing in and out of the control room?

      d) For non-DCS systems, do they appear to maintain 'log sheets' and record routine inspections? For DCS systems, do they appear to look at trends as part of routine operation?

Appendix C
Energy Maturity Matrix

	Strategic Aspects		
	Top Management Commitment	**Energy Policy**	**Objectives and Targets**
5	Actively supports a comprehensive strategy.	Regularly review of plan and policy. Part of wider business strategy.	Well defined long-term and interim targets, and delivery plan.
4	Lacks support of a formal policy.	Formal policy available.	Defined interim targets and delivery plan.
3	Lacks support of draft strategy from management and key personnel.	Unadopted policy set by departmental head.	Defined target over next 10 years and delivery plan.
2	Informal policy supported by staff.	Only guidelines.	Defined 5-year target, no delivery plan.
1	None.	None.	None.

	Strategic Aspects		
	Long-Term Plans	**Short-Term Planning**	**Reporting Procedures**
5	Quantify and evaluate reduction prospect for 100% of energy use.	Approved 1- and 2-year funds of short-term plan for 125 per cent energy reduction target.	Comprehensive and regularly for various audience.
4	Quantify and evaluate reduction prospect for 75 per cent of energy use.	Approved 1- and 2-year funds of short-term plan for 100 per cent energy reduction target.	Regularly to shareholders and staff.
3	Quantify and evaluate reduction prospect for renewal and refurbishment.	Quantified short-term plan fund for 75 per cent reduction target.	Occasionally, often on positive news.
2	Plan without energy reduction opportunity.	Quantified short-term fund for 75 per cent reduction target without detail.	Prompted by business needs. Positive news only.
1	None.	Insufficient projects to meet 50 per cent of target.	None.

Management Aspect		
Site Champions	Devolution of Responsibility	Organising
5 Formally trained. Half-hourly data available. In charge of several sites.	Comprehensive and regularly reviewed.	Integrated into management structure. Clearly defined.
4 Formally trained. Half-hourly data available. In charge of own site.	All key staff for all department exists.	Energy manager accountable to a member of management team.
3 Limited training to implement policy. Half-hourly data available.	Written responsibility for some staff.	Energy manager report to ad hoc committee.
2 Plan to appoint champion. Half-hourly data available.	Unwritten responsibilities	Part-time energy manager with limited authority.
1 None.	None.	None.

Management Aspect		
Human Resources	Identifying Opportunity	Communications
5 Proactive long-term investment with full management support.	Formal process on all new projects. Decision based on life cycle costs.	Formal at all levels and awareness measured.
4 Provided after well-argued proposal by energy manager.	Staff to identify on new projects. Life cycle not considered	Formal at all levels and awareness measured
3 Limited success on occasional proposals.	Staff notified on proposals. Dependent on capital cost.	Formal but awareness not measured.
2 Unclear and lack of expertise.	Staff identify informally. Marginal savings. Usually rejected due to capital cost.	Ad hoc basis.
1 None.	None.	Ad hoc basis.

Implementation Aspect		
Information System	**Review of Energy Performance**	**Investment Information**
5	Set targets. Monitor consumption, faults and quantify savings and budget tracking.	Regularly. Compared against internal and external benchmark. Ideas sought after.	Monitor past savings and continuous opportunities for investment.
4	Monitor and targets reporting based on sub-metering. Savings not reported.	Frequently. Monitor consumption and cost data. Routine analysis..	Potential proposals presented. Insufficient information results in delays or rejection.
3	Monitor and targets reporting based on meters. Ad hoc energy cost for budget purpose.	Occasionally. Regular cost checks with exception reporting. Limited analysis.	Available information not in correct format or not easily assessed for viable projects.
2	Cost reporting for internal use based on invoice.	Review based on revenue cost. Limited exception reporting.	Insufficient information to proof previous investment is beneficial.
1	None.	None.	Little or no available information to support funding.

Implementation Aspect		
Appraisal Method	**Procurement**	**Project Funding**
5	Full discounting method using internal rate of return and ranking priority.	Life cycle cost for 100 per cent of goods and consideration of alternatives.	Competes with other investment. Benefits other than cost benefit considered.
4	Discounting method using specified discount rates.	Life cycle cost for 75 per cent of goods and consideration of alternatives.	Competes with other investment. Have to meet stringent requirement on ROI.
3	Undiscounted appraisal methods used, e.g., gross return on capital.	Life cycle cost for selective goods with high carbon impact/ implication.	Only considered when very short-term returns are evident.
2	Simple payback criteria are applied.	Commitment to sustainable options but no documented evidence.	Funding available with low-risk project with payback less than one year.
1	None.	None to low carbon options.	None.

People Aspect		
Awareness	**Promotion**	**Motivation**
5 High awareness level throughout the organisation.	Regular organisational based campaigns using existing information channel.	Formal and informal communications by energy department.
4 Most major users aware of potential and opportunities to save energy.	One-off energy campaign tailored to the organisation.	Energy committee the main source and direct contact with main users.
3 Some awareness of energy saving potential and how to achieve it.	Various information via organisation's information channels.	Ad hoc committee chaired by senior departmental manager communicate to major users.
2 Awareness in place but patchy.	Informally via association and published literature.	Informally between engineer and a few users.
1 None.	None.	None.

People Aspect		
Training	**Momentum**	**Market Awareness**
5 Continuous training for all technical and operation staff.	Integrated into all management system for continuous improvement.	Continually keeping abreast with current development via scientific literature and other sources.
4 Internal training to major users following training needs.	Partially integrated into existing management system.	Regularly monitoring current development via scientific literature and other sources.
3 Information via professional and technical journals.	Temporary impact.	Keeping up with current development via scientific literature and other sources on ad hoc basis.
2 Induction contains energy reduction but no formal training.	Passing phase by end users.	Investigate on current development when project is imminent.
1 None.	None.	None.

	Operational Aspects		
	Existing Plant and Equipment	**Operational Knowledge**	**Operational Methods**
5	Majority of equipment incorporates energy efficiency, is correctly commissioned and well maintained.	All staff understand their roles in energy efficiency and minimising energy use.	Operation methods and settings for energy efficiency defined and implemented.
4	Equipment is energy efficient, well commissioned and maintained.	Staff are aware of how they affect energy use and take all good housekeeping measures.	Operating methods for energy efficiency defined and implemented.
3	Most equipment is not specifically energy efficient but is regularly maintained.	Most good housekeeping practices are adhered to.	Targets set against realistic budgets and maintained through financial procedures.
2	Equipment is not energy efficient, undergoes periodic maintenance.	Energy saving techniques are adopted where they can be accommodated.	Targets set by default through budget setting procedures.
1	Energy performance has not been considered.	No consideration is given to energy efficiency.	No targets set.

	Operational Aspects		
	Maintenance Procedures	**Documentation and Record-Keeping**	**Plant and Equipment Replacement**
5	Formal appraisal on all equipment and fabric element. Results acted upon where necessary.	Complete description and detailed schedules of system, control and operation.	Selection to suit application. Considers life cycle, energy use and energy saving.
4	Regular survey on all equipment and fabric element. Action taken on most defects.	Detailed description and reasonable schedules of system, control and operation.	Selection to suit application. Considers life cycle and energy use.
3	Regular survey on all equipment and fabric element. Action taken dependent on budget.	Basic description and basic schedules of most system, control and operation.	Selection to fit for purpose. Likely to consider life cycle and energy use.
2	Survey prompted by failure or safety considerations. Action taken on major defects.	Minimal description and schedules of some system, control and operation.	Energy efficiency data obtained as part of selection process.
1	No survey carried out.	None.	No consideration of energy efficiency.

		Monitoring and Targeting	
	Operational Requirements	**Data Sources**	**Administration**
5	Data competently analysed promptly. Data used promptly in appropriate detail.	Detailed records on changes to occupancy, temperature, humidity and working practices.	Readings taken as planned, collated and combined with relevant business records.
4	Data analysed and used in adequate detail.	Regular records on changes to occupancy, temperature, humidity according to shifts.	Regular readings taken are collated and combined with relevant business records.
3	Budgetary figures used based on usage and adjusted for changes in base data.	Data calibrated. Routine records on changes to temperature, humidity.	Frequent readings taken are collated and combined with relevant business records.
2	Budgetary figures used based on usage.	Records based on bills from suppliers.	Occasional readings taken are collated and combined with relevant business records.
1	None.	None.	None.

		Monitoring and Targeting	
	Analysis	**Outputs**	**External Audits**
5	Usage is normalised, energy targets assessed against business needs.	Report contains technical, financial data and highlights impact of uncertainties in the analysis.	Instruments calibrated. Database accuracy and fuel price checked. Trends and anomalies analysed.
4	Usage analysed against fuel costs, building usage etc. and against previous periods.	Report contains technical and financial data for comparison with previous periods and budget	Instruments calibrated. Database accuracy and fuel price checked.
3	Usage analysed against fuel costs, building usage, etc.	Report contains technical and financial data for comparison with previous periods.	Database accuracy checked. Ad hoc cursory check on report and compared with previous year.
2	Occasionally usage analysed against fuel costs, building usage, etc.	Report contains technical and financial data for the period.	Ad hoc check on database accuracy. Ad hoc cursory check on report.
1	None.	None.	None.

Source: Adapted from BRESCU (1995, 2001) and NIFES Consulting Group (2002).

Appendix D
Further Reading

Business Strategy

Grant, R.M. 2009. *Contemporary Strategy Analysis*. 7th edition. Hoboken, NJ: John Wiley and Sons.

Sloman, J., Hinde, K. and Garratt, D. 2010. *Economics for Business*. 5th edition. Harlow: Financial Times/Prentice Hall.

Energy Studies

Savage, S. 2009. *The Flaw of Averages: Why We Underestimate Risk in the Face of Uncertainty*. Hoboken, NJ: Wiley.

Vesma, V. 2011. *Energy Management Principles and Practice*. 2nd edition. London: British Standards Institution.

Management

Hope, J. and Player, S. 2012. *Beyond Performance Management: Why, When, and How to Use 40 Tools and Best Practices for Superior Business Performance*. Boston, MA: Harvard Business School Press.

Kaplan, R.S. and Norton, D.P. 1996. *The Balanced Scorecard: Translating Strategy into Action*. Boston, MA: Harvard Business School Press.

Kaplan, R.S. and Norton, D.P. 2004. *Strategy Maps: Converting Intangible Assets into Tangible Outcomes*. Boston, MA: Harvard Business School Press.

Kaplan, R.S. and Norton, D.P. 2008. *The Execution Premium: Linking Strategy to Operations for Competitive Advantage*. Boston, MA: Harvard Business School Press.

Organisational Dynamics

Ariely, D. 2010. *Predictably Irrational: The Hidden Forces That Shape Our Decisions*. New York: Harper Perennial.

Buchanan, D.A. and Huczynski, A.A. 2010. *Organizational Behaviour*. 7th edition. Harlow: Financial Times/Prentice Hall.

deRond, M. 2012. *There Is an I in Team: What Elite Athletes and Coaches Really Know about High Performance*. Boston, MA: Harvard Business Review Press.

Goffee, R. and Jones, G. 2006. *Why Should Anyone Be Led By You? What It Takes To Be an Authentic Leader*. Boston, MA: Harvard Business School Press.

Goleman, D. 2011. *The Brain and Emotional Intelligence: New Insights*. Amazon Kindle.

Goleman, D. 2011. *Leadership: The Power of Emotional Intelligence – Selected Writings*. Amazon Kindle.

Heskett, J. 2011. *The Culture Cycle: How to Shape the Unseen Force that Transforms Performance*. Harlow: Financial Times/Prentice Hall.

Ludeman, K. and Erlandson, E. 2006. *Alpha Male Syndrome: Curb the Belligerence, Channel the Brilliance*. Boston, MA: Harvard Business School Press.

Index